THE
SCOT IN HISTORY

BY
WALLACE NOTESTEIN

GREENWOOD PRESS, PUBLISHERS
WESTPORT, CONNECTICUT

PREFACE

THE reading that resulted in this book was started at
a time when those two happy hunting grounds, the
British Museum and the Public Record Office, were
unavailable for studies in seventeenth-century parliaments.
When it looked to a worried lover of Britain as if the worst
possible might happen, the reading of Scottish history and
literature seemed an anodyne. I was naturally interested in
Scotland. My mother was a Margaret Wallace and her
mother a Janet Bruce, both of them descended from Lowland farmers. My people on both sides were Presbyterians
and I grew up in a stronghold of Presbyterianism. It was a
surprise to find that whenever one touched Scottish history
from the Reformation on, one was at once looking out on
what seemed a familiar landscape. Never had I realized
until I began this reading how much Scottish Presbyterian
codes and ways of doing things and of thinking about them
had been carried across the seas and even as far as Ohio. I
read a paper on Scottish character at my alma mater, the
College of Wooster, but that paper only set me going. So
many questions occurred to one about Scottish character,
and questions usually go back to history for an answer. How
did Scottish character come to be what it is? That the subject was full of pitfalls needs no saying, but it was challeng-
ing. Surely it was a subject that needed consideration. Many
books there are dealing with national character but none
that I know of that undertakes to trace such character his-
torically. Probably some German has written a book of that
kind about his people but it is unknown to me.

Scottish history and character led inevitably into comparisons with English history. Those comparisons I could
not resist. Comparative history is as treacherous a ground
upon which to walk as the history of Scottish character. I

remember a rainy August in Gloucestershire when Carl Becker and I sat by an inn fire, or walked when we could, and talked interminably, comparing English and French history. The trouble was neither of us knew enough of the other's subject. That is nearly always the case. Nevertheless books of comparison should be attempted. This is not really a book of comparison but the reader who will look at the Index under the headings "England and Scotland, comparison of as to": and "English and Scots compared as to": will see that several comparisons have been made.

I would like to hope that this book will lead to other and better ones about national character in history and about comparative history.

For an understanding of national character a thorough knowledge of modern psychology would have been useful, and I am utterly unknowing in that subject. Friends have told me that it is a field in which a little knowledge is a dangerous thing and that enough knowledge would require years of study. Nor do I know much of recent sociology and I suspect that acquaintance with it would have been helpful.

In considering character I have had to stick pretty closely to the main line of Scottish history. That indeed is no simple subject. It is full of old controversies that still engender heat, more heat than those of English history, perhaps because the Scots still enjoy their old quarrels. About the Reformation, about Mary Queen of Scots, and about the Jacobites, the fires die down slowly. I have not tried to walk delicately between disputed matters, but have said my say, as an American layman, a long way off from old wars. One would be utterly fair, but who succeeds in that effort?

If the book is that of an American amateur in Scottish history, that may not be wholly a disadvantage. He may be able to look on Scottish history as a professional would not. It is possible that one who does not know the subject with that intimacy in which the historian finds his happiness may nevertheless discover points of view worth consideration.

Preface

It will be seen throughout this volume how heavily it depends upon various books of Hume Brown and especially upon his *Scotland before 1700 from Contemporary Sources.* W. L. Mathieson's books have been useful at many points and those of C. S. Terry, R. S. Rait, and James Mackinnon. Harry Scott Graham's *Social History of Scotland in the Eighteenth Century* has been my authority for certain aspects of that century. I. F. Grant has been indispensable for medieval history. The series of little books called "The Voices of Scotland," by Eric Linklater, Edwin Muir, Alexander McLehose, Sir John Orr, and others, has given me many suggestions and confirmed some of my own impressions. I have gone to original sources as far as that was possible. It has been a delight to become more familiar with the early poets and chroniclers of Scotland. Many other books which have been useful are mentioned in the text.

While most of the narrative and a considerable part of the interpretation of the narrative can be found in the standard works, I believe that the analyses of character are largely my own. For them and for the comparisons with England I must take the blame.

My friend the late William Allan Neilson, who shared with me an old weakness for Scottish ballads, read an early draft of the book and gave me wise suggestions, especially as to the Scottish poets. H. W. Meikle of the National Library of Scotland was kind enough to go over an early draft and point out errors. Neither he nor Mr. Neilson saw the final draft and neither can be held in any way responsible for any word said. My wife, who once taught English composition and who still enjoys fitting words and sentences into their appropriate places, read most of the last draft and encouraged me to go ahead and publish. Then she did more than can be fairly asked of a wife, she went over the proofs.

New Haven, Connecticut
14 August, 1946

CONTENTS

INTRODUCTION

TO a student of English history Scottish history seems full of sound and fury and without that continuity of development that gives significance. There is little evolution of Parliament, no accretion of common law, no rights slowly won for the subject from the king. It seems a narrative full of isolated episodes rather than of great symphonic movements. One grows tired at length of murders and battles and of escapes to the moors.

But the Scot is more interesting than the history of his country. He has become a character in the world, more important and more significant than the size of his land or its story would justify. From the days of Sir Walter Scott on, the world has been eager to read about him, to see him in his habitat, and to talk with him. The Scot has made effort to see him unnecessary, for he has himself gone to all parts of the world and allowed strangers to find out about him. He can be induced to sing the bonny songs of his country; if you press him, he will recite Burns; and he can quote on almost any subject from the wisdom of Sir Walter Scott. It was a good while ago that he made the discovery that in no part of the globe was his Scottishness a handicap, and he has availed himself of that discovery. When continentals and Americans rail against the British they are likely to make an exception of the British of the north. The Scot is accepted as a friendly, even kindly chap, who will fit into the scene wherever he happens to be. He is a braw lad, a judge of good whiskey, a member of the club. He is seldom without personality and color.

But he is more than that. He has proved himself on a hundred battlefields and on a thousand ships in every outpost of the British Empire. He is a disciplined creature who can stand when all about is falling, who can fight when the day seems lost.

Yet that is exactly what he was not, in the old days. A good fighter, yes, but not disciplined. We need go back not more than five centuries to find Scotland a land of much barbarism mixed in with some civilization. Indeed only three centuries ago Scottish life was pretty uncivilized, the people unbroken to law, passionate and often cruel. What has happened in the intervening years? How has the blood-thirsty and often treacherous Scot become the highly respected and worthy citizen of today?

This is a theme which concerns us. The development of Scottish character is a subject I propose to consider in this book. It is possible, or I hope it is, to think of the history of a nation in terms of how the character of the people found form in events, or conversely of how what happened to a people, or what they thought happened, made them what they are.

Of course events are not all that make a nation. The original stocks and the overlays of stocks have much to do with national character, more possibly than anything that happens to the people. Furthermore, on the other side of the picture, the events in the history of a nation are not by any means wholly explained by national character, because other nations with other codes and ideals may impinge upon a country and change its history and its economic status in such a way as to affect the daily life and eventually the character of a people.

Thus when we try to explain Scottish character in terms of the history of Scotland, or to explain Scottish history in terms of national character, we are dealing not with exact factors and equations but with unknowns and variables. To be sure, the historian has always to do with unknowns and variables to some degree, but in this type of analysis he is reckoning with peculiarly inexact factors, and his effort is attended with obvious dangers.

If we are to show the influence of Scottish character upon the history of the country and the influence of the history upon the character, we shall have to observe the way the Scots behaved in some of their great struggles and how a series of events and economic conditions affected the life of the people and so their character. It will be helpful to make comparisons with England at these same points, because the English were their near neighbors and went through the Reformation and the Civil Wars at about the same times. It would of course be desirable to make comparisons with other nations in western Europe but that cannot be done in a book of this size and is beyond the competence of its writer.

These are perilous paths to follow. National character is a vague subject at best and one upon which much nonsense has been written. Yet surely it is the duty of the inquisitive student of the past to concern himself with national character and its manifestations and, if possible, with explanations. For such an examination Scotland affords an excellent opportunity. The country is set off by itself, separated by water from every other nation save England, and pretty sharply separated from England, not only by the Cheviots and the Tweed, but by racial stock and history and traditions. Scottish nationality as much as that of any country can be regarded as the product of its history, and its history as the continuous unfolding of Scottish character.

I have already suggested that the inheritance of qualities from racial stock is never to be forgotten. The Gael had certain rather definite characteristics and the dominant stock of Scotland, even in the Lowlands, was Gaelic. That Gaelic stock was modified by the Anglian immigration and by a considerable admixture of Normans. Along the west coast and in the islands there was a large Scandinavian influx. Men of Scandinavian stock were to be found along much of the coast line and especially in the north. The Gaelic qualities in the Scot betray themselves from the days of Malcolm Canmore to those of Sir Walter Scott. The Anglian stock was strongest along the eastern fringe of Scotland from Berwick northward; and there one may still meet the hardheaded acquisitive Scot who knows how to raise cattle or to make bargains. The Norman nobility who filtered into Scotland affected the court life and gave Scotland some of those restless potentates who were always starting wars against their neighbors. But one of those Norman families was the Bruce family who came originally from the village of Bruys in Normandy, and it might be guessed that some of that organizing power which distinguished Robert Bruce was derived from his Norman ancestry. The Scandinavian element may have furnished some of the seafarers and travelers to far countries that we find among the Scots. But these are risky speculations, as the stocks were to be greatly mixed. What is safe to say is that the Gaelic influence in Scottish character has always been evident, and the Anglian influence can almost certainly be observed in certain parts of the country.

Those different elements in the Scottish make-up might never have been thoroughly welded together had not invasions from the south hammered them into a nation. So history modified what Scotland had by inheritance. Scotland was unified by its enemy. There were many different stocks from the Lowlands and the Highlands with Bruce at Bannockburn. At the end of that day it looked as if the Scottish nation were on its way to a great future.

But Robert Bruce was hardly in his grave when the English invasions began again, part of the Four Hundred Years' War between England and Scotland. The English marched north again and again, burning farmhouses and abbeys and towns. Invasion after invasion impoverished the country, and there were no strong kings to save it. Scottish kings were slain or died in early life and left regents or youngsters to rule the realm, thus giving the restive nobles chances to be at each other's throats. That long period of near-anarchy had its effect upon Scottish character. It set civilization back and made less possible those virtues that go with gentility. Scotland relapsed into something close to barbarism. What a different story Scotland might have had but for the ambitions of English kings and the mischances of the Scottish royal family!

Introduction

With the Reformation, history comes in again as a factor modifying Scottish character. It was touch and go whether John Knox's and Andrew Melville's brand of Calvinism was to prevail in Scotland or not. Had not Elizabeth of England assisted the Protestant cause Scotland might have remained as Catholic as Ireland. The effect of continued Catholicism on Scottish character is interesting to imagine. It was a special type of Calvinism that Knox and his successors imposed upon the Scots, a harsh religion, full of thou-shalt-nots, an Old Testament religion with little brotherly love or tolerance in it. But that hard Presbyterianism did more than any other factor to create the disciplined Scot of today, the Scot of stern moral convictions and sober conduct.

Scottish character was modified again by the Civil Wars, which were fought with all the bitterness and intensity of the earlier wars. There were as many shifts of parties and almost as much treachery as in the old days. It is true that when Cromwell conquered the country and imposed English government upon it things were a great deal better and there was a semblance of justice, as the Scots themselves had to recognize.

The Covenanting troubles of the reigns of Charles II and James II, the bloody suppression of the fanatics of the west, had direct effect not so much upon Scottish character as upon Scottish traditions. Rothes and Lauderdale managed to make a large body of Scottish martyrs out of sectarians. But those martyrs were remembered, and when Presbyterianism came into its own with the Revolution and William and Mary, they became the martyrs of the Kirk of Scotland and their sufferings, the scenes at their executions, their last words, became part of the lore of the whole Church of Scotland. Presbyterianism took over bag and baggage martyrs whom the main body of the Church would not have recognized, and gained for itself a martyr tradition. Indeed the Covenanters have become a national tradition and part of the story of Scotland. Traditions do affect national character and there can be little doubt that the Covenanting tradition increased the capacity of the Scots to stand firm in whatever sect of Presbyterianism they had elected to join. The great secession of 1843 is in the good Covenanting tradition.

Then just when Scotland was on its feet, with a profoundly significant national character of its own, came the Union (1707) with England and the end of the Scottish Parliament and of the symbols of sovereignty. Scottish prosperity and opportunity were greatly advanced but Scottish political nationality was ended. The Scots played second fiddle to England. That necessarily affected Scottish character. The Scots were cut off from their old history and heritage and in some degree from their traditions. A proud people, they became more and more defensive in their outlook. English civilization, English moderation, could not but affect them and lessen the barbarism and violence left over from the Middle Ages and from the wars of the seventeenth century. English prosperity and English ties with a new world gave them much to occupy them. They found themselves sharing the prestige of the British Empire, and that was good. But Scotland no longer stood where she did, and the Scots were ill at ease.

Thus at many points Scottish character has been modified by the history of the country.

How Scottish history is itself a revelation of Scottish character will be a more difficult matter to set forth. Yet the way Scotland fought its wars against a stronger nation to the south was a revelation of Scottish capacity to endure and suffer defeat and more defeat and still hang on. The way the Reformation was carried through in Scotland by John Knox and Andrew Melville is another illustration of Scottish character and furnishes interesting comparisons with the English and their Reformation. No less interesting indications of that character appear in the course of the Scottish Civil Wars. There again the comparison with England is fruitful. And the struggles of the Covenanters in the time of Charles II reveal aspects of Scottish character that are typical and very different from the English.

Introduction

The Scot knows that his national character is tied up with the history of Scotland. Perhaps because his country has been merged into a larger unit, he looks yearningly toward his past. No nation lives more upon its past. Walk the streets of Edinburgh, poke down into the wynds off High Street, gaze at the Gothic monument on High Street and the Neo-Gothic on Princes Street, survey Calton Hill with its memorial to Thomas Muir and those political reformers whom Scotland wronged, mount to the castle and go round the rooms where every window has a story, loiter through Holyrood still haunted by Mary and Rizzio, or scramble up Arthur's Seat and look away over Edinburgh, and you will realize that the ancient capital of Scotland is a museum. Edinburgh stands on her hills, custodian of the past. She is a fit symbol of a people who have lived upon the past because they have little else of national pride to live upon. The Parliament is no more, the king of Scotland dwells four hundred miles to the south, even if he occasionally visits at Holyrood and in the Highlands. About all that is left politically of Scotland is her law, her Kirk, and her General Assembly where the great of the land meet once a year and thresh out churchly matters. It is the past that ties Scotland together, that interests a people who have somewhat lost their excuse for being Scots. How intense is that craving to find themselves in the past has been discovered by theatrical managers in Glasgow and Edinburgh. They have only to put on a play dealing with Scottish history to pack the house. The adventures of Bruce, the fortunes of James IV, the ups and downs of Mary Queen of Scots and of Bonnie Prince Charlie are rather old stories by now, but the Scots seem never to have too much of them. The Scots are a part of all that they have met.

Their national experience has been a hard one. Little wonder that they seem at bottom a dour and serious-minded people. They are familiar with defeat and lost causes. The boys and girls of Scotland have been brought up on stories with unhappy endings. Sir William Wallace led the uprising of the people against the English but was finally defeated and his hiding place betrayed. Though it is more than six hundred years since he was executed at Smithfield, statues of him are to be seen in town squares, atop hills, and even deep in a forest. His pictures adorn cottage walls. The Bruce had to hide himself in the western mountains and islands and watch spiders until at last he prevailed at Bannockburn. Flodden Field, Halidon Hill, Pinkie Cleuch, and Dunbar are incidents in English history but major battles remembered with pain by the Scots. There was also Glencoe for them to remember and The 'Fifteen and The 'Forty-five. What a lot of Highland blood was wasted for the Stuarts, for Scotland's "rightful king"! Scots still sing, "Will Ye No Come Back Again?" though few of them would wish the Stuarts to return. Scottish ballads and music deal with defeat and longing. The sweetest Scottish songs are those of saddest memories.

Even the landscape seems to the American tourist to have a sadness about it. The motorist on his way north leaves behind the ordered fields and set trees of the south. His road is between bare hills and grassy moors; past poor stark villages; he looks upon clouds that are gray and only now and then reveal the diffused rays of the sun. Even when one moves over the fallow lands between Glasgow and the Border, the cold stone of the farmhouses bearing the marks of patching up through the ages, the funereal spruce on the hills, the walls that have been broken down and put back many times, all seem to speak of the long struggles for survival. The ruins of Linlithgow with its lawns sloping to the water, with its chambers of kings now open to the winds, with its tower where Queen Margaret waited for the return of her husband from Flodden, and in vain; the palace of Dunfermline where Scottish kings once drank the blue-red wine above the deep glen; the streets and quads of St. Andrews and the gray sea wall; the three-pronged Eildon hill, the open choirs of Melrose, all remind one of lost battles and lost causes. Other nations have their ruins but Scotland's are strangely associated with defeat and disaster.

Introduction

The Scot expects the worst to happen. He is experienced in making his escape and coming back to fight another day. He is willing to wait for that other day and not to give up even if it is lost. What matter if the Southrons broke down his fences and burned his byres and homestead and drove away his herds. He would hide in the hills and when the English went home would return and rebuild and prey upon them for their sheep and cattle.

His long record of struggles with the Southrons has put him on his guard. And he is so today, watching the situation with a wary and cautious eye. Yet he thinks well of himself. In his heart he believes that no people since the Athenians have so much to their credit and he might, in a pinch, leave the Athenians out. He is British, yes, and he will sing "There will always be an England" but he murmurs to himself, "As long as Scotland is there."

Scotland is there, for him, even if it has become merely a northern province of Britain. He remains a Scot, a citizen of what has been no mean nation. Upon his face and in his speech and in his way of doing things and even of thinking is written his character, a fixed and definite character that has come out of long national experience.

PART I
THE EARLY SCOTS

I

THE WILD SCOTS

JUST before the battle of Bosworth Field between Richard III and Henry Richmond it was suddenly discovered that the English crown was missing. The Bishop of Dunkeld, who was at the English court, suspecting his servant, McGregor, of the theft, examined him and guessed by his countenance that the man knew the whereabouts of the crown. Thereupon he delivered McGregor to the English king. McGregor was brought before the English lords and was questioned. He answered: "Sir, and it be your Grace's pleasure to give me leave I will show you the verity wherefore and why that I took your crown and thought to have had the same with me. Sir, ye shall understand that my mother prognosticated when I was young . . . that I would be hanged as the rest of my forebears was before me; therefore I thought on her sayings and took her to be a true woman, yet I thought it should be for no little matter that I should die that death. It should not be for sheep nor cattle nor horse nor mares, as my forebears did, to steal and be hanged for. But I think it a great honor to my kin and friends [to die] for the rich crown of England that so many honorable men has lately died for, some hanged, some beheaded and some murdered. . . . By my father's soul, Sir, give me credence, if I had it in Scotland in Blair-in-Athol, there should never one of you have seen it."

At these words of this Highland man that could not speak good English, says Robert Lindsay of Pitscottie, the English lords laughed and made them so merry and rejoiced at his speaking that they obtained him grace from the king's hands and a remission of that fault and sent him back with a safe conduct to Scotland.

The story, whether true or not, tells something about the

English and more about the Scots. To the English lords the Scots were a rude people in the north. Not too much blame should be attached to the stealer of a crown, when he was a Scot; no doubt he came of a long family line of thieves, and his aspiration to fulfil his mother's prediction in a big way indicated ambition to excel in the family profession. They found him frank and oncoming and were ready to laugh at him as just another Scottish thief and, laughing, to forgive him.

The Scots could not all regard cattle theft as a serious sin. For getting away with cows and horses had been customary along the Border and in the Highlands since the earliest days. You might he hanged for it, but if you were, you stood a chance to become a hero in a ballad that would be sung by all the lasses in the country. The thieves of Liddesdale and Annandale were famous in medieval Scotland and indeed down to the reign of James VI.

> Of Liddisdale the common thieves
> So pertly steals and reifis   *robs*
>   That nane may keep
> Hors, nolt nor sheep.   *cattle*
> Nor yet dare sleep
>   For their mischiefs.

Many of these thieves such as Johnny Armstrong and Jamie Telfer survive as heroes in the minstrelsy of the Border. So long as they robbed the English rather than the Scots they were deemed brave and gallant men by the makers of ballads and songs. They were finer figures than the highwaymen of eighteenth-century England. Even those rough customers who broke the long-established laws of England were held up as romantic figures and when they were hanged London turned out in numbers and strong men shed the expected tears.

The cattle- and horse-lifters were a feature of life in parts of Scotland from the early Middle Ages down to the first part of the eighteenth century. But they furnished only a minor part of the infractions of the law. The dark wynds of Edinburgh and of the lesser towns were always the scenes of stabbing, and in many instances the murderer was not traced down or punished. The reader of Scottish history is always appalled at the lawlessness of the old days in town and country. He wonders if the records can exaggerate, and then he discovers that local records are of the same kind. That impressive moral dignity with which the modern Scot manages to clothe himself, that otherworldly gravity which so becomes him, are genuine enough. Yet those worthy people of the north whose virtues are always being sung by their descendants in the new world and at home were extraordinarily careless about the lives of people they did not like or with whom they happened to quarrel. They were indeed careless of their own lives and ready to take up a quarrel on small excuse.

We must remember of course that no medieval people were overcivilized, that lawful and orderly proceedings are the result of a very slow development of good government. The English in medieval times did not, for all their courts and assizes and itinerant justices, manage to put down crime. But even to them the Scots seemed a wild lot. Aildred of Rievaulx, who was the venerated head of an abbey in a glen among the Hambleton hills in northeast Yorkshire, and thus not so far away from the Border, makes Walter Espec, founder of the abbey, speak of the "worthless Scots." William of Newburgh, who lived only a few miles from Rievaulx, spoke of the Scots as a barbarous race. The more famous William of Malmesbury, far in the south, wrote of the "rust of Scottish barbarism." It was naturally assumed that a traveler going to Scotland was imperiling his life. After the king of England had sent a daughter north to be married to the Scottish king, he sent a physician to look after her health and safety. That physician found her seriously mistreated and, when he protested, happened to fall suddenly ill, and died.

The French, who deemed themselves of a higher degree

of civilization than the English and who tried to think of the Scots as allies, regarded them nevertheless as a far northern people who were rough and unaccustomed to the amenities of life.

For that matter the Scottish historians themselves, who had in some cases been abroad and perhaps studied in Paris, looked upon their own countrymen as boorish and wanting the polish of the French. The English they disliked so much that they were loath to compare their own people to them, although they constantly betrayed a sense of inferiority.

The lawlessness of their own people the early Scottish writers do not often allude to. The Scots were so used to their own lawlessness that they did not recognize it.

It was not until modern times that the Scots came to realize the wildness of their ancestors. Sir Walter Scott, who may be fairly called one of the greatest of inquirers into Scottish antecedents and who did most to interpret the history of his country to the world, was aware, as few before him, of the failings of his own people in respect to law and order. When he was scribbling away at his *Chronicles of the Canongate* he paused to drop a line to a friend and told him that he set to his tales like a dragon. "I murdered McLellan of Bomby at the Thrieve Castle; stabbed the Black Douglas in the town of Stirling; astonished King James before Roxburgh; and stifled the Earl of Mar in his bath, in the Canongate. A mad world, my masters, this Scotland of ours must have been. No fear of want of interest; no lassitude in those days for want of work.

> For treason, d'ye see,
> Was to them a dish of tea,
>   And murder bread and butter."

Sir Walter was not overstating the case.

Such episodes make up a child's history and give him as bad dreams as modern gangster films, but they leave the historian unsatisfied. Who can remember all the ins and outs of those everlasting family quarrels, who cares to remember? The historian seeks some theme such as can be imposed upon history by reflective men, and no theme is given him. There is no unity to be searched out, no such developments as make the story of England a pleasure to think upon. The English had quarrels; they had indeed murders of kings now and then, and of other great men; the vale of the Severn is marked with the battlefields of the Wars of the Roses. But the historians of the English have been able, without wresting truth or forcing facts, to transmute baronial quarrels and the deaths of kings into matters of significance in the rise of liberal institutions. They do not have to impose philosophy upon history; the philosophy is there to behold. When the historians of Scotland have sought to find deeper meanings and long developments they have sometimes become metaphysical.*

To say that the Scots were far behind the English in the use of orderly processes is not so much to condemn them as to state a fact which needs explanation. And to explain we have to consider the geography of Scotland. One needs only to look at a relief map of the country to realize how divided up the nation is by mountains and lochs. The Grampians cut north Scotland off from the Lowlands, and everywhere lines of ridges bar one district from its neighbor. Long inlets of the sea, firths and lochs that are often dangerous to cross, segment the country. Inverary, for example, is a short way from Glasgow by air, but by road or the sea it is a long journey round. In the old days the roads were few and far apart and the sea was the only available highway. Storms were likely to come up quickly and unobserved from behind the high cliffs that bounded the firth, so that sea travel was a constant risk. It will be recalled that the lovely Rosabel would, against all warnings, cross the gloomy firth, because her lady mother sat lonely in the castle hall. The lovely Rosabel would cross, storm or no, and though the fires flared

* Yet some deeper meanings must be there, and I suspect that such economic historians as I. F. Grant are finding them.

over Roslin Castle to guide her boat her fate was that of so many who risked the sea passage. The inlets of the sea and the sharp-edged mountains not only split Scotland into fractions but afforded fastnesses in the hills out of reach of the king and his officers.

We have said that the Grampians cut off the north of Scotland from the south. The Highlands are behind the line of the Grampians, to the north of the Clyde and the Forth. The Lowlands include the territory north of the southern hills to and beyond the Forth and a narrowing strip of the east coast almost as far as Aberdeen. Now up to a very modern period in Scottish history, let us say roughly to the second half of the eighteenth century, the Highlanders were one nation, or a series of nations, and the Lowlanders were another, even if they were all members of a single kingdom. The Highlanders could not prevail against the Lowlanders and the Lowlanders made little impression upon the men who lived in the northern mountains, not to speak of those who inhabited the islands on the west coast. Lowlanders could not reduce the north to order nor could the king of Scots exercise more than a nominal sovereignty over that part of country. It was too easy for the Highlanders to retire into the inaccessible parts of their domain. And the great lords of the north had power of life and death over their subjects.

The very nature of the topography of the Highlands stood in the way of an orderly government of Scotland, as well as the fact that the people were Gaelic and thus different from the mixed stock of the south; and what was more important, they were a primitive folk. They were divided into clans that were usually at odds with one another. They were loyal to no authority but to their immediate chiefs. To them the king of Scots who moved between Edinburgh and Stirling and Perth and St. Andrews was hardly more than an exalted Lowland chief who was to be resisted whenever their particular chieftain called upon them.

The people of the south and east, the Lowlanders, were

8

better at accepting government. Gaelic they were in considerable part, as we have noted, and most of them spoke Gaelic up to the sixteenth century. But their stock had been so interfused with Angles, Flemings, Normans, and Scandinavians that they were more susceptible of taking on orderly government. The Anglian element, a better one than many English historians have assumed, had been a wholesome influence upon the Lowlands; Queen Margaret, wife of Malcolm Canmore, had done much to bring English ways and manners into the Scottish court; and the monastic establishments had also had an Anglicizing effect. It was somewhat later that Norman influences began to touch the Scottish court and the people. With David I (1124–53) and with Alexander II (1214–49) and Alexander III (1249–86) it looked as if the kingdom of Scotland might be consolidated into one of the most significant and flourishing realms in western Europe.

Yet there was always weakness. The nobles were a restive lot looking out for their own and intriguing, whenever the chance arose, against the crown. Though the various stocks in Scotland had been pretty well amalgamated into a nation, the Highlanders were still a people to themselves and in the western Lowlands there were groups that still were more attached to their feudal lords than to the realm.

It may be said, however, that if Scotland had been all of Lowland people, it might have submitted to the processes of orderly government as early as the English. The Highlands and the Lowlands were not sharply separated; the Highlanders were always drifting over into the Lowlands and bringing with them their wild ways. The Lowlanders despised the Highlanders, but, living in close proximity to them, were affected by them the more easily because the basal stock was the same.

There is a further fact to be remembered in considering the Lowlanders and comparing them with the English. They had many resemblances to the north English, the English of Northumberland, Cumberland, Westmorland, Durham,

9

Lancashire, and Yorkshire. It may be asserted confidently that the Lowlanders were more like the north English than those in turn were like the south English. There was a great deal of Scandinavian blood in north England, as in western Scotland, left not only from the Danish invasion but from the inroads of the Norsemen into the western Pennines.

It is always an amusing game to suggest to a Northumbrian or to a Yorkshireman that Scotland begins at the southern border of Yorkshire. He is at once resentful, for his ancestors have been fighting against the Scots for the better part of a thousand years. Yet there is some truth in the suggestion. The north-country English have the dourness and steadfastness of the Lowlanders. They are equally keen on the brass, equally thrifty in dispensing it. Both Lowlanders and north-country English have lived in a comparatively unfertile country of many hills and have had to seek out and create wealth where the visible means of support were few. Both are quicker on the uptake than the people of south England. The reader will recall the story of the English schoolboy who was questioned about the coming of the Angles into Britain and who answered that the acute angles went north and the obtuse angles stayed south. Both north-country English and Lowlanders have the same type of practical intelligence, though the former are perhaps less interested in intellectual matters. Both have a talent for mechanical contrivances and between them they have done much to furnish the modern world with inventions. Both have a willingness to find out about their fellow human beings, both have the same virtuosity in making friends.

But the north-country English have this advantage over the Lowlanders, that they have long been connected with a great nation, share a tradition of orderly government, and have a long experience of success; and they are in consequence less provincial and more sure of themselves. They have long been a part of a thoroughly unified nation and, if they are more apt to violence than the people of the south

and now and then betray traces of an old Scandinavian fury
not quite forgotten, they are nevertheless men experienced
in submitting to government and taking part in it. A long
while ago they took on English discipline. The Scots never
really acquired a sense of discipline till they were joined with
the English at the beginning of the eighteenth century.

II

THE FUSING OF THE SCOTS

IN order to deal with Scottish character in the days before the Reformation, it will be necessary to recount in this chapter in bare outline the early history of Scotland up to the Wars of Independence and then to discuss in general the period between these wars and the Reformation, say from 1314 to 1561.

The long period from 844 to the death of Alexander III in 1286 was a time of progressive acquisition of territory by the king of Scots and, toward its close, of progressive prosperity, unification, and civilization.

In 844 when there was no kingdom of England and the kingdom of Wessex was struggling with Danish invaders and King Alfred was soon to appear, Kenneth MacAlpin, King of the Scots, who lived north of the Clyde and Forth, conquered the Picts who were farther north and west and became King of Scots and Picts. That made him overlord of most of Scotland north of Stirling. In 1018 Malcolm II won Lothian, the country to the south and east of the Forth, an English settlement that had been part of Northumbria, and soon added Strathclyde (the west coast of Scotland south of the Clyde and including Cumberland and Westmorland that later were to be part of England). By these conquests the Celtic north of Scotland imposed its rule upon the English part of the country that was destined eventually to become the dominant region. Malcolm III, known also as Malcolm Canmore (1057–93), ruled the greater Scotland now won, during the same time that Edward the Confessor, Harold, William of Normandy, and William Rufus ruled England. By marriage with the Saxon Margaret, who with her brother had taken refuge in Scotland, he gave the Anglians a chance to impress themselves upon the nation. Anglian ways prevailed at court and Angles escaping from Norman England settled in the country. With them came Flemings who found homes in the burghs and became a considerable element in the town population, adding large numbers of skilled men to the resources of the country. All this migration went down ill with the Gaels of the north who had originally conquered the south and who saw themselves outweighed by it. The center of power was to move south and the south was to prove itself a steadying element in Scotland.

With the twelfth century, with the reigns of David I (1124–53), Malcolm IV (1153–65), and William the Lyon (1165–1214), came Norman leaders into Scotland to exercise their powerful influence upon the country. The Bruces were given two hundred thousand acres in Annandale, the De Morevilles and Fitzalans became hereditary constables and seneschàls of the realm, the De Morevilles gaining much of northern Ayrshire and the Fitzalans much of mid-Ayrshire and Renfrewshire. David, "the beld [paragon] of all his kin," did more than increase and solidify the influence of the Normans; he remolded the Church, established new bishoprics, founded abbeys and encouraged them, and enforced tithes upon the people for the upkeep of the churches. To burgesses and merchants he gave special privileges, confirmed to burghs the right of choosing their own officials, and did what he could to stimulate fishing and weaving. He talked, we learn from the "Lament" preserved in Fordum's chronicle, to priests, knights, monks, to rich and poor, to citizens and pilgrims, to tradesmen and peasants, making each one think that he had his interests at heart. "For he did his utmost to draw on that rough and boorish people toward quiet and chastened manners; so much so that he looked after not only the great affairs of state, but all things down to the very least . . . in order that he might by his example, stir up the people to do likewise." He was successful. "Hence all the savageness of that nation became meekness, and was soon overlaid with so much kindliness and lowliness, that, forgetting their inborn fierceness, they bowed their necks under the laws."

At the very time when England was caught in the civil wars between Stephen and Matilda, Scotland was moving toward civilization. David seems to have been aware of the great influences affecting the Continent—St. Bernard, the religious revival, the development of the Cistercians, and the Third Crusade—and kept Scotland in the current of European movements. For the moment it looked as if Scotland might become a more flourishing kingdom than England.

The results of his work were evident in the next century. The seventy-two years that made up the reigns of Alexander II (1214–49) and of Alexander III (1249–86) have been called the golden age of Scottish history. Alexander II added to the territories of the crown. He conquered the hitherto unsubdued land of Argyle, the rough, hilly country to the north of the Clyde along the western sea. Alexander III continued his work. He was able to gain the Hebrides off the west coast and the Isle of Man. His conquests did not please the Gaelic Picts in the north, who resented the influence of the south but were unable to make head against the now strongly established kingdom.

Alexander III's court was increasingly dominated by Normans who had come from England. Normans held the chief offices and Normans set the pace. They were not a force for unification, and during his minority Alexander had his hands full with them. It took no prophet to foresee that the Scottish kings had the same problem ahead of them as the English kings had had, that of keeping the upper hand. As he grew older Alexander maintained and strengthened the hold of the central government. Under his strong rule the outlook for Scotland seemed good. Anglians and Normans and Gaels were intermarrying and a Scottish nation seemed in the making.

The Fusing of the Scots

Then it was, at the end of Alexander's reign, that the English, who had been casting jealous eyes northward, interfered to ruin the future of the country.

The close of Alexander III's reign had been overcast with troubles that seemed in retrospect a portent of the unhappy centuries ahead. One after another Alexander's children died until he was left with only one granddaughter, the Maid of Norway. He summoned at Scone a council of thirteen earls, eleven bishops, and twenty-five barons (of whom eighteen were Norman) and induced them to recognize his granddaughter as heiress of Scotland, the Hebrides, the Isle of Man, Tynedale, and Penrith. It was not long after that he rushed off one stormy night, crossed the ferry of the Forth and, against all advice, rode in the night along the high cliffs of the eastern coast, in a hurry to go to his new young wife. Next morning his body was found at the foot of the cliff near Kingshorn. His granddaughter, the Maid of Norway, was brought back across the sea to take the throne but died on the way.

> When Alexander, our king was dead
> That Scotland led in love and le,   *peace*
> Away was sons of ale and bread   *abundance*
> Of wine and wax, of gamyn and glee.   *wassail cake, games*
> Our gold was changed into lead,
> Christ, born into virginity,
> Succour Scotland and remede   *remedy*
> That stad [is in] perplexity.   *placed*

Throughout Scottish history the recorders and chroniclers, who are seldom accustomed to mark significant dates, recall the death of Alexander as a turning point in Scottish history.

Scotland was left with three claimants to the throne, each of an important family: Robert the Bruce, John Balliol, and Henry Hastings. What was worse, the claims of all three were almost equally good. It was the chance of the powerful and ambitious Edward I of England. He insisted on constituting himself arbitrator and decided in favor of Balliol, pledging him to fealty for the kingdom of Scotland. Balliol eventually rebelled, was defeated and deposed.

At this point there appeared out of Elderslie, west of the then little town of Glasgow, a Lowland knight, William Wallace, who rallied the people of Scotland against the English. Only a few of the nobles joined his standard. It was rather an uprising of the people. Wallace was surprisingly successful at the start, defeated the English forces sent against him at the battle of Stirling Brig, and constituted himself Guardian of Scotland. Edward moved against him, defeated him at Falkirk, drove him into the mountains, and finally captured and executed him at Smithfield in London. Scotland seemed destined to go the way of Wales, to become a part of the kingdom of England and to be ruled and exploited by the English governors. Wyntoun tells us that the governors ruled so

> That Scottis men micht do na thing
> That ever micht please to their liking.

The English, says Wyntoun, mistreated the wives and daughters of the Scots, took away their horses and dogs

> or anything
> That pleasant ware to their liking.

At long length Robert the Bruce, grandson of the claimant, took up the cause of Scotland, partly because he found himself an outlaw for murdering the Red Comyn in Dumfries Kirk. For years, from recesses in the mountains and from islands off the south coast, Bruce kept up what seemed a losing fight. He learned patience, how to retreat that he might fight another day, how to control his forces until the time struck, how to change his plans suddenly. His learning was rewarded. At Bannockburn (1314), just south of Stirling, he defeated Edward II and gained the independence of

16

Scotland. Bruce was able to give the country peace and order and good government.

But the peace did not long outlast his reign. Hardly had he been laid away in Dunfermline Abbey when the wars with the English began again; they went on with intermissions through the fourteenth and fifteenth centuries, and the early part of the sixteenth. The English would invade the country as far as the Forth, burn towns and destroy monasteries, country churches, and farm buildings. Their invasions were particularly hard on the Scots because the city of Edinburgh and so many of the important towns of the realm were between the Forth and the Border, near enough to the English to be easily attacked.

One who reads the story of these wars is always surprised that the Scots were not completely conquered. Had the English not been so busy in wars with France and later in those internal struggles known as the Wars of the Roses, they might have been able to make Scotland a dependency. It seemed fortunate for the Scots that they had the "auld alliance" with France, yet that was not always an advantage, for the French when hard pressed demanded that the Scots make war on the English.

Scotland was not conquered but her back was nearly broken. Edward had started a train of events that destroyed the possibilities of the northern realm.

He had, however, done something else, for which he has never been given due credit. He had hammered the Scots until he had made them one nation in feeling, had given the great common people occasion for patriotism. Whatever their ancestry, Gaels, Picts, Angles, Normans, or Norse, they became one people united in hatred of the Southrons. A few of the great nobles might still look across the Border or even to France but the people were Scots and their heroes were Wallace and Bruce.

From the death of Bruce in 1329 to the Reformation, there is not much narrative history worth recounting here. Certainly it would not be worth while to go through the history

17

reign by reign. What does concern us is the general state of the country, since it has relation to Scottish character. That state might well be called semi-anarchy. The chaos called feudalism, which seemed to be on its way out in Scotland sooner than in England, returned and persisted much longer than in England, persisted indeed down to the reign of James VI.

The anarchy and revival of faction were considerably due to the weakness of the kingship. When a king mounted his throne he might start off well, as James I and James IV. But there was always the temptation to go to war with England, a temptation that was seldom resisted, although those wars were so unsuccessful that the king of Scots might well have adopted it as a general principle that wars with England were to be avoided. Much of the time France was at war with England and wished the support of her traditional ally; at other times, at many times indeed, Border troubles, cattle and sheep raids, produced irritation that led easily to small invasions back and forth. Furthermore the English kings had not forgotten Edward I and still cherished the dream of reconquering Scotland.

In those wars the Scottish king stood a good chance to be killed (James IV) or captured (James I). If he were captured, he might be held a long time in England and then ransomed at heavy cost. If he were killed or died at an early age, his infant son succeeded to the throne, one of the nobles assumed the regency, and then began all those struggles between various changing groups of nobles that make up so much of the history of Scotland from the death of Bruce to the reign of James VI.

When the king was not at war with the English he was often engaged in fighting one or another combination of nobles. Now the Douglases, the Humes, and the Hepburns of the southwest, now the Campbells and the Macdonalds of the west, now a lord of Athol or of Crawford in the north would summon hundreds and sometimes thousands of retainers and march in force against the king. So common were such wars that they were hardly called rebellions and did not seem to fall under the heading of treason. Rebellious nobles were all in the day's work of the king of Scots. Nobles who were defeated were likely to be killed in battle or put to death when captured, but putting them to death was not so much a punishment for treason as the natural and usual way of disposing of the defeated.

The combinations of nobility were many and infinitely diverse. There was a considerable body of families on whom Bruce in his long effort to win support in the years before Bannockburn had bestowed great stretches of land: the Douglases, for example, an increasing family who spread out over Scotland and who were never more happy than when engaged in conspiracies against the king. Under the manrent usages of the time a feudal lord was bound to take up the cause of any wronged subordinate, and that custom led to unlimited occasions of feudal war.

Broadly speaking, the restive part of Scotland was along the southwest border, with Galloway and the surrounding country as a continuous center of disaffection, and in the west and north. The northern lords could easily retire into the far parts of the Highlands if they found it necessary. The east coast of Scotland, from the Border to Fife, the lands of the Angles, and the middle of eastern Scotland from the Border to Perthshire, usually stood by the king. But no rule held absolutely. If the king were a minor, and a particularly rebellious group of nobles had gained control of his person, then it would be the more settled portions of the country that were resisting the sovereign.

If the king was able to overcome one combination of nobles arrayed against him, there was soon another combination. The picture shifted not only from year to year but sometimes from month to month. It was easy for the defeated to secure themselves behind lochs and mountains and await a more favorable situation.

The troubles of the Scottish kings were not unlike those of the earlier kings of England. Henry I, Henry II, and King

19

John all of them had on their hands a powerful Norman nobility who got out of hand at the least opportunity and whose recreation it was to turn against the king. It was old habit from Normandy. But eventually, between the time of Edward I and the Wars of the Roses the English nobility was forced to acquiesce in a strong kingship. That nobility found out that treason was a serious matter and that the king was too strong for any combination of rebellious nobles.

Moreover the English kings, beginning with Henry I, or indeed with William of Normandy, developed a centralized government. That government, from the time of Henry I and Henry II, reached out its tentacles through the country by sending forth royal judges and sheriffs who enforced the king's peace and brought crime under the surveillance of royal officials. In Scotland the kings sought, through establishing sheriffs of great lords and through giving special commissions of justice to great lords, to maintain justice. But there was no closely integrated system of justice as in England.

We may put it that feudalism was slowly broken down in England by a series of laws and enactments imposed by self-willed and vigorous kings. William I, Henry I, Henry II, and Edward I held the feudal barons in check and set up machinery which continued to hold them in check. But Scotland did not have the luck to have such kings. Robert the Bruce was a strong king and James I and James IV might have been strong kings but had short shrift. The Stuart line which came in with the marriage of Bruce's daughter Marjory to Robert the Steward won eventually great loyalty from Scotland but was not made up of strong characters. James VI alone succeeded finally in becoming master in his own house.

In England the nobility learned to some degree to work together in Parliament. It is true that sometimes they used Parliament as a means of checking the king, but such checks were legal and strengthened the powers of the Parliament and so of the government. It is true that the Wars of the Roses at the end of the fifteenth century showed how near the government of England might come to degenerating into anarchy. Things were much worse in Scotland. There the nobles never became a class with a mission and duties toward the state. There were family alliances, there were occasional combinations of western nobles with northern. But the combinations were so shifting that they meant little. The nobles were individuals heading groups of retainers. They did not combine to put down or limit a bad king by exacting promises from him of good behavior. They were creatures who fought for their own hands, treacherous men without scruples, capable of turning against those with whom they had been most closely associated. "There is nocht ellis bot ilk man for hym self," said the author of *The Complaynt of Scotland*, written in the mid-sixteenth century. "Thou [the nobility] art the special cause of my [Scotland's] ruin, for thou and thy sect professes you to be nobles and gentlemen, there is nocht ane spark of noblenes nor gentrice [gentility] among the most part of you." That was only too true. If the nobles ever had a feeling of noblesse oblige, they were unskilful in revealing it. Rather they were wolves who combined to hunt in packs.

They were not even patriotic. It is true that they followed the king again and again in wars against the English. But there was hardly a war against the hated southerners in which some of the Scottish nobles did not either underhandedly or openly support the king of England.

III

AN UNDISCIPLINED PEOPLE

SCOTLAND had been fused into something like a kingdom. Had it not been for the failure of direct heirs and for Edward I's ambitions in the north, it might well have become a nation of European importance. It is more than conceivable that feudalism might have been undermined by careful government and that anarchy might have been replaced by order. That was not to happen. The Scots missed that training in obedience to a sovereign and that experience of local government which might have made them a disciplined people. The centuries between Bannockburn and the Reformation showed how much they wanted discipline.

Even earlier than in that period the English had been taught discipline. The Norman kings imposed their stamp upon England, gave it strong government, and took over Anglo-Saxon forms of local government and improved upon them. The Normans came to Scotland too, but as individuals and families, willing to attach themselves to the crown and to receive lands from it. Restless spirits "born for many men's undoing" they had long been in Normandy, and restless spirits they continued to be in Scotland, with no strong master to use them for his purposes. As trained servants of a wise and strong-minded king, they might have shown all their talents and power of initiation. As nobles on their own, seeking their own, they revived and continued the worst features of feudalism.

The Church in Scotland should have been an influence for order. The English Church proved an element of strength to the kingdom. The archbishop of Canterbury was almost another king ruling in his own sphere and bringing about regular and systematic control of the Church. But when

22

Scotland gained an archbishop he was not very different from other bishops and never enjoyed the prestige of the archbishops of Canterbury and York. Nevertheless the Scottish Church was, up to the end of medieval times, a support of the crown and a force for peaceful and orderly government. In 1473, when James III began naming to ecclesiastical preferments, the Church became the prey of the new prelates who were usually cadet members of noble families and little different in their selfish aspirations from other members of those families.

It is usually true that the burghers of a nation may be reckoned on as a factor for law and order. Your burgher has learned by experience what he can do and cannot do. He conforms to codes; he seldom breaks over into lawlessness. The Scottish burgher was one of the most dependable elements in Scotland even during the fearful time between the Wars of Independence and the Reformation. For the Scottish burghs, in spite of all they suffered from the English invasions of the country, were becoming better organized and more prosperous. They were acting in many cases for the common good, and were showing an ability to take orders from the central government. They were conscious of their own importance and were developing an enterprising middle class that could not long be denied some share and weight in the affairs of the nation, a weight that was to become evident at the beginning of the Reformation.

The tenant farmer who in England was serving on juries and performing various local functions had nothing to do in Scotland which would have taught him the arts of government on a small scale and given him the benefits of discipline. Too often he had to leave his work to fight in the forces of some neighboring lord who was on the warpath.

The influence of the Continent ought to have been a factor for discipline, as it was in England. We have heard much of the French gift for form and for orderly arrangement. French words sometimes in England led to distinctions that sharpened and clarified English custom. Now the French

23

came to Scotland, soldiers in numbers, and courtiers now and then. It is hard to see that they did more for the country than create irritation and leave behind them some words and phrases connected with cooking and the household.

But what about the Lowlanders? They were near neighbors of the English, they were in a certain degree English in origin and in some part Fleming. They were indeed the most steady-going people in Scotland and betrayed at times a sense of discipline. Yet the tendencies toward civil war and anarchy, the winds in the west and in the Highlands "blowing misrule through Scotland," were too much even for the Lowlanders. They could not but be affected by those fierce and impetuous people who lived near them and who followed the impulses of their unstable chieftains. They were possibly even more affected by the restive Normans who had taken over so much of the land and influence in the Lowlands.

Few influences there were then making for discipline and many feudal factors that worked against it.

Wherever one looked at the Scottish picture in the long period between the Wars of Independence and the Reformation, the want of order and good government showed itself. The natural passion of the Scottish nature was given an outlet by the violence of the time. The revenge, cruelty, inconstancy, and treachery that show themselves in a time of anarchy flourished so widely that one might have thought those attributes were characteristic of the Scots, and the English of the time did indeed think so.

It has been said by a score of modern writers and by many writers of medieval times that the Scots were a violent people, that there was about them a passionate quality. Whether George Buchanan in the middle of the sixteenth century was the first writer to speak of the *praefervidum ingenium Scotorum* I do not know. Certainly he did use the phrase *Scotorum praefervida ingenia* and it has been used in the first form many times since. In another part of his writings he called them "inclinable to passion." Now George Buchanan was himself one of the greatest of Scottish scholars

24

and one of the most discerning, and he had had the advantage of foreign travel—he had been much on the Continent and had been educated there—and he was able to see his own people in a kind of relief. Somewhat earlier the historian of Scotland, Hector Boece, had written of his countrymen: "They are right ingenious and able as well to letters as other virtues and corporal exertion of the hands, right hardy and ready to all jeopardies both in war and peace, in such manner that nothing may be difficult to them, if they lived temperately." He went on to suggest that the Beginner of the World left them bare of wines knowing that that commodity, while necessary to other peoples, was harmful to the Scots. Boece would not have approved of whiskey as the standard drink of the Scots. He might even have advocated prohibition for his passionate countrymen. They were given to overhastiness, said Leslie, a wise Catholic bishop, in the early days of the Reformation. We think of the Scots as above all a cautious people, yet Bishop Leslie's judgment fits in closely with what one comes to believe about the Scots who cross the stage in the two centuries before the Reformation. Lindsay of Pitscottie, that racy and picturesque chronicler of Scots affairs, declared that his countrymen could not endure justice or punishment, nor could they suffer their neighbors to live in peace. Few who have read the chronicles, who have examined the beginnings of Scottish civil disturbances and wars, or who have studied the Scot in the sparse intervals of peace in those days would disagree. The biblical injunction, whatsoever thy hand findeth to do, do with thy might, needed not to be pressed home as a text in the north. Impetuosity was natural to Scots.

Now impetuosity in a time of disorder may show itself in unpleasant forms. The passionate man, if not disciplined by custom and law, is likely to seek revenge upon his enemies. The craving for revenge is one of the last sins to be removed in an ordered world. There are many instances of how strong that craving was among the medieval Scots. When the Bishop of Caithness, north of the Highlands, oppressed his people with taxes, they caught him (1222) and roasted him to death. The Scots were overbent to revenge, declared Bishop Leslie, and he said that the children in the Hebrides were brought up to remember old family quarrels. Hector Boece wrote that the Highlanders would keep injuries in their minds till they had recompensed them. Sir Richard Maitland wrote a poem in the mid-sixteenth century that expressed the natural human aspiration for revenge.

> Though I be sweir to ride or gang,   *loath*
>   There is something I wantit lang,
> Fain have I wald,   *would*
> And them puneist that did me wrang,   *punished*
> Though I be auld.

In another poem he wrote:

> Yet, or I die   *ere*
>   Some sall them see   *shall*
> Hing on a tree till they be deid.   *hang, till*

If an old man failed to accomplish his revenge on them that did him wrong it was the least his son or grandson or great-grandson could do to remember those wrongs and seek a time when the victim was unsuspecting to avenge the family.

> We are the men that all the warld does style us,
> Remembering ill and give no thanks for good,

declared one of the makers of the satirical ballads of the early Reformation.

The passionateness of the Scots in a time of disorder resulted sometimes in cruelty and even in pleasure in cruelty. When James I executed his enemies, the Duke of Albany and his sons, Walter Stewart and Alexander Stewart, "the deaths of these noblemen were so far from breeding any distaste in the common people that . . . they flouted at their fall, reproached their insolencies, delighted in their execution; and as much without reason railed on them when they were dead as they had flattered them being alive." A sense of pity for human tragedy was not among the notable characteristics of the common man anywhere; it is indeed a product of a highly civilized world. Drummond of Hawthornden tells how one Macdonald of Ross, "a thief flesht in all murthers," punished a widow who had threatened to report him to the king, by nailing horseshoes to the soles of her feet. James I caused Macdonald to be shod in the same cruel way, and then made him "shorter by the head." But the prevalent cruelty can best be illustrated by the "letters of fire and sword" issued in 1528 in the name of the crown to the sheriffs of six northern sheriffdoms, to six neighboring nobles, and to "all the free-holders, barons, captains of clans, and gentlemen," commanding them to invade the Clan Chattan "to their utter destruction by slaughter, burning, drowning, and other ways, and leave no creature living of that clan except priests, women and bairns."

A passionate people is likely to be inconstant. Grafton, the printer, who disliked the Scots wrote of them:

> But that people of their proper nature
> Hath, even from the first, been so untoward,
> So unsteadfast, inconstant and unsure.

Inconstancy flourishes where there is no strong government, where each noble is on his own. The Scots were always starting a war, going off lightly to battle, and then withdrawing and fighting someone else. The nobles, as we have already noted, were breaking their alliances and forming new ones and breaking those. So frequently did they change sides and then quarrel with their new friends that it is almost impossible for the modern reader to keep track of the shifts of policy and of alliance. Alexander, Duke of Albany, wrote the sage Drummond of Hawthornden, was a "man who delighted in nothing more than in changes and novations." In that respect he was no different from hundreds of other Scottish nobles of pre-Reformation times and even after.

Inconstancy is not far removed from treachery. People who change sides easily are likely to be regarded as treacherous. A passionate folk when unrestrained by use and custom, when anarchy is all around them, are easily led into treachery. In the indignation of the moment they forget old promises and act suddenly. "I have read in histories written by Englishmen," wrote John Major, "that the Scots are the worst of traitors, and that this stain is with them inborn." Major doubted if the Scots were more treacherous than the English but he did not seem eager to argue the point. In one of the satirical poems written at the time of the Reformation, the author speaks of the false and filthy traitors: "So generally are we of strangers styled." He goes on to tell how the Scots are railed upon and reviled for treasons manifold. Such railings were unfair, of course, the writer asserted. There was hardly an English writer from the days of Edward I on that did not mention the treachery of the Scots, and hardly an English person in those times that trusted them. But the English were their enemies in war and could hardly be expected to speak lovingly of them.

The records of the Scots themselves, the stories in the Scottish chronicles, prove that treachery was not uncommon. In many instances they would promise quarter to enemy soldiers and, when those soldiers surrendered, would promptly execute them. They would make up quarrels with old enemies and suddenly break again into violence against them. Such episodes are to be found in English and French chronicles, but hardly on such a scale as in Scottish annals. The pictures in Froissart and De Comines of Frenchmen at war are not heart warming, but there was probably less trickery and double-dealing than in Scotland. It is true that I have read a great deal less in French records than in Scottish and cannot be too sure of my comparisons. I have at one time or another read the English chronicles of the same centuries pretty thoroughly, and I would say that treachery was less

common among the English, even in the dreadful period of
the Wars of the Roses, than among the Scots. In both England
and France there was growing up a notion of chivalric courtesy in war. There was a knightly ideal to which many warriors in those countries were coming to conform. Occasionally
in Scottish history of the centuries just before the Reformation one runs into examples of that ideal, but they were rare.

William Dunbar, one of the greatest of the Scottish poets,
wrote:

> The sugarit mouths, with minds therefra,
> The figurit speech, with faces twa,
> The pleasant tongues, with hearts unplain,
> For to consider is a pain.

No doubt the "faces twa" could have been found in any court
and in any country. Dunbar was a disappointed poet who received less favor from the court than he had hoped for. But
he was not wholly wrong in his suspicions.

The most famous case of treachery concerns James II and
the eighth Earl of Douglas. The Douglases had long been a
family almost as powerful as the Stuarts and they had been
abler men. James II was afraid and jealous of their power.
While the earl was away in Rome the king had attacked his
lands, taken some of his fortresses and killed many of his tenants. When Douglas returned there was a reconciliation, but
Douglas made an alliance with the Earls of Crawford and
Ross, looking possibly to future rebellion against the king.
At any rate the king invited him to visit him at Stirling Castle
and gave him a safe conduct. For two days and nights the
king entertained him. After supper on the second day he demanded of him that he break his alliance with Crawford and
Ross. Douglas replied that neither might he nor would he
break it. The king struck him with a dagger and the men
around him finished the earl off.

The treachery provoked resentment and James did what he
could to put a good face on the story. Yet such episodes were

too common in Scotland to gain more than passing notice, save from the family or families injured. It would be easy to fill this chapter with similar stories.

A time of disorder and anarchy brings the worst of a people to the fore. The English with their constant invasions of Scotland had been partly responsible for the unlovely exhibitions of Scottish passion. We must not suppose, however, that all Scots of those days were revengeful, cruel, inconstant, and treacherous. No doubt there were straight going, truthtelling, faithful Scots aplenty. They were not as likely to figure in the narratives of the time. Those who did figure so largely, the undisciplined and passionate creatures of an unhappy age, were the ancestors of a people that was to prove among the most disciplined in Europe.

IV

THE SCOTS AS WARRIORS

THE good Sir James Douglas, who followed Bruce's dying instructions and carried the heart of that hero on a crusade, was reckoned to have been in encounters against the English fifty-seven times and against the Saracens and other infidels sixteen times. His record was perhaps no better than that of many other Scots who went soldiering over the Continent of Europe and fought for the French, for the Germans, for the Swedes, and for the Russians. Scotland produced in large numbers the species fighting men, no doubt because the Scot had gained so much experience in fighting at home and on the whole enjoyed the trade.

Their habit of war was so ingrained that their heroes were naturally warriors. The songs of the men of the Western Isles, Buchanan tells us, were in praise of valiant men. One of the chroniclers gives us a pretty picture of young women singing of the great battle of Harlaw (1411) fought between the men of the west Highlands and the men of the Lowlands.

Fighting involved qualities the Scots admired, courage, endurance, and loyalty to leaders.

The Scots were brave soldiers. Better men of war, said Hardyng who hated them, were not under the sky. One of the earliest of English chroniclers declared that the Scots had no fear of death, and a Spaniard observed of them that they would as soon die as be enslaved, and that they accounted it sloth to die in bed, "deeming it glorious and manly to slay or be slain." Even today one meets Scots whose boast of their ancestors is that they did not die in their beds. John Barbour in *The Brus* states the matter clearly:

And thryldome is weill wer then
    deid;   *thralldom, worse, death*

31

For while a thryll his lyff may leid,	*thrall*
It merrys him, body and banys;	*mars, bones*
And dede anoyis him bot anys.	*death, once*

The Scots admired endurance. The ability to stand up to hardship and pain was a virtue with them as with the Spartans. Wyntoun tells us of William the Ramsay through whose helmet and head a spear was driven. A priest was brought in to shrive him, but another Ramsay put his foot on the man's head and pulled out the spear by main force. The man who was supposed to be dying sat up with good cheer. The English Earl of Derby, who was present, could not help exclaiming, "Lo! stout hearts of men!" In all the stories of the Bruce his patience and endurance are exalted. "His mishaps, flights and dangers, hardships, weariness, hunger and thirst, watchings and fastings; nakedness and cold, snares and banishments; the seizing, imprisoning, slaughter and downfall of his near ones, and—even more—dear ones, . . . no one now living, I think, recollects or is equal to rehearsing."

Loyalty in warfare was one of the great virtues. The Scottish code of loyalty was no doubt an outgrowth of the principles of feudal loyalty. But it stemmed also out of the fierce loyalty of clansmen to their chief.* Barbour in *The Brus* reverts again and again to the virtue of *leavte* or *lawte* [loyalty],

Through leaute liffis men rychtwisly.	*lives, righteously*
With a vertu of leavte	
A man may yet sufficyand be;	
And bot leavte may nane haiff price.	*without, have, praise*
Whether he be wicht or he be wyss	*strong, wise*
And where it fails, na vertu	
May be of price, na of valu.	

* It may seem to the reader inconsistent to talk about Scottish loyalty when I have already mentioned their inconstancy and treachery. Yet there is no real inconsistency. They were inconstant in sticking to the combinations into which they had entered. They were treacherous toward enemies with whom they had made peace. To their own chiefs and feudal lords they were marvelously loyal.

It was not a virtue learned from the Church or from the priest. It was a quality pre-eminent above those Christian virtues which the Scottish poets and historians seldom exalted.

Loyalty was a Highland virtue but it infected all Gaels whether Highland or Lowland. It was a virtue of the Angles on the east side of Scotland, who had brought from their old homes on the Continent the tradition that it was a disgrace to return from battle if the leader was missing. The story of many a Scottish skirmish in the Middle Ages is the story of men standing and dying with their leaders, and also of leaders risking their lives for their adherents. Bruce is pictured as dismissing his supporters and taking on a particularly difficult assignment for himself. If the leader and his immediate supporters were killed, the rank and file sometimes thought it no disgrace to slip out of battle. Loyalty meant that you helped as long as you could.

The weakness of the code of loyalty was that men were dependent upon their leadership. When Bruce was ill, his men became discouraged.

> For folk for-outen capitane,   *without*
> . . .
> Sall nocht be all so gud in deid
> As thai ane lord had thame to leid.
> . . .
>   For when that he
> Is of sic will and sic bounte,
> That he dar put him till assay   *to trial*
> His folk sall tak ensampill ay
> Of his gud deid and his bounte,
> That ane of thame sall be worth thre
> of thame that vikkit chiftane has   *unskilful*

The Scottish hero was nearly always accompanied by his *fidus Achates*, who remained near him and fought by his side. Bruce's friend was Sir James Douglas, the good Sir James.

All men lufyt him for his bounte;   *loved*
For he wes off full fayr effer.   *behavior*
Wyss curtais and deboner   *wise, generous*
Larg and luffand als wes he,   *liberal, kindly*
And our all thing luffyt lawte.   *over*

No less notable was the devotion of the guid Graeme, Sir John Graham, to Sir William Wallace, as celebrated by Henry the Minstrel. When Wallace found the body of Graham after the battle of Falkirk, he kissed him and uttered a long eulogy:

In thee was wyt, fredom and hardines:
In thee was truth, manheid, and nobilnes;
In thee was rule, in thee was governance;
In thee was virtue withouten variance;
In thee lawte, in thee gret largnes;   *bounty*
In thee genetrice, in thee was stedfastnes.   *gentility*

The Scottish methods of warfare were of an old feudal type. The great lords were summoned and they summoned their retainers, who obeyed the summons with speed. They brought their own equipment. Each man carried his food on his back. Froissart, who visited in Scotland, describes the way the Scots went to war. "They bring no carriages [wagons] with them, . . . neither do they carry with them any provisions of bread or wine . . . they have no occasion for pots or cauldrons, for they dress the flesh of their cattle in the skins, after they have taken them off, and, being sure to find plenty of them in the country which they invade, they carry none with them. Under the flap of his saddle, each man carries a broad plate of metal, behind the saddle a little bag of oatmeal. . . . They place this plate over the fire, mix with water their oatmeal, and when the plate is heated, they put a little of the paste upon it, and make a thin cake . . . which they eat, to warm their stomachs; it is therefore no wonder that they perform a longer day's march than other soldiers." Thus the problem of a commissariat hardly existed for the Scots.

But the weakness of the system was of course that these retainers, who were always willing to go to war at any summons, did not expect to stay long. After ten days or two weeks or so they were ready to go home. Go home they would, whether the war was finished or not. Hence their leaders had to make sudden forays, burn and capture and move back again. They could not plan campaigns. Nor could they count too much upon surprising their enemies. The summons to arms had to be widely given out, and in many cases the enemy learned of the summons and where the clans were to meet. Once the troops had come together the leaders, if it were a matter of an expedition into England, were likely to rely upon what information they had of English forces near the Border and would proceed south in such a way as to avoid them. They would burn and steal and try to return before the English forces could find them out.

Battles were in the best feudal manner, and the leaders led in the actual fighting. They were often on horseback but sometimes on foot. They used spears and, when they dismounted, carried swords and battle-axes. They were surrounded by their special retainers who fought to protect them, but the leaders hoped to meet and fight with the leaders of the enemy forces. The battle raged round the leaders and it was necessary that they should maintain themselves. When the Douglas was seriously wounded at the battle of Otterburn he directed his friend to conceal his situation and bestow him by a bracken bush and fight on. The result was a victory for the Scots who did not know till the battle was over that their leader was dead.

There was little strategy about the fighting. Occasionally the Scots made plans to draw the English or whatever enemy they were meeting into a trap. Sometimes they chose the field with a careful eye to the terrain, picking a hill with a stream in front and hills or woods at the side. When they knew that the enemy had far superior forces it was the strategy of the Scots to retire northward, burning farms and villages as they went, knowing that the English would soon find the problem of food a difficult one and turn south again. In emergencies the Scots could always draw off to the Highlands where it was almost impossible to follow them. But if they were actually forced into battle their main reliance was upon the élan of the first attack.

Wallace and Bruce each of them made use of strategy. At Stirling Brig Wallace drew part of the English army across the narrow bridge of which he then gained control, thus cutting off the forces that had crossed. In another battle he attempted strategic movements but was defeated by the greater numbers of the enemy and by their steadfastness. At Bannockburn Bruce is said to have set stakes in the low ground in front of his army to confuse the English cavalry. His own cavalry he held in reserve and they were able at the right moment to ride down the English bowmen. The army of camp followers, who appeared on the horizon and frightened the English with the illusion of another army coming against them may have been a stratagem.

But in general the English used more strategy than the Scots. They had learned by experience the dangers of the fearful direct assault made by the Scots and used flanking methods and cavalry against it. Their archers they held usually on a flank until after the Scots had made their charge, and those archers proved often a decisive factor. Flodden and other battles were won by the better plans of the English.

In the matter of prisoners the customs of the Scots varied much. In some engagements great courtesy was shown to prisoners and they were even allowed, if English, to go back to England on their promise to reappear. Often noble prisoners were kept for the ransom money that might be won. But in too many cases, especially in the struggles of the Scots with one another, when groups of nobles and their retainers were fighting, the prisoners were almost at once beheaded. In some instances they were promised safety and the promises broken. Blind Harry tells us that when Sir

William Wallace captured a batch of English "knaves" he
made them draw the spoil to Clyde's forest and then hanged
them on trees. Blind Harry was a romancer, but what is important for us is not the truth of the story but the conduct
he was ascribing to his hero.

The code of Wallace about making peace, as Blind Harry
tells it, was no better than that about prisoners. The English
sent Wallace's uncle to propose peace. Wallace listened to the
proposal and opposed it, but his friends supported it, and it
was decided to make peace for a season. Wallace was home-
sick for the town of Ayr, went there in disguise, and presently
killed a fencer in combat, thus starting up the war again.
Lord Percy complained to Wallace's uncle, and Wallace
agreed not to violate the peace while he stayed with him. But
he was soon away and found easy excuse for attacking an
English convoy.

The Scots were often defeated. What is extraordinary is
that they lost so many battles and still were able to retain
their independence. After Otterburn in 1388 there was not
a battle of importance won by the Scots against the English down to the Reformation. Homildon Hill, Flodden Field,
and Pinkie were decisive victories for the English, victories
in which the well-known families of Scotland suffered losses
they never ceased to remember. They had met defeats earlier,
as at the Battle of the Standard in 1138. Falkirk where Wallace was crushed had been a fearful blow. About that battle
the admission was made:

> Na never wes sene befor that day
> Sa haly vincust the Scottismen.   *wholly vanquished*

Yet for all these defeats and enormous losses in lives and
property the Scots did not seem to look upon war as a bad
or unnecessary thing. The Douglases caused a great deal
of the trouble in Scottish history, turning against the king
and against everyone else to whom they had promised support. But in the old couplet engraved upon the sword which

37

the dying Bruce gave to the good Sir James Douglas, there was nothing but praise for the Douglases, since they were so warlike:

> So mony good as of the Douglas been,
> Of ane sirname were never in Scotland seen.

War was a glorious thing, even beautiful. The recognition of beauty was not characteristic of the Scots but they knew the beauty of an army, even of an English army. Barbour thus describes the English army:

> Their spears, their pennons, and their sheildis
> Of licht illuminit all the feldis,
>   . . .
> And cote-armure of seir colour,   *severe*
> And hauberks that were white as flour
> Made them glitterand as they were lyk
> To angellis he, of heavenis rik.   *high, kingdom*

On the other hand Barbour, it has to be said, makes Bruce in his old age thank God for the time given to repent his spilling of so much blood. Now and then a Scottish poet regrets the disunity of his country, and behind that regret there must have been sorrow for the continuous or almost continuous warfare. Yet neither the poets nor the Scottish historians pause to exalt the times of peace. Contemporary writers say little about the success of their kings such as Robert the Bruce and James IV in maintaining peace and order in the country. It is the later historians who lived in the sixteenth and seventeenth centuries that began to emphasize the blessings of peace and of strong royal government.

One wonders what the people thought. They were so brought up in the old tradition of clan wars that they probably complained little. A man's job was to hunt and fish and raise oats and barley and go fighting for his lord. Wars meant that cattle and sheep might be driven home and were therefore part of one's occupation and method of making a living.

Something of the general opinion about war may be seen in the heroes of Scotland. The two warriors who fought against England, Wallace and Bruce, had earned their places as the heroes of the country. No doubt Henry the Minstrel and John Barbour in their long epics had a considerable part in establishing them as the national heroes. Yet we may be sure that the two men were chosen as the central themes of long poetical narratives not only because they had so great a part in freeing their country but because they were fit examples of what the Scots regarded as heroic and admirable. Nearly all peoples in their early stages and often much later exalt their leaders in war. The historians of Scotland from the Wars of Independence to our time have united, all of them I think, in exalting Wallace and Bruce. Few men have escaped so well from the historians' desire to reverse the judgments of their predecessors.

Now what were the ideals exemplified in these two national heroes, as indicated in the epics about them? Both were of powerful physique, men who could single handed bring down three or four foes sent against them. The stories of the exploits of Wallace are of course beyond belief. He was not his best unless attacked by four or five men at once. Both men were miracles of energy. Bruce, however, was a man also of guile. His testament expresses somewhat his outlook on war. I give it partly in translation.

> On foot should be all Scots war,
> By hill and moss themselves to fight.
> Let wood for walls be; bow and spear
> And battle-axe their fighting gear.
> That enemies cause them no dread,
> Let them keep all their stores in strait places
> And burn the plains them before,
> Then shall they [the English] pass away in haste,
> When that they find nothing but waste,

39

With wiles and waking in the night
And much noise made on height,
Then shall they turn with great fright
As if they were chased with swords awa.
This is the counsel and intent
Of good King Robert's testament.

It was the policy of a weaker nation, and a wise policy.

The Scottish heroes were tough specimens and often tough customers, at least in the epics given up to their glorification. Wallace appears to have killed every Englishman who started an argument with him. He killed one of his own supporters who was lagging in retreat. Blind Harry makes out that Wallace divined that the man was lagging behind out of treachery, but when the English found his body they seemed unaware that he had been acting on their behalf. As for Bruce, it will be recalled that one of his early deeds was to kill his rival, the Red Comyn; moreover he committed the murder within the holy precincts of a kirk. It is to be said for Bruce, however, that on many occasions he showed consideration for others. Indeed he showed traces of a gentleness which seems strangely out of keeping with his time.

The Scots did not withhold their admiration for a hero because he was unsuccessful. Wallace was hanged at Smithfield in London, his body dismembered and scattered, and his cause utterly lost for years. James IV, who by his want of judgment involved himself in war with the English, against the advice of his nobles and against the pleadings of his English wife, and who suffered in consequence the unparalleled disaster of Flodden, won for himself nevertheless by his courage a place hardly deserved among the heroes of Scotland. The Scots were accustomed to heroes that had suffered defeat, even to unwise heroes who brought defeat upon themselves. One who suffered in a good cause was welcomed into the Scottish Valhalla. The Scottish ideal on that subject was perhaps best put by Alexander Montgomerie in his long allegorical poem, *The Cherry and the Slae* (published 1597):

The Scots as Warriors

Who speeds but sic as high aspires,
Who triumphs nocht but sic as tryes
   To win a noble name?
Of shrinking what but shame succeeds?

      . . .

I put the case, thou nocht prevailed,
   So thou with honor die;
Thy life but not thy courage failed,
   Shall poets pen of thee;
Thy name then, from fame then,
   Shall never be cut off,
Thy grave ay shall have ay
   That honest epitaph.

The question of courage versus due caution was dealt
with by Barbour in *The Brus*. There were two extremes, he
asserted, overboldness and cowardice. Each of them should
be avoided. Boldness mixed with wit, that is, intelligence,
was really valor. Bruce had lived by that principle. When he
saw that he was badly outnumbered he told his men to get
away in three companies and then took pains to guard the
rear that the "flears" might escape. But he could be very bold
and hold a ford against many, when he thought it feasible.
It was often a close decision what was best to do, and the
narrator of Bruce's career realizes that men must not be too
lightly accused of cowardice.

No one was braver than the good Sir James, known by the
English as the Black Douglas. He raided his own castle which
had been in the hands of the English, held a feast there and
then burned it down. It was the episode known as the "Douglas larder." But Sir James could also slip away in a hurry to
avoid capture. It was better, he said, to hear the lark sing
than the mouse cheep.

At one time and another Barbour has a good deal to say
about cowardice, but its ill results rather than its obliquity
are what he emphasizes. The same is true of Lindsay of
Pitscottie, when he tells the story of the flight of James III
after the battle of Sauchieburn. James was not all that could

be desired in a king. He had shown himself fond of music and the arts, and the weakness thus revealed was a clear indication to his nobles that he could not be depended upon in the day of crisis. The king recognized his own weakness, eschewed his pleasures, and determined to be a worthy sovereign. But the Lords of Argyll and of Angus and those everlasting troublemakers, the Humes and the Hepburns, guessed that the king would not long stand up against them. The lords who were fighting with him knew as well as his enemies that the king was weak spirited, and planned the battle in such a way as to keep him in the background. But the Humes and the Hepburns came on fast and the thieves of Annandale rushed forward shouting, until the king "raid [rode] his way."

The rest of the story cannot be left out, whether true or not. "But he spurred his horse at the flight speed, coming through the town of Bannockburn. A woman perceived a man coming fast upon horse, she being carrying in water, came fast away and left the pig [pitcher] behind her." The king fell off his horse before the mill door and was so bruised with his fall, being heavy with armor, that he swooned away. The miller and his wife dragged him into the mill and not knowing who he was, cast him into a nook and covered him with a cloth. The king revived and asked for a priest, to make his confession. The miller and his wife asked him who he was, and he answered: "This day at morn I was your king." "Then the miller's wife clapped her hands and ran forth and cryed for a priest. In this mean time a priest was coming by (some says he was my Lord Gray's servant) who answered and said, 'Here am I a priest; where is the king?' Then the miller's wife took the priest by the hand and led him in at the mill-door; and how soon the said priest saw the king, he knew . . . him and kneeled down on his knees and speired [inquired] at the king's grace, if he might live, if he had good leechment [medical care]. He answered him, 'he trowed [believed] he might—but he would have a priest to take his advice and give him his sacrament.' The priest answered, 'That shall I do hastily,' and pulled out a whinger [dagger]

42

and struck him four or five times even to the heart, and syne got him on his back, and had him away. But no man knew what he did with him, more [nor] where he buried him." Such was the fate of a weak king.

Weakness of spirit was not confined to kings. Alexander Scott [*floruit* 1548–68], in a poem called "The Jousting and Debate betwixt Adamson and Syme," shows the two contestants urging one another into combat but somehow failing to join battle:

> Will shortly to his horse he slydes,
>   And says to Syme by name,
> Better we baith were buyand hydes   *buying*
>   And wedder kins at hame,   *wetherskins*
> Nor here, up at Dalkeith this day.

Will was a cousin in spirit of Andrew Fairservice in *Rob Roy,* a servant who, when blows were being dealt, slipped out of the way. There was the timid Scot, as there are timid men in all countries, and Sir Walter knew about the type. But such Scots were comparatively rare.

V

THE WOMEN

IN his rhymed chronicle Wyntoun tells a story of the siege of Berwick. The Scottish defender of the castle promised the English to surrender it by a certain time if he were not rescued by Scottish forces, and in token of that promise he yielded his two sons as hostages. But when the time came to yield he was still hopeful that he might be rescued. One of his sons had been drowned. The besiegers sent word that unless the castle were at once surrendered the other·son would be publicly executed outside the castle gate within sight of his father and mother. At this point a woman comes into the picture. The Scottish mother urged the father to stick fast to his determination not to give up. She was young, she told him, and was able to beget more bairns. As for her son, he would die with honor to his country.

It is in such stories, some of them no doubt mythical, that women enter the chronicles. In the dim centuries before modern times we have to rely a good deal for our knowledge of Scottish women upon casual references and incidental allusions, and they do not afford a firm basis for generalizations. The poets and ballad makers serve us better, for, although the stories they tell are often less authentic than those told by the chroniclers, they reveal attitudes toward women as well as the attitudes of women and thus throw a little light upon Scottish character.

In this chapter I shall deal with Scottish women from the early days down to the Reformation and a little beyond that, indeed, down to the Union of the Crowns in 1603. What the writers of the sixteenth century said and thought about women is so much in line with earlier thought that we can make no distinction between medieval times and the late sixteenth century.

44

The Women

From the earliest days it would appear that women shared much of the work with the men. The Highland women, eighteenth-century travelers tell us, did the work in the fields while their husbands hunted and fished and fought with their neighbors. That famous traveler, Thomas Pennant, was revolted by the servitude of the Highland women who had to do all the heavy carrying and farm work. It is a reasonable guess that the drudgery left to the women had not been less in earlier centuries. In the Lowlands women also shared in the work and could be seen in the fields with the men. Their labor was needed as it was in pioneer America. Wherever women worked with men in Scotland or America, their relative position tended to improve.

Women were indeed known to help their men in battle. When the poet Barbour in *The Brus* describes the siege of Berwick he tells how the women gathered the spent English arrows and ran with them to the men fighting on the walls. Whether Barbour in his description of the siege was historical or not hardly matters. That women should take so nearly an active part in the battle seemed not in any way surprising to him. Everyone remembers the story of the lady at the skirmish of Ancrum Moor who fought beside her lover until both her legs were gone and then fought upon the stumps.

Women were not too subordinate in matters of love. In Robert Henryson's exquisite poem, "Robin and Makyne," merry Makyne begged the shepherd, Robin, to have pity on her. Had she not loved him for two years or more? Robin was at first not interested, and by the time that he was Makyne had ceased to desire him and was laughing and singing while he "sighed sair." The chronicler Fordun tells a tale, how Martha, really Marjory, the heiress of the Earl of Carrick, was out riding one day with her attendants when she came upon a gallant knight, Robert the Bruce. A comely young man he was, and she besought him to stay and hunt with her, but seeing him unwilling, she compelled him to go home with her and within a few weeks married him, thus adding the territories of Carrick to those of Annandale which the Bruces possessed. The enterprising young woman became the mother of the great Bruce.

Now these stories fit in well with those of the female share in courtship that one finds in modern Scottish novels and plays. The Scots women were not shy, they really knew their worth, and were likely to say what was on their minds. Bunty pulled the strings sometimes in the old days as in the modern. There is less evidence than one would expect of parental control of marriage. The young people were seldom hindered of their hopes by wilful parents. The young people knew what they wanted. It is possible that they had long known. In the Gaelic story of Deirdire which Alexander Carmichael published in the *Transactions of the Gaelic Society of Inverness* we have the woman taking her full part in the matter that concerned her most. The lovely Deirdire, who had been brought up in seclusion away from men, was finally found out by friends of King Connachar and plighted to him. She and her maidens are out one day behind the house enjoying the scene and drinking the sun when they see three men passing by. Deirdire recognizes that the three are the sons of Uisne and that Naoise is "taller than the men of Erin." The three brothers hurry on, but love for Naoise is so implanted in the heart of Deirdire that she cannot resist going after him. She gathers up her garments and pursues. She cries out to him but his brothers assure him the cry is that of the lake ducks of Connachar. She cries again but the brothers say it is the cry of the gray geese. At her third cry the brothers say it is the cry of the lake swans. But Naoise turns back and the two meet and there are kisses. "From the shame that was upon Deirdire she was going into glowing blushes of fire while the trembling hues of her ruddy cheeks were moving as fast as the tremulous leaves of the aspen tree of the stream." "Naoise bethought to himself that he never saw in bodily form a drop of blood so lovely as this; and Naoise gave a love to Deirdire that he never gave to thing of vision or to living form but to herself alone."

The story is not unlike that of the heiress of Carrick. Indeed

46

Deirdire, whose story is possibly two thousand years old, behaves like some of the heroines to be met in the plays and stories of Barrie.

The great ladies of Malory and of the French romances for whom gallant knights went riding in quest of glory did not exist in Scottish poetry. There were no Guineveres and Enids. The two Scottish poems that come nearest to presenting love stories of the chivalric type were *The Kingis Quair*, written probably by James I, and "Squire Meldrum" by Lyndsay of the Mount. Yet neither of those poems really belongs to the chivalric type. In *The Kingis Quair* the speaker, i.e., the king, who is a prisoner in England, chances to look down from his terrace in the castle and sees in the garden below a lovely woman. At once his heart, his will, his nature, and his mind "are changit clene richt in another kind." But the king threw no glove, he entered no tournaments wearing her colors. Rather he set forth in fresh verse what a woman might be in a man's life. There was no courtly love in the medieval Scottish tradition but intensity of feeling for one woman. Nor is Sir David Lyndsay's "Squire Meldrum" a story of courtly love in the French romantic manner. Squire Meldrum was an historic person whom Sir David had known and whose adventures he related, no doubt with exaggeration. In the story the squire, who had fought in France and at sea and then had returned to Scotland, came in his journeyings to the castle of a young widow who received him openhandedly. Next morning early she entered his room and gave him little chance to resist her wooing. It was not long after that she was bearing him a child and arranging to marry him as soon as the Pope would give her a dispensation (the two being related). The episode is romantically handled, and yet Lyndsay treats the lady neither as a highly romantic character nor as a naughty creature, but as a delightful and natural woman who did not conceal her liking and who furnished a pleasant interlude in the life of his friend and hero. The lady was married against her will to another. Meldrum remained loyal to her.

Yit wald my Ladie luke, at evin and morrow
On my legend at length, scho wald not mis   *she*
How for her saik, I sufferit mekill sorrow.
Yit give I micht at this time, get my wis,   *if, wish*
Of hir sweit mouth, deir God, I had ane kis.
I wis in vaine, allace we will dissever.
I say na mair; sweit hart, adew for ever.

This was no Guinevere and Sir Launcelot business, adultery on the grand scale, but a case of Scottish true love crossed.

That true love is no less in the marriage relation. Few poets, I think, have done as well as the early Scots in expressing their deep feeling for their wives. There is so much allusion to the loyalty of women to their mates and to the affection of husbands that I cannot begin to quote as much as I should like. But I must repeat part of a poem that has often been quoted:

My heart is heich above,
   My body is full of bliss,
For I am set in luve
   As weil as I wald wiss;   *wish*
I luve my lady pure,
   And she luvis me again;
I am her serviture,
   She is my soverane.

She is my very heart,
   I am her hope and heal;
She is my joy inwart,
   I am her luvar leal;
I am her bound and thrall,
   She is at my command.
I am perpetual
   Her man, both fute and hand.

The thing that may her please
   My body sall fulfil;
Whatever her disease,
   It dois my body ill.

The Women

My bird, my bonny ane,
  My tender babe venust   *graceful*
My luve, my life alane,
  My liking and my lust.
                    •   •   •
And then is all the sorrow
  Furth of remembrance,
That ever I had afforow   *before*
  In luvis observance.
Thus never I do rest,
  So lusty a life I lead,
When that I list to test
  The well of womanheid.

Here is none of that Scottish sentimentality about love that
is so easy to find in the nineteenth century. Profound reflection on the meaning of married life has gone into the poem.
"She is my joy inward," says the lover. Whoever put it better!
That each is bound in servitude to the other is an observation
out of experience. "The well of womanhood" carries the implications that there were in women unfailing resources of
tenderness.

The affection for partners in and out of marriage, and
usually within marriage, was expressed in language that was
charming and sincere and unworn. Women were to be cherished for homely virtues.

    . . . my own sweet thing,
  My joy and comforting,
  My mirth and solacing.

The comfort and ease that women could bestow was the
theme of much verse. They commanded loyalty for the best
of reasons.

    Faithful, constant and bening   *benign*
    I sall be while the life is in me,
    And luve her best attour all thing,   *above*
    Baith fair and gude and womanly.

49

Love could be on a very high plane. But lovers could be soft too. Blind Harry in his delineation of the character of Wallace and in his narrative about the ladies around Wallace does manage to impart to the hero a kind of softness about women that reminds us of nothing so much as of some of the heroes of modern Scottish novels. Women could be soft too, yielding themselves lightly to the brave or the strong.

The Scottish poets were not given to euphemism. Arbuthnot in the *Maitland Quarto MS.* wrote:

> The blithest thing in bour,
> The bonniest in bed.

Sir David Lyndsay was equally plain spoken:

> What pleasure micht a man have more
> Than have his lady him before,
> So lusty, pleasant and perfite,
> Ready to serve his appetite.

I find less than I expected in Scottish literature about the virtue of faithfulness upon the part of husband or wife, a subject common enough in medieval writing. David I and his elder brothers, who preceded him in the kingship, were praised by Fordun because they did not shock modesty by wenching. Lindsay of Pitscottie suspected that James IV might have done better at Flodden Field had he not spent the days before the battle in an amour with Lady Heron of Ford, who was believed afterward to have given information to the English. Pitscottie breaks out into unusual indignation: "I believe the stinkand adultery and fornication had a great part of their evil [ill] success."

Chastity was indeed a virtue about which the Scottish chroniclers and poets had surprisingly little to say. The episode of Squire Meldrum and the fair chatelaine and the poet's objective attitude toward what happened have already been noted. Wallace was, next to Bruce, the most honored of Scottish heroes, and yet Blind Harry who created the Wallace of myth, shows him visiting his leman. It is true that later he

follows history by marrying his hero off to a Lanark woman.
Those damsels who entertained heroes were not wicked in
the eyes of those who wrote about them. I do not remember
a woman who was regarded as thoroughly wanton in all the
Scottish writing of medieval times. The sins of those who
yielded to love's enchantments were not avenged by public
opinion nor by the fates. The overweening emphasis upon
morality which we associate with the modern Scots is curiously missing in medieval Scotland.

Even the Scottish priests were not too concerned about
moral problems and the behavior of their parishioners. If
one may judge from the satires about them, and from some of
the more authentic records, they were often keeping paramours openly and, like good family men, looking after the
interests of their sons.

It would be wrong to imply that there was no public opinion whatever about morals before the Reformation. Many
passages could be assembled to show that good people were
expected to be chaste. But it was no great matter if kings and
great men and others were not. Certain understood codes it
was wise not to violate. The principle that those who kiss
should not tell was clearly set forth in a poem by Alexander
Scott.

> To play, syne hald your peace,   *then*
> And counsel keep, for hurting of their name.

The subordination of women to their husbands is a standard medieval theme in the literatures of France and England
and indeed in the literatures of western Europe. It is of
course to be found in Scottish literature too. Arbuthnot, who
wrote some of the most thoughtful and beautiful verse about
women did speak of them as

> To man obedient
>   Even like ane willow wand,
> Baith faithful and fervent,
>   Ay readie at command,
> They luif most leill, though men doe fail.

Lyndsay treats the subjection of women in a conventional way. Even queens, he says, should be under subjection. All women, like birds in a cage, should be kept in "thirlage."

The patience of women under the rule of trying husbands is a favorite medieval theme and the Patient Griselda of the ballad appears in many forms in many places. That virtue is mentioned by Scottish poets too but less is made of it than in most literatures.

I come now to women in society, in their relations to their fellow beings and what was expected of them in those relations. In such a discussion I must distinguish between the women of fairs and markets and the ladies whom poets apostrophized. To judge from the ballads and the early metrical tales the young women were often a lively lot. Aeneas Silvius, the Italian traveler who toured Scotland in the reign of James I, described Scottish women as comely and pleasing but rather free in their manners. They were often more than lively, they were hoydenish. It is unfortunate that the two poems, "Christis Kirk on the Green" and "Peblis to the Play," cannot be readily put into English, for the reader would be easily convinced that the young women were not always of the quietest behavior. They seem to have taken part in all the fun that was going on at markets and fairs and in taverns, and that fun was fast and furious. They were not afraid to ape their betters.

> Kittock that clekkit was yestrene   *hatched*
> The morne will conterfeit the Queen.
> And Mureland Meg that milkes the cows,
> Cleggit with clay abone the howis,   *muddied, above, thighs*
> In barn nor byir she will not bide
> Without her kirtill taill beside.   *train to her gown*

They were able to give and take, says another poet:

> Sum taunting words they have per quair   *by rote*
> That service them in all mateir.

The Women

That is a nice bit of observation about a type of young woman who has mastered a certain art of easy repartee.

What was called hoydenishness in women of the fairs and taverns corresponded possibly to what was known as merriness and gayety in the ladies whom the poets praised.

> That pleasant sort are all comfort
> And merriness to men.

So they were. The lady who welcomed Squire Meldrum to her castle may not have been of the type of Caesar's wife but she was evidently the personification of merriment and gayety.

Closely related to gayety was spiritedness. One can infer the admiration for that quality not only in comments of the poets but in the story of the Countess of Buchan who left her home and castle and rushed through dangers to put the crown on the head of Bruce, because that had been the right of her father's family. The lady who when her husband was killed in battle continued to maintain his cause against his enemies and to defend her castle against them is to be found in chronicles and more often in ballads.

> Sen that be women douchtie deidis were
> done,   *since, by, deeds*
> Baronis be blythe and hald your hartis abone   *high*

Beauty and graciousness were always features admired in women but the Scottish poets asked more. Some of them praised wit in women, by which they meant knowledge; they extolled wisdom and even broad-mindedness.

> Suppoise scho seme offendit,   *she*
> When men dois hir constraine,
> That fault is sone emendit,
> Her mynde is so humaine.

By "humaine" I think the poet means that she has a breadth of understanding to accept control lightly, that she is above small pride.

One virtue expected of women in medieval times and in other times was to be religious. It became women to be more devoted to the Church than were men. And devoted they were, as for example, to go far back, Margaret, the wife of Malcolm III, whose good deeds were set down by her chaplain and biographer. In Lyndsay's satirical writings we find women under the influence of the priests. But in general Scottish women of the earlier period do not seem given over to piety. There was no other queen especially devoted to such observances as Margaret's. Nor was the Lady Wallace especially devoted to the Church, nor the wife of Bruce, nor the daring Countess of Buchan. The women in the ballads watch for their husbands to return from battle, but little is said about their prayers for the interposition of the Deity. Rather they seem realists, awaiting bad news.

The Scottish women were abundantly able to take care of themselves. But there were times when they needed special consideration. In Barbour's story of the royal Bruce there is a touching illustration of consideration for a woman. Bruce's army was on the march when the king heard a woman cry, and, asking the reason, was told that it was one of the washer-women who followed the army, and that she was in the pains of childbirth. Bruce ordered a tent set up for her and women sent in to help her and commanded that the army should not move forward until she had been delivered of her child.

> For certis, I trow, there is no man
> That he ne will rew upon woman.   *have pity*

VI

POVERTY AND CHARACTER

THE character of a people is naturally affected by the economic conditions to which over a considerable period they have been subjected. To some degree the generous virtues flourish where there is constant and widely distributed prosperity, and the faults of selfishness accompany continuous poverty. Prosperity, to be sure, breeds such unpleasant traits as self-satisfaction, arrogance, want of initiative, and sheer laziness. Poverty sometimes makes necessary mutual helpfulness and neighborliness and even self-sacrifice. Yet the observer cannot but believe that when men and women have some margin of ease and comfort of living the virtues of disinterestedness are likely to blossom. On the other hand when over a period people are desperately hard put to it, when they are driven merely to keep hunger and cold away, they easily become mean and grasping and have little gratitude even to those that help them. They become constricted in their outlook, seeing neither beyond their street nor beyond the next day. They have neither time nor energy to indulge the imagination. That wonderful gift of making new connections, of reaching out beyond the immediate scene, of interpreting the situation, seems to be bestowed upon those who have some leisure and range of movement. It is when men see themselves in wide relations that disinterestedness and idealism most easily flourish.

If a country is on the upgrade, if ease and prosperity are touching more and more people, if new groups are emerging from bitter servitude into the independence that prosperity gives, then we can expect talent to make itself evident, we can expect to see men exercising imagination and developing human sympathies. It was so in the time of Elizabeth and in the days of Victoria. The prosperity of a few will not be enough to enlist that body of men necessary to stimulate one another and set a movement going. Out of many individual imaginations working not too far from one another are born discovery and literature. Thus that there should be some political unity, or a nation conscious of itself and of its experience, is an advantage to the operation of the imagination.

These principles, which may be disputed by some of my readers, deserve at least to be kept in mind tentatively as we shall follow the ups and downs of Scottish history and the various expressions of character. They deserve to be remembered in considering not only what did happen but what might have happened. They have relation to the economic condition of Scotland pictured in this chapter.

Scotland had, it will be recalled, an early golden age, from the time of David I (1124–53) to Alexander III (1249–86). The country had become unified politically; larger and larger groups of people were doing rather well; there was a center to Scottish life in a court that had some pomp and circumstance. There was as yet neither much leisure nor much national consciousness nor much chance for reflection. Had the golden age continued, had Alexander III been succeeded by men of a similar type, it is possible that there might have been a flowering of talent and that poets and biographers might have appeared in due time. Such a possibility was cut off by the Wars of Independence and by the invasions that followed.

Instead of moving toward a great age, Scotland was destined to go through hundreds of years of disunion and poverty.

She was not a fertile country in any case. I have already adverted to the relief map of Scotland in order to indicate how divided up the country was. But one can well look at such a relief map to show how small was the proportion of good valley land. From the air much of Scotland must look like the involutions and convolutions of the brain, fold after fold of elevations. Between the Clyde and the Forth, running southeast to the hills that guard the Border, between the Lammermuirs on the east and the hills of the southwest, there was a long stretch of good land, some of the best in Scotland. North of the Forth in Perthshire and Fifeshire and more narrowly along the east coast as far north as Aberdeen were good slices of piedmont land. And all through the mountains in the north were valleys that sometimes contained long narrow strips of comparative fertility. But when one adds together all the valley land of Scotland it comes to very little in the total area. Indeed when one compares the farm land of Scotland with that of England, one sees why the country was so much poorer. England had, to be sure, her Pennine range in the northwest, but even in that hilly region there was really more land worth grazing than in most of the Highlands. The Yorkshire moors in the old days were capable of carrying many sheep while a considerable proportion of the Highlands was too steep and rocky to support even sheep.

Scotland's wealth in the early days consisted in her fish and game, her cattle and sheep. From the earliest days fish were a standard commodity in Scotland. The lochs and firths were full of them. Fishing was the surest way to make a living. Herring and salmon were most often mentioned but there were many others. So many fish were caught that the Scots could not only supply their own needs but export to England and to the Continent.

But fishing was at all times a dangerous occupation. The lochs were narrow, winds came up suddenly from every direction, and the shores nearest were often precipitous. A man had to have skill of boats, skill of winds and currents, skill of fishing tackle, and be able to endure the hardships of wind and wave and rain. He needed to know where to find the fishing. In other words he had to be a man of some "ingine" or natural talent.

The hills and mountains were full of game, deer, birds, and various kinds of fur-bearing animals, the skins of which furnished one of Scotland's chief exports. Tracking and catching these animals required bodily agility and a knowledge of animal habits as well as of terrain.

As for the raising of cattle and sheep, all the hills of the southwest as well as the Cheviots, the Lammermuirs, and the Pentlands offered grazing country. Where the hills were steeper and the cattle could not go the sheep would clamber. The problem of the Scottish sheep and cattle men was to keep their wealth. In a country where feudalism still prevailed and where there was little general organization of justice, driving off cattle and sheep was almost one of the recognized sports of the time. You appealed to your feudal overlord to help you regain your stock; in that foray to regain what had been lost your lord and his fellow retainers were not unlikely to bring back more if possible than what had been driven away. Sheep and cattle were a primary source of wealth and the maintenance of a capital in that form required active men who were ready to ride at any time of day or night and ready to ride into combat.

> Broken keep and burning farm
> Taught his fathers strength of arm;
> Feud and fight from gate to gate
> Showed them how to nurse their hate.

All along the Border were peel castles, narrow round towers built with walls from six to eight feet thick, almost unassailable points, to which men might retire when hard pressed.

Sheep raising was an occupation that must have occupied the life of many men. The shepherd figures in Scottish life as in few countries. He was celebrated in many poems. He was often pictured as a wise, reflective type of man, and so he may have been. He had to be an active, alert person and at the same time he lived much to himself out on the hills alone.

Scotland had mineral resources and was tapping them in the Middle Ages. The pursuit of blackstones, or coal, went on from an early time along the Tay and the Forth. While there was a considerable use of coal, peat was the more common fuel.

Scottish agriculture was at its best in the fertile plain of the Lowlands called Lothian, and yet even there it was what might have been expected in medieval times. The people had possibly been long moving from a pastoral to an arable economy. There was no such carefully developed system of manors as in England. The Normans had not conquered Scotland and "were not in a position," says I. F. Grant, "to work out their theories in Scotland, as they had done in England." That meant that the relationship between classes was more fluid. It is also probably true that there was between landlords, tenants, and bondmen a greater degree of loyalty than in England. "In Scotland more than elsewhere into the purely feudal relationship had crept something of the greater warmth and fervour of the simpler and more ancient bond of union of the clan."

There was not always as much security. Under the general Scottish system the farmers gained no such permanent rights over the lands they worked as the copyholders in England. In many instances they were given short leases which meant that they had little encouragement to develop and improve their holdings. There were many different kinds of farming in Scotland but the infield and outfield system was the common method in Lothian and in many other parts of the country. The infield, Grant tells us, was the best land, or that nearest the farm. It was held by "run-rig," that is, in intermixed strips, where were grown barley and oats and sometimes peas and beans. The outfield was given up to pasture, one small portion of which might however be plowed this year and another small portion the next. The system was of course wasteful and inefficient, as similar strip systems were in England and on the Continent.

The English at a later date accused the Scottish farmers of being shiftless about their farming and asserted that one could see Scots plowing with their coats on. In many in-

stances the farmers seem to have left the hard work of the
fields to the laborers. John Major declared that the farmers
tried to rival the lesser gentry and brought up their sons to
live in the country and to follow war. One does not get from
him a picture of intelligent and zealous farmers.

But Major, who gives one a sense of being an observant
and fair person, may be telling the truth. It is amazing that
the Scottish poets have almost nothing to say about the joys
of cultivating the fields. One passage in Henryson is the only
one of the sort that I have seen.

> Moving thusgait greit mirth I tuke in mynd,   *in this manner*
> Of lauboraris to se the besines,
> Sum makand dyke, and sum the pleuch can
>   wynd,   *making, plow*
> And sawand seidis fast from place to place.   *sowing*
>   . . .
> It was greit joy to him that luffit corne
> To se them laubor baith at evin and morne

Henryson was a Fifeshire man and he lived in a fertile
county, where the laborers might be seen in numbers. It is
to be feared that old habit made many farming people less
keen about the land than about fighting. They liked to be
off in the train of an overlord for a spell of warfare. War
was more exciting than field work. With so many wars
going on, the Scot was often a returned soldier, and the
returned soldier has often found it hard to settle down to
everyday effort.

The violence of the time was no help to the farmer. "In
those days," says a chronicler, "there was no law in Scotland, but the great man oppressed the poor man, and the
whole kingdom was one den of thieves. Slaughters, robberies,
fire-raisings and other crimes went unpunished and justice
was sent into banishment, beyond the kingdom's bounds."
Much of the best farming land, as we have noted, was close
to the English border within easy range of the invading

Poverty and Character

parties that came across from Northumberland. Lyndsay of the Mount speaks feelingly of the effect of war upon the wretched farm laborer:

> Oppression did so loud his bugle blow
> That none durst ride but into fear of weir   *war*
> Jok-upon-the land that time did miss his mair.

He lost not only his mare but his cows and his sheep; his barns were burned and his fields overrun. It was little wonder that the farmers became careless in their work. To farm at all must have required long patience.

The Wars of Independence and the many wars with England that followed, as well as the struggles of the nobles with one another, injured not only the farmers but the merchants in the burghs. In an earlier day, from the time of David I to that of Alexander III, the Scots had been doing rather well. Aildred of Rievaulx, who wrote the life of David I, pictured Berwick as at that time a flourishing town, doing an import and export business. The Scots sold abroad salmon, herring, and other fish, hides and skins, wool and coarse woolen cloth, and imported wine and wood, spices, pepper, alum, ginger, almonds, figs and raisins, onions, garlic, honey, olive oil, thread for nets and linen thread, deals and knives, cooking pots, wax and soap. The import and export business was not so good in the long period from Bruce to Knox; yet merchants did venture forth and sometimes did rather well. In the "Thrie Tailes of the Thrie Priestis of Peblis," one of the fathers paints a picture of a successful merchant who started in a small way,

> With hap and halfpenny, and a lamb's skin;
> And purelie ran fra toun to toun on feit,   *poorly*
> And that richt oft wetshod, werie and weit   *wet*

He bought a horse and then a cart, and moved into town. He grew rich and went to sea and bought a ship of his own. He had a silver basin in which to wash, and three thousand pounds in his cupboard.

> Riche wes his gounis with uther garmentis gay—
> For sonday silk, for ilk day grene and gray.
> His wyfe was cumlie cled in scarlet reid   *red*

The priest was telling a fancy tale but no doubt he knew Scottish bourgeoisie who had put ships to sea and done well. Few merchants in the Scottish burghs prospered in any such way. They had little capital on which to build up large enterprise. What capital they had consisted in buildings and goods likely to be destroyed by the English in their raids. That they managed even to maintain themselves during the long period of wars and anarchy is worth remark. A great deal of the business of the Scottish burghs was farming the burgh lands. The Scot was learning against great handicaps to thrive in a small way. It was a skill his descendants were to inherit.

The Scots may be compared with the English in this respect. Through their near monopoly of wool the English learned at an early date that whatever taxes were put upon them by an acquisitive government, they could raise prices and make a profit. Their long experience with the woolen trade and much later their start over other nations in large-scale industry taught them that they could succeed without counting costs closely. They never calculated as closely as the Scots. They did not need to do so.

The poverty of the Scots impressed their neighbors to the south, who were so largely responsible for it. The Spaniards, the Venetians, and the French who sojourned in north Britain also commented on the miserable hovels of the peasantry and the lightly built dwellings in the towns, upon the ill-kept fields and upon the prevalence of beggary. The French knights who had come over to Scotland to march against England exclaimed: "We have never known till now what was meant by poverty and hard-living." It became customary to pity and despise the poor and miserable Scots. Aeneas Silvius writing in the reign of James I (1424-1437) speaks of the poor people whom he saw begging at the church doors and being given blackstones for fuel. He tells us that the towns had no walls and that the houses were constructed for the most part without lime, that is, of mud. In the country, he says that the roofs of the houses were built of turfs and the doors of hides. Other foreign writers speak of the houses as possessing but a single room and no floors, and often a pile of dung in the middle of the room. The arrangements for sleeping and eating seemed to the English, whose own at that time would appear crude to us, to be incredibly primitive. English travelers as late as the seventeenth century were shocked at the sanitary arrangements in the houses of the Scottish farming people, even in homes that were fairly commodious. The poorest whites in the American South are probably better provided with sanitation than were common folk among medieval Scots.

What increased the appearance of poverty was the clothes of the men and women, skins of animals and coarse colored fabrics thrown loosely about them. Scotland was a comparatively cold northern country but the people had apparently accustomed their bodies to the cold and wore clothes that did not cover them adequately.

The French Froissart, from whom we learn so much of interest in late medieval times and who has given us the story of the wars between France and England, was deeply impressed by the poverty of Scotland. "You will never find a man of worth [means]," he wrote. "They are like savages who wish not to be acquainted with anyone and are too envious of the good fortune of others, and suspicious of losing anything themselves, for their country is very poor."

The poverty of Scotland was a problem to Sir David Lyndsay, who wrote in the early sixteenth century. He knew no fairer people nor men of "fairer ingine." Why then were they so poor?

The Scot in History

The fault is not, I dare well take in hand,
Neither in the people nor the land.

He concluded that the land lacked labor and the people
"governing." There was a want of justice, of policy, and of
peace.

Great commodities Scotland had, he asserted, fish in the
sea and cattle on the mountains, metals both gold and silver
in the mountains, and precious stones. He was right about
the commodities, save that he overstated the amount of gold
and silver to be found. But it is clear enough that the people,
save in the hill country of the southwest and of the north,
had enough to eat, if not a great variety. It was a small
population, probably less than half a million, that needed
to be supplied, and there must have been at least as much
game and fish as today. Aeneas Silvius wrote: "These people
were poor but had plenty of flesh and fish to eat." Etienne
Perlin, the French traveler, says almost the same thing, that
the Scots were poor but had plenty of provisions. They had
milk, butter, and cheese, and some fruit but not many veg-
etables. Bread they had not enough of, and it was poor
bread at that; oatmeal cakes served instead. The Scot was
used to a spare diet but he made his food go a long way. His
poverty consisted in wretched housing and inadequate cloth-
ing and in his poor equipment for his work.

But the picture was not wholly dark. Conditions during
the fourteenth, fifteenth, and sixteenth centuries were almost
static. There was, nevertheless, increasing prosperity in the
Lothian country to the southeast, prosperity that could not
be wholly prevented, in spite of English invasions. It was in
the Lothians that the Angles had settled, and though they
had for a time been overcome by the Gaels, they were able
to make their influence felt and to give the Lowlands much
of the special character it eventually attained.

Furthermore, there was a class on the rise in Scotland,
coming up in spite of the bad times, and that was the serf
class. One gathers that the serfs were winning their freedom

64

as early as in England, indeed a bit earlier. Now the striking thing about England is that by mid-sixteenth century
there were practically no serfs left. The descendants of the
servile class were paying money instead of rendering services
and had become freemen. In this respect England was far
ahead of the rest of Europe, save the Scandinavian penin-
sula. Scotland was also ahead. Within a century after the
Wars of Independence, to be ultra-conservative in statement, by the reign of James I (1424–37), there were hardly
any serfs left in Scotland.

The disappearance of villeinage in England meant the
rise of a widespread middle class, and with that the emergence of talent. The enterprise, the initiative, the daring,
the imagination of the Elizabethan Age are connected in
some degree with the large body of freemen on the upgrade.
Since the emancipation of the villein class in Scotland had
come even earlier than in England, there ought to have been
something resembling the Elizabethan Age in Scotland. It
was prevented by anarchy and the English invasions.

Yet it is true that the late fifteenth and the early sixteenth
century saw the emergence of some of the greatest of Scottish poets. I am not thinking so much of the anonymous
ballad makers, whose skill in poetical narrative of a certain
kind has never been excelled, but of such poets as Dunbar,
Robert Henryson, Gavin Douglas, and Sir David Lyndsay.
Those men and other poets whose works have been lost to
us showed a thoughtfulness and an ability to interpret the
human scene they knew that is far beyond the reach of most
of the later Scottish poets. It is true that they all drew upon
the classical writers for themes and characters but they said
much that was original and Scottish. Had Scotland had some
peace and general prosperity it is hard to say how long and
important might have been her poetic efflorescence. The
theater might have gained a start. Other forms of art might
have appeared. Scottish initiative might have shown itself
in many ways.

Due to the poverty and violence of her people Scotland

missed many possibilities. Poverty made for violence and violence for poverty. People who took out their fierce energies in struggles with one another and with their neighbor to the south had little energy left to improve their state of living and to develop those arts which would have made living more seemly and beautiful. They missed those comments on human experience which great writers and artists might have offered them. They missed in large degree the Revival of Letters and all the wealth of Greek and Roman reflection on living. They missed a Reformation of an English type that was indeed a kind of Renaissance of the individual. In its stead they had a Reformation that turned the Scottish mind from an intellectual and imaginative consideration of human affairs to a Hebraic and rigidly moralistic outlook upon living.

Their poverty cost them much. It was positively injurious as well. It emphasized the less pleasant aspects of life, the meanness, the roughness, the parochialism.

VII

A NATIONALISTIC PEOPLE

NATIONAL feeling was slow to emerge anywhere in western Europe. Men had been accustomed to be loyal to their feudal overlords. The conception of a nation had to make its way politically and to gather feeling about it. The French did not begin to feel themselves Frenchmen until almost modern days. The English first displayed nationalism in the reign of Henry III when the king was distributing his favors to the incoming Frenchmen. There was a flashing up of English feeling in Parliament in the reign of Edward I when the Pope was taking money out of England. But it was with Henry V's successful wars with France that the English began to gain a strong sense of patriotism. The defeat of the Spanish Armada in the late days of Elizabeth made patriotism a significant feature of English character.

The beginnings of national feeling in Scotland were a little later than in England. Many factors operated against the rise of nationalism in the north. The Scots had been several peoples originally, like most nations, and were only with difficulty welded into one. Even when that welding had been accomplished politically, the various peoples remembered old loyalties and fought for them, as at the battle of Harlaw. The Highlanders were a people unlike the Scots of the south and east, and the Norse of the west coast and of the Isles were a breed of their own. There were smaller loyalties to chieftains and lords that seemed more vital than any conceivable national loyalties.

It will be recalled that the Scottish nobles continued long after Scotland had been unified to rule over their own little principalities and to make combinations against the king whenever it suited them. Naturally they constituted an element that interfered with the growth of national feeling. We have seen that some of them were Normans with estates in both England and Scotland, men who looked toward two kings and could not be wholly Scottish in their attitudes. That divided allegiance continued until rather a late date.

In most countries patriotism tended to gather about the person of the king. Henry V and Elizabeth were sovereigns of England who commanded loyalty and whose persons seemed the embodiment of the State. The Scots were not so fortunate. After Robert the Bruce there was no king of Scotland whose fame and personality drew the Scots to him as Henry V and Elizabeth drew the English to them by their success and vividness. James I and James IV might conceivably have done so had they lived. But the Scottish kings reigned too briefly to be successful, and had too many enemies with famous old names. The kingship was not able to accumulate prestige around it or win glory or surround itself with religious sanctions. Scottish feudalism was an enemy to more than political unity; it was foe to the quality of kingship and to that patriotism that needed personalization.

It is usually a threat from outside that rouses national feeling and so it was in Scotland. If the Scots were a little later than the English in the first awakening to national feeling, they were more deeply affected by that awakening than the English. The Wars of Independence against England made the Scots realize that they were one people and implanted patriotism in them. The two personalities of that struggle were men singularly fitted to gather national feeling about them. Wallace, it will be recalled, never won much support from the natural leaders of Scotland, the nobility, but in some way rallied the common folk of Scotland to his standard. We know so little about him that it is hard to say just what his special quality was. It must have been something more than courage and daring, of which he had much. That he could bring men from the Lowlands, from the Highlands, and from the Western Isles to serve under him suggests that he had some largeness of outlook. That the clergy supported him indicates some belief in his disinterestedness. He had an intensity of purpose that appealed to his countrymen. His victory at Stirling Brig gave the first hope to the oppressed Scots that they had had for a long while. His defeat at Falkirk, his lonesome underground movement, his capture and cruel execution, none of them lessened the feeling of the Scots for him. His career was easily the stuff out of which legends are made.

We know more about Bruce and he was as well fitted as Wallace to be a Scottish hero. Courage he showed and infinite patience, and he rallied at length forces from the various parts of the Lowlands and from the Highlands to his standard at Bannockburn. There the Scots stood to fight for "wife and child and freedom." Bruce was successful and made Bannockburn the name that Scots best remembered. Bruce's Testament became a kind of primer of Scottish policy.

The two men came to be heroes of youth. In a time when there were no novels to affect the ideals of the young, the epics about Wallace and Bruce must have been the inspiration of youth. Those lasses who sang at their work about the battle of Harlaw no doubt could recite stories about the Bruce and Schir William Wallace. There were to be new heroes in later times, John Knox, Andrew Melville, Montrose, and Sir Walter Scott, but none of them took the place of the wight Wallace and the guid King Robert.

Scottish patriotism gathered around the names of two heroes and around an abstract word—freedom. Freedom might have meant many things. To the Scots in their long struggle against English domination it meant one thing, independence. It was the freedom that Edward I had tried to take away from them. His military men had given them experience in what it was to be a subordinate nation. "Chains and slavery" they had found it, though it was Burns long after who used those words. The historians of Scotland who began early to develop elaborate fictions about her past were on firm ground when they told of Scotland's demand for freedom. Freedom was the magic word of Scotland's long story. The Scots did not mean freedom of the individual as against the king, as the English meant, but freedom as against a foreign potentate, and particularly against any English king. In 1318 the earls, barons, and free tenants declared: "While there exists a hundred of us, we will never submit to England. We fight, not for glory, wealth or honor, but for that liberty which no virtuous man shall survive." The early chronicles were full of a fierce feeling for liberty. But poets express such things best, and it was Barbour, in *The Brus*, who exclaimed:

> Alas! that folk that evir wes fre,
> And in fredome wont for to be,
> Throw that gret mischance and foly,
> War tretyt than so wikkytly,
> That thar fays thar iugis war: *foes, judges*
> What wretchedness may man have mar?   *more*
> A! fredome is a noble thing!
> Fredome mais man to haiff liking;   *makes*
> Fredome all solace to a man giffis.

George Buchanan, the great Scottish humanist, was guilty of boasting when he wrote:

> The Scot alone could freedom boast!
> The Goth, the Saxon, and the Dane
> Poured on the Scot their powers in vain—
> And the proud Norman met a foe
> Who gave him equal blow for blow.

Buchanan went on to assert that only the Scots were able to hold the Romans in check. The historians were pushing freedom a long way into the past.

It has to be admitted that the patriotism of the Scots was not wholly a virtuous enthusiasm about themselves. The elements were mixed in it, and a chief one was hatred. Ralph Sadleir, writing in 1543 to the English king, declared: "Such malicious and despiteful people, I think, live not in the world,

as is the common people of this realm, specially towards Englishmen, as I have well found and proved since my coming
hither." Sadleir in his daily movements in Edinburgh had
chances to sense Scottish antagonism, and he was not given
to overstatement. The Scots hated the people with whom
they had fought so many wars.

It is unnecessary to go over the story of why they hated
England. The reasons appear in the chapters behind and the
chapters ahead—so many byres destroyed, so many towns
burned by the invaders from the south. Yet the fault was not
all on one side. The Scots occasionally came to the support
of France by thrusting down into Northumberland. Furthermore the good old game of stealing cattle went on from both
sides of the Border. It was indulged in as much by Scottish
Douglases as by English Percys, as much by the thieves of
Liddesdale and Annandale as by the English reivers of the
Middle Border.

When Johnny Armstrong, who had been a law to himself
on the Border, was captured by the king of Scotland, he
pleaded for his life, setting forth his good deeds in spoiling
the English. He would have stolen meat and malt from England as long as he lived.

> She [England] suld have found me meat and maut,   *should*
>   And beef and mutton in a' plentie.
> But never a Scot's wife could have said
>   That e'er I skaithed her one puir flea.   *harmed*

No Scot had suffered from his raids. Was he not a patriot?
Patriotism was not enough; he was condemned to be hanged,
and exclaimed bitterly:

> To seek het water beneath cauld ice,
>   Surely it is a great folie.

Johnny Armstrong was well hanged. That the ballad makers
and probably the men of Liddesdale and Annandale and

many other Scots this side of the ill-reputed dales were on his side was to be expected. Why should the king of Scots hang so great an enemy of the English? Johnny Armstrong, and another reiver, Jamie Telfer, became the heroes of ballads, and they and their fellow reivers were part of the story of Scottish antagonism to the English. Cattle thieves and their admirers also serve in developing patriotism.

The Scots did not keep all their hate for the English. Now and then their national feeling was roused against the French. Traditionally, of course, the French were their friends, who had supported them against the English. Was there not the Auld Alliance and tender allusions to it? Yet sometimes the Scots grew weary of those friends. When the French soldiers came to the assistance of Robert the Second, the Scots began to murmur and say, "What devil has brought them here? or who has sent for them? Cannot we carry on our wars with England without their assistance? . . . We neither understand their language nor they ours. . . . They will very soon eat up and destroy all we have in this country, and will do us more harm, if we allow them to remain amongst us, than the English could be in battle. If the English burn our houses, what consequence is it to us? We can rebuild them cheap enough, for we require only three days to do so, provided we have five or six poles and boughs enough to cover them."

When in the early sixteenth century it was a question of bringing in the Duke of Albany from France to be governor of the country during James V's minority, the answer of the chancellor, according to Lindsay of Pitscottie, was that the duke knew not the "nature of our country, nor our laws, nor execution so well as our own lords that is born and gotten in Scotland and has our language; therefore my lords I think it best for me to choose one of our own lords who understands us and we him and kens the qualities of Scotland."

The Scots had some notion themselves, then, of the qualities of Scotland. They thought they kenned them. Would that

72

they had tried to say what they believed those qualities to be!

One of them was obviously patriotism. No one would have denied that to the Scots. It was not rooted in reverence for old institutions, nor was it love for Caledonia stern and wild. It was as yet little more than a passionate dislike of intruding enemies and devotion to warriors who had fought against them. It was not yet emotion sublimated into something higher. It did not rouse the poets. When the "makars," the poets, Dunbar and Henryson and Lyndsay came along, and the ballad makers of the early sixteenth century, they had almost nothing to say about freedom or love of country.

Today the Scots have as much feeling for their ain folk as any people in any time, a feeling that has nothing to do with hate. Their love of country is broad and deep, grounded upon experience of use and wont and faith in them; upon experience of many ups and downs of fortune; upon memories of men and deeds and confidence in future men; upon recollections of castled summits and highland glens, even of ballads and songs.

VIII

TRAITS INBORN

IN this and the following chapter I am going to deal with
certain characteristics of the Scots to be found in the
days before the Reformation. It is impossible to classify
those characteristics in any strict fashion. In this chapter I
shall deal with qualities of the Scottish people that in general
seemed to be natural to them from an early time. In the
following chapter I shall mention certain qualities of the
Scots that can be more readily explained by their circumstances and their history. But I would not press the distinction. Who knows whether a certain characteristic of a people
is part of their racial inheritance or a result of their environ-
ment and of what has happened to them? It is easy to believe
that often a national characteristic was inherited and yet accentuated by circumstances. It is hardly possible that any
trait of a people is wholly the result of their history. I am
making a distinction that is convenient for purposes of treatment and may have some validity.

It has been said again and again that there is something
"clean contrair" about the Scots. The reader will have observed earlier that they were given to the fantastic and yet
were realists. I have already commented on their cruelty
and treachery and now the time has come to say that they
were also a kindly and friendly people. We cannot examine
the episodes of Scottish history in the days before the Reformation without realizing that with their continuous warfare
and savagery there was an oncomingness and warmhearted-
ness about them toward their fellows. The Scots indeed
thought of themselves as the "kindly Scots." Caius Julius
Solinus, writing in the third century A.D. had called them
"affable and kind to their own people." The whole clan system
was based upon mutual kindness and consideration. It had

given a friendly personal quality to the feudal relationship. Bishop Leslie, no mean or partisan observer of his countrymen, tells us of the hospitality of the nobility who lived deep in the country in their castles. "With glad will and freely they use to lodge kin, friend, and acquaintance, yea, and the stranger that turns in to them. A slandrous thing they esteem it to be to deny this and a point of small or no liberality." We may fairly assume that the customs of the nobility were imitated by the lesser fry, so far as they had facilities. Hospitality was part of the code of the Highlanders as far back as we know anything about them. In 1498 Pedro de Ayala had called the Scots partial and hospitable to foreigners. That agreeable sense of being welcomed that foreigners felt in Scotland was not a delusion. The warmth of manner can be recognized in the early metrical romances, in the ballads, and more particularly in the historical narratives. One can read the English chroniclers at length and find nothing of the sort. But in Scottish narratives one is always coming upon pleasant and even dramatic scenes of meeting. The woman who welcomed the hard-pressed Bruce to her house, not knowing that he was the king, is an example. The Scots were glad to meet one another; they made a fuss about people. They liked to do favors and to praise one another. When not suspicious of the stranger, they would use the bonny word to make him feel at home or would help him on his way. They liked their fellows, unless for their own or family reasons they happened to dislike them. The come-hitherishness that is mentioned in modern Scottish writing is no new characteristic of the Scots.

They were an emotional people. The narratives of Scottish history are crammed with scenes of "greeting," that is, weeping. Alexander Lindsay the fourth Earl of Crawford, known as the Tiger, and more commonly as Earl Beardie, from his long beard, made an alliance against James II with the Earl of Douglas and Macdonald of the Isles, Earl of Ross. When the king sent for Douglas and stabbed him Earl Beardie broke into rebellion. Through treachery he was defeated at the battle of Brechin. Abandoned by his friends he finally came bareheaded and barefoot before the king. The earl, who was liable to death for his rebellion, made his "wriesome" to the king, appealing to Scottish history and recounting in detail the deeds of his famous predecessors who had ever "lost their lives for the liberty and welfare of this realm." He went on: "Finally it is neither the fearful enduring of my dearest spouse, nor the greeting of my bairns, nor the lamentable sobbing of my friends, nor yet the heirship of my lands that moves me so mickle as the decay of our house and lamentable change and fortune of the noblemen of Angus with the rest of my adherents, whose lands, lives and goods stands in danger for my cause." Lindsay of Pitscottie goes on to picture the scene that followed the earl's appeal. "When the earl had ended, the nobles and gentlemen of Angus that came in his company to seek remission, held up their hands to the king most dolorously crying mercy, till that sobbing and sighing cut the words so sair that almost their prayers could not be understood, through the which there raise sic ruth and pity among the company that men could scarcely contain themselves from tears and mourning. And so every man began to implore the king's Majesty for respite to the earl and his assistars." It is not surprising that the king was unable to resist their pleas.

Such scenes of open weeping can be found throughout the records of medieval Scotland. The royal Bruce, his friend the good Sir James Douglas, Wallace, and other heroes were easily moved to tears. There is no suggestion that such tears were unworthy of strong men. They fell to weeping much as did the Greek and Trojan heroes in Homer.

What seems more purely Scottish was the predilection of the poets for the fantastic. Throughout medieval Scottish poetry there is a note of the utterly unrestrained, the unreal, the wild and eerie, some blending of other worlds and this, something utterly topsy-turvy. To be sure there was a good deal of the topsy-turvy all through medieval literature, and this world and the next were strangely and amusingly mixed up. Yet the Scots of medieval times seem to be more imaginatively fantastic than continental writers. The purely fantastic may have some old Gaelic roots. It is to be found in the Scottish poets from Dunbar down to modern times. Two poems by Dunbar deserve mention: "The Dance of the Seven Deadly Sins" and "The Little Interlude of the Droichis [dwarfs]." It is impossible to quote these at length because the language is too medieval to be understood, but the reader will perhaps tolerate a bit of quotation. In the "Dance of the Seven Deadly Sins," Mahoun, that is Satan, gives a dance in hell. The harlots with their haughty ways come in but Mahoun does not laugh until the priests appear with their bare shaven necks and then all the fiends laugh and make jibes against them. Boasters, braggers, and bargainers pass in pairs, flatterers, backbiters, and gossips go by. But no minstrels or gleemen were present, for they were not allowed in hell.

Then cryed Mahoun for a Heleand padjane,	*pageant*
Syne ran a feynd to feche Makfadyane,	*then*
Far northward in a nuke,	*nook* or *corner*
Be he the correnoch, had done	
schout,	*coronach* or *war-cry, shouted*
Erschemen so gadderit him abowt,	*Irishmen, gathered*
In Hell grit rowme they tuke.	*great*

"The Little Interlude of the Droichis" is ascribed to Dunbar, but not certainly, and was evidently a fragment of a play. The Blind Dwarf had been with fairies to find out marvels. His great-grandfather had struck the devil and made him howl. His grandfather when he danced made the world shake. He had ten thousand ells of plaid in his doublet.

And yit he wes of tendir youth,	
Bot aftir he grew mekle at fowth,	*in size*
Ellevin myle wid mett was his mowth,	*in measure*
His teith wes ten myle squair.	

•

He wald upoun his tais up stand,   *toes*
And tak the starnis doun with his hand,   *stars*
And sett thame in a gold garland,
   Aboif his wyvis hair.   *above, wife's*

In another place I shall quote a poem about God and the Highlander, and I could cite several poems of the same extravagant quality, the like of which is not to be found in English verse, but seems to be pure Scots. I may say in parenthesis that these fantastic poems seem to make a little fun of Highland men.

Yet along with the fantastic went a certain logic and realism. Erasmus was not the only foreigner to note the Scottish capacity for making fine distinctions and reasoning from them. Scaliger commented upon the skill of the Scots in dialectic. Alexander Scott writing in mid-sixteenth century, or a little earlier, noted this characteristic of his people:

   For lymmer lads and little lasses lo,   *impudent*
Will argue both with bishop, priest and friar.

With the disposition for dialectic went a realism that is astonishing in a people so fond of the fantastic. There was always the Scot who recognized the possible and the impossible, who refused to struggle against the inevitable. Wyntoun declared that men could often make amends for their trespasses, but in warfare when they did not follow orders, "In the neck follow the pain."

The Scots were superstitious, the Highlanders even more so than the Lowlanders. Witches, warlocks, fairies, brownies, and water kelpies figured in their daily lives. The persecution of witches came indeed later, in the last part of the sixteenth century and during the seventeenth century, and proved how dangerous a thing superstition may be. It cannot be said, however, I think, that the witch persecutions were worse in Scotland than in England. Like the English the Scots were affected by comets, and things seen in the sky, monsters, and warring armies, portents of wars to come.

In this chapter I have been confining myself to the period in Scotland between Bruce and the Reformation. But one instance of superstition that belongs twenty-five years after the Treaty of Edinburgh might have happened much earlier or much later, with different personnel and a different religion. In 1585 a pestilence was raging in Scotland. When the extreme Protestants gained the upper hand in Stirling, the pestilence there stopped at once, "not by degrees or piecemeal, but in an instant, as it were." The thieves of Annandale, those old hands at lifting goods, ransacked the pest lodges in the fields about Stirling and carried away the clothes of the infected, "but were never known to have been touched therewith themselves, or any others that got or wore the clothes." Their immunity was believed to be nothing less than the finger of God. "Let mankind advert and admire it." It required an unusual act of faith to believe that the Supreme Being was so pleased with the success of the Presbyterians that he preserved the robbers of the dead and dying from infection.

Kings and great men going forth to battle were in the chronicles pretty sure to be warned of the outcome, though they seldom heeded the warning. There are two famous stories in Scottish history that concern kings and are really much alike, and have a certain Scottish quality. James I, one of the stronger of Scottish kings, roused many enemies after his return from his imprisonment in England. It was well known that Sir Robert Graham was conspiring against him. As he crossed the Forth from Edinburgh on his way to the Christmas festivals at Perth, a woman of Ireland who called herself a soothsayer "cried with a loud voice, saying thus: 'My Lord King, an ye pass this water ye shall never turn again on life.'" One night shortly after at Perth a squire told the king that he had dreamed that Sir Robert Graham should slay him. The king himself had a dream that boded ill. One evening he was "occupied with playing at the chess, at the tables, in reading of Romans, in singing and piping, in harping and in other honest solaces of great pleasance and disport, when the woman of Ireland appeared at the door of the king's

79

court, and said she had something to tell the king, 'for I am the same woman that not long ago desired to have spoken with him at the Lithe [Forth], when he should pass the Scottish sea.' " The king sent word that she should come the morrow, and the woman went away saying: "It shall repent you that ye will not let me speak now with the king." Before morning Sir Robert Graham slew him.

The story of James IV is similar. Against the advice of his nobility and the urgings of his queen he was about to go to war against the English. It was just before Flodden in 1513. Lindsay of Pitscottie's story bears quoting, whether true or not, because it reveals an attitude.

"There came a man clad in a blue gown in at the kirk door with a roll of linen cloth, a pair of bottouns [long boots] on his feet . . . with all other hose and clothes conforming thereto. But he had nothing on his head beside red yellow hair behind and on his cheeks, which went down to his shoulders, but his forehead was bald and bare. He seemed a man of fifty-two years, with a great pikestaff in his hand, and came fast forward among the lords, crying and speiring [inquiring] for the king, saying he desired to speak with him, till at the last he came where the king was sitting in the desk at his prayers. But when he saw the king, he made him little reverence or salutation, but leaned down gruffling on the desk before him, and said . . . 'Sir King, my mother has sent me to thee, desiring thee not to pass at this time where thou are purposed, for if thou dost, thou wilt not fare well in thy journey, nor none that passes with thee.' " By the time the man had spoken these words, the evensong was nearly done and the king thought upon the words, "studying to give him an answer." "But in the mean time, before the king's face and in presence of all his lords that was about him for the time, this man vanished away and could in no ways be seen nor comprehended, but vanished away as he had been a blink of the sun or a whip of the whirlwind."

This story George Buchanan also tells as he heard it from

Sir David Lyndsay, the poet and a member of the court and a more trustworthy man than most. Sir David had been present on the occasion. The story has a touch of magic in it, and especially in the Scottish language which I have had to modernize.

It will be seen by any reader that there is an "out" to both these stories, i.e., a rational explanation. The woman from Ireland who warned James I and the squire might both of them have known of the plans of Sir Robert Graham, no great secret. As for the man who warned James IV, he may very well have been set on by some of the men around the king. by some of the nobles indeed who had no heart for the campaign, and he may have managed to make his exit before anyone noticed where he went. To the Highlanders and many Lowlanders both stories would have carried supernatural implications. To the more hardheaded Lowlander there was a rational explanation.

Now there are countless Scottish stories of that type, stories which may be taken as illustrations of the supernatural, if you have a mind, or of this earth, if you so please. How far this blending of the supernatural and the rationalist is characteristic of the Scottish character in the Middle Ages I would prefer not even to guess. But the blend of the two is interesting, because so many stories of later Calvinistic Scotland are of the same pattern. The horse on which the minister was riding refuses to go forward along a certain road; the rider against his will yields to the horse and takes the other road, and thus saves himself from flood or from men who were waiting to murder him. Was there in the Scot a strong desire for the supernatural and an ever-present leaning to the rational?

The curiosity of the Scots has a long history and was surely one of the most inborn of Scottish traits. The men who lived in deep glens between the mountains had little to see but their neighbors and turned their keen scrutiny upon them. In the poems of Dunbar there is that intense interest in those about the court and all their doings. The characters in the Scottish epics and metrical romances and in the ballads are always probing to find out. It was in the early sixteenth century that Henryson hit off his fellow Scots in these lines:

> Displeis you not, my gude maister, thocht I   *though*
> Demand your birth, your facultie and name,
> Why ye come heir or where ye dwell at hame.

Here we may recognize the modern Scot who talks to one on railway trains and asks questions, often personal questions, which the traveler unused to Scotland might resent. The Scot has long been interested in the stranger as well as in his neighbor, his place of living, his status in life, his occupation, and his success in it. He can hardly be turned aside from making inquiries.

The Scot did not take his pleasures sadly. He enjoyed this world. He had delight in "luvis'" observance in the home, in watching the domestic creatures of house and byre, in looking beyond the byre to the fields. The Scottish poets did not miss the pageant of the country. Green meadows, singing birds, flowers of May, water running over white stones, the stars on a winter night, moved them to expression that was, I think, more than conventional.

Not all the Scot's pleasures were so quiet. He loved merriment with his fellows. The insistence upon merriment is to be found throughout Scottish literature and much in the medieval literature.

> Now, let ilk man his way avance,
> Let sum ga drink and sum ga dance,
> Minstrels, blow up ane brawl of France,   *dance movement*
> Let see who hobbles best.

There are two medieval Scottish poems, "Peblis to the Play" and "Christis Kirk on the Green," that express merriment, wild, unrestrained, almost fantastic merriment. I cannot quote them at length because they were written in the old Scottish tongue. "Christis Kirk on the Green" begins

> Was never in Scotland heard nor seen
>> Sic dancing and deray,   *noise*
> Neither at Falkland on the green,
>> Nor Peblis at the play,
> As was of wowers, as I ween,   *wooers*
>> At Christs Kirk on ane day:
> There come our kitties washen clean
>> In their new kirtillis of gray,
>>> Full gay,
> At Christis Kirk of the green
>> that day.

It is impossible to pick out any single stanza in "Peblis to the Play" that gives a sense of the wild hilarity of the young people assembled for fun. Suffice it to say that the young men and women carried on in a noisy and indecorous way and that the young women were quite as boisterous as the young men and courted the indignities done to them. It is rough peasant merriment, and I do not know whether it is peculiarly Scottish or merely peasant.

The poet Dunbar urged the value of merriment.

> Be mirry, man! and tak nocht far in mynd
> The wavering of this wretchit warld of sorrow.
>> . . .
> Be Blyth in hairt for ony aventure,
> For often with wysmen it hes been said aforow,   *before*
> Without glaidness availis no tressour.

In another poem Dunbar wrote:

> Now all this time let us be merry,
> And set not by this warld a Cherry
>> Now while there is gude wyne to sell;
> The Cheil that does on dry Bread wirry,   *worry*
>> I give him to the Devil of Hell.

Dunbar praises Edinburgh as the merry town, full of joy and bliss, of play and pleasance. Sir David Lyndsay in his *Ane Satyre of the Thrie Estaittis* expressed delight in immediate pleasures:

> But give us leave to sing,
> To dance, to play at chess and tables,
> To read stories and merry fables,
> For pleasure of our King.

The poets, many of them, liked to recall festivities when gentlewomen dressed up, and when everyone went to see Robin Hood and Little John bring in birchen bobbins (knots of leaves). Before the Reformation and even for a good while after it was in progress, the people in borough and in country liked to have tournaments where young men rode at the lists and where young women, dressed in their best array, asked young men to ride in their livery. Sometimes the boroughs arranged to set bonfires going and to have "clerk plays," "As wes the custom in our elders days." Robin Hood and his merry men had a great hold in Scotland, as in England, and were given up reluctantly.

Sometimes the merriment was a bit forced. The Scot recognized that life was fleeting and danger lay in wait at every turn of the road. This life had many miseries, winter nights were long and cold, and "good lusty simmer with flowers" was too brief.

The Scot, and not only the Highlander, loved to consider the evils of this world; but not for long.

> When I have done consider
>   this warldis vanitie
> Sa brukill and sa slidder,   *brittle, slippery*
> Sa full of miserie,
> Then I remember me
>   That here there is no rest,
> Thairfore apperantlie
>   to be mirrie is best

Traits Inborn

It was "auld Maitland," Sir Richard Maitland of Lethington, who wrote these lines, and he wrote others that complained of the disappearance of merriness.

> Whair is the blythness that hes beine
> Baith in burgh and landwart sene,   *country*
> Amang lordis and ladyis schene,   *fine*
> Daunsing, singing, games and play;
> Bot now I wat not what they meine,   *know*
> All merines is worne away

Sir Richard declared that he had seen no mummers this year, and that kirkmen all dressed soberly and went no more into the choir. In another poem he commented upon the evils of the time and then continued:

> And yit I think it best that we
> Pluck up our hairt and mirrie be,
> For thoch we wald ly doun and die   *though*
> It will us helpe na thing

Maitland can hardly be called merry. He is gloomy about the whole outlook and says desperately, let us be merry anyway. And that is Scottish too. The brooding melancholy that we think of in Scottish character is chiefly to be found after the Reformation. Yet there were Lowlanders enough before then who were haunted with the cares of this world and the fear of death. They were the kinsfolk of the Yorkshiremen to be found in the Brontë novels. The Brontë characters never looked forward to any merriness. But the Scots were ready to recall past pleasures and to await and expect new days of gayety. Since this world is so bad and the next fearful, let us, said their poets, extract every bit of pleasure from it that we can.

IX

TRAITS INDUCED

IN this chapter I am going to continue the discussion of Scottish traits that appear before the Reformation, dealing now with those that seem in some degree to have developed out of the situation and history of the country. But it will be evident that the distinction between the traits natural to the Scots and those arising out of their situation and history is a tentative one.

We think of the Scots as a naturally religious people, and we assume that they have always been so. A cursory exploration of the Scottish past before the Reformation inclines one to the view that the Scots had been less affected by their Church than might have been expected. The whole medieval world of western Europe was of course religious. But as one reads Scottish chronicles and the poets one is a little surprised at the want of zeal for the Church. True it is that one early chronicler says that Scots were unwarlike and given to religion, but his testimony about their unwarlike character is so out of keeping with what we know of them that his comment on their piety may be taken with some grains of salt. Kings did endow abbeys, as David I, who proved a "sair saint" to his people because of his gifts to the Church. Queens did live devotional lives, as Margaret, wife of Malcolm III. Monastic establishments were spread over the fertile valleys along the Border and along the Forth. But few of the leaders of the country took religion to heart. The kings in general, almost all of them, were essentially secular beings, and few of them lived long enough to acquire the piety characteristic of old age. In the whole history of Scotland from Wallace to Knox, there were not more than three bishops that impressed the country with their godliness. The saints, who were a common feature of the medieval land-

scape, were rare in Scotland. The warrior class, that is the
nobles and their retainers, suspected the religious of being
weak and effeminate.

The poets indeed uttered religious ideas in abundance, but
those ideas were mostly part of the standard patter of the
times. The poets indicated other points of view. William
Dunbar in analyzing his fellow poet, Kennedy, represented
his attitude as distinctly secular:

> I will na priestis for me sing,
>   Dies illa, dies ire;   *irae*
> Na yit na bellis for me ring
>   Sicut semper solet fieri,
> Bot a bagpipe to play a spring.

The poets were of course full of the miseries of this world and
assumed that those miseries were to be compensated for by
the felicities of the next. Yet Dunbar in pagan fashion
lamented the deaths of his poetry-writing friends, the makars,
and ended every stanza: "Timor mortis conturbat me."

Alexander Arbuthnot [1538–83] felt that he had come upon
an evil age and wrote:

> Religioun now is reknit as ane fabill
>   . . .
> All houpe of heven is hauldin vanitie
> And hellis paine is comptit poetrie

No doubt most people still believed in heaven and hell in a
vague sort of way, but there were other matters that concerned them more.

The notion of God as the All-Comforting and All-Loving
was not Scottish of the old time. The Scottish poets of the
early days were more interested in nature, in flowery meads
and the changes of the seasons, than they were in that constant interposition of the Deity harped upon in more modern
Scottish writing.

If this be true, one naturally asks why. Was the want of

zeal for the Church partly the result of the fact that a Roman Christianity had been imposed upon Celts who looked back to their Culdees and their Celtic forms and had never been wholly won to the religion of Rome and of England? Was it partly because the Norman Church had never spread itself over Scotland as over England? So much of Scotland was thinly populated, villages were so far apart, that in many places no church buildings were erected and no priests sent to look out for the men behind the mountains. An archbishopric was organized late, and the bishops, it will be recalled, were most of them cadets of great families who were less interested in religious matters than in family power. No such effort or skill was put into ecclesiastical organization as in England. It was as if the Church trusted to the many monasteries that were set up, and they were most of them located, as we have seen, in the south. In England the king and the Church worked together to maintain order and to do away with anarchy. In Scotland the bishops were increasingly associated with the nobles.

By the early sixteenth century the Scottish Church was losing what hold it had. It was not so much pushed out by the Reformers; it was dying of its own weakness and corruption. Sir David Lyndsay devoted his satirizing abilities to showing up the abuses and evils of the Church and the sins of its priests and bishops. A performance of his *Satyre of the Thrie Estaittis* before the king and court drew no rebuke, nor did it produce a visible sensation. Bishop Leslie, who stayed by the Catholic Church and opposed the Reformers, admitted its abuses. Both early and late the Scottish Parliament showed itself unfriendly to the Church. But the ease with which a minority overturned the Roman Church and set up the rule of the Calvinists is perhaps the most convincing evidence that the Church had lost its hold upon the people.

All this has to be said with reservations. We have few records left and we know too little of the Church in Scotland before it began to be under fire.

Traits Induced

In one respect at least the Scottish religion before the
Reformation has a similarity to that imposed upon Scotland
by the Calvinists. The Scot was already on familiar terms
with his God. He was not afraid to speak up to the Lord. In
Robert Henryson's poem the sheep cries to the Lord:

> Lord God, why sleepis thou sa long?
> Walk, and discern my cause groundit on richt.

In his *Satyre of the Thrie Estaittis* Sir David Lyndsay makes
the character Verities say:

> Get up, thou sleepis all too long, O Lord,
> And make some reasonable reformation
> On them that does tramp down thine heavenly word,
> . . .
> O Lord, I mak Thee supplication,
> With thine unfriends let me not be oppressed.
> Now, Lord, do as ye list.
> I have na moir to say.

And now I come to the theme of Scottish democracy in the
medieval time. There was not much democracy in theory.
That a man's a man for a' that and a' that had not occurred
to poet or chronicler before the sixteenth century. Dunbar complained that men were always coming up in the
world, and despising the nobility, men whom nature made to
bear a pack. Gentlemen were a special race and it was to the
credit of Sir William Wallace that he was "cumyn of gentlemen."

> His father wes a manly knycht
> His modyre wes a lady brycht.

There was no John Ball in Scotland to ask

> When Adam delved and Eve span
> Who then was gentleman?

89

There was, to be sure, allowance for rise in rank by bravery in war. In Wyntoun's chronicle John Comyn and Simon Fraser are addressing the Scottish army before the battle of Roslin in 1303.

> The simplest now our host within
> Has gert gentilis of his kin.   *made*

That passage is long before Shakespeare's version of Henry V's address to his men on St. Crispin's Day. Common men can by courage make themselves into gentlemen.

It is to be noted further that there was no Peasants' Revolt such as that of 1381 in England. Now and again we gather that all was not well with "Jok-upon-land" and that the priests were taking away his last cow and horse. But we hear little of oppressions by the landowners and nothing of widespread and even general discontent, or of little rebellions breaking out here and there. In saying this we must be careful, for we really know little about Scottish manorial life and shall never know much, because the documents are missing. But we have seen already that the servile class gained its freedom in Scotland at an early date. It will be recalled further that the manorial system had not been organized with any such thoroughness as in England. It is true that the feudal system lasted much longer in Scotland. Men were tried for their lives in Scottish lords' courts up to the middle of the eighteenth century. But Scotland was not set off in compact manorial units as England was, units that settled the exact status of everyone in the country. The near-by manor house in England and especially in the south of England tended to keep everyone in his fixed position. Castles and the homes of landowners were farther apart in Scotland, as in the North Riding and in Westmorland and Cumberland, and men were less in awe of the lord. In England the manor house next the church and in the village was a continuous barrier against any possibility of the breakdown of the class structure.

The feudalism of the Highlands, indeed the whole clan

system which was characteristic of the Highlands and over-
lapped into the Lowlands wherever there were Gaelic influences, was not so much a force for democracy as an influence against too great subordination of the individual. There
was a ladder in the clan system but with no lower rungs;
there was no fearfully depressed class at the bottom. Clansmen fought and lived with their chiefs and were in theory related to them. We find in medieval Scottish poetry the pride
of the chief in his young men and their pride in his prowess
and power. Men so joined in kinship and fierce loyalties to
one another must have exercised some freedom with one
another. When we begin to learn about the Highlands in
early modern times we find that men fought gladly for their
leader and stood little in awe of him, and we may fairly assume that such was the situation in medieval times. Men engaged in a common warlike task and thrown much together
needed no doubt stern discipline, but those pictures of the
clansmen which we get impress us little with that discipline
but rather with the free and easy relationship of the men to
their chief. If there was no clan, there was a group who
adhered to some great noble, held land from him, and fought
for him when fighting was called for. They looked to him as
a leader and he saw to it that they were protected from harm
and even from poverty. There was a man at the top of the
ladder and a few men near him probably and the rest were
on the middle of the ladder. That was far from social democracy but it was not a highly aristocratic system. Few individuals felt crushed down under it. Men had some chance to
become persons of importance, especially if they were coura-
geous in battle.

The ballads ought to give us some hint of a democratic
outlook, although few ballads, it must be remembered, go
back earlier than the sixteenth century, and furthermore the
ballads have to do mostly with the Border men and in particular with Border reivers. The simple lassie in the song has kilted
her coat of green satin up to the knee and has gone off with
Lord Ronald Macdonald, his bride and his darling to be.

That is an old story in ballads, of course, more possible in Scotland than in most places. Lord Ronald was probably an impoverished younger son of a great family and Leezie Lindsay could afford a green satin skirt and was perhaps the daughter of a well-to-do farmer. A poverty-stricken younger son might have been fortunate to marry Leezie with her satin skirts. Furthermore ballads often express desire rather than fulfilment; the theme of King Cophetua and the beggar maid is very old. There were many Leezie Lindsays who looked no doubt upon the handsome younger sons, and songs that suggested possibilities of marriage above status might have been more often sung than realized in practice.

When we turn to the poets we find little trace of even incipient democracy. Yet Alexander Scott in discussing love remarks that the passion makes noble ladies subject to baser men:

> For luve to hieness has no heid.   *highness, heed*

He goes on to assert as a proverb

> That men and wemen less and mair
> Are cumd of Adame and of Eve,

and continues:

> So though my liking were a lady,
> And I no lord, yet not the less,
> She should my service find as ready
>   as duke to duchess.

This was carrying the right to love pretty far for the sixteenth century.

In *The Complaynt of Scotland*, written in the middle of the sixteenth century but based upon a French original, the matter of blue blood was analyzed and it was declared that if a surgeon should draw part of their (the nobles') blood in a basin, it would have no better color than the blood of a plebeian or of a mechanic arts man.

Such democratic sentiments were uncommon. But the poems of the time, although they assume no democracy of outlook, do breathe a broad humanity and occasional pride in the common man. There was still order and degree in a country that was long to remain feudal, but the common man was respected.

The Scots were deemed proud. The earliest records of the Highlanders comment upon their fierce pride. But the Lowlanders were not far behind them. Foreigners who visited Scotland at an early date pronounced the Scots vain and ostentatious. It has been observed that the Scottish farmer loved to play the gentleman and was inclined, we are told, to leave all menial jobs to his laborers. The Scot loved to make a brave show. "A filthy thing they esteem it and a very abject man they hold him that goes upon his foot any voyage," wrote Bishop Leslie of the Border men, and he went on to indicate that his fellow countrymen would economize on household equipment and spend their substance on fast horses. Such men were not unknown in other countries, and it may be that Bishop Leslie was attributing to his fellow countrymen a kind of pride that was characteristic of many peoples. In a famous Scottish ballad the man of the house wishes a new cloak and his thrifty wife talks him out of it.

Tis pride that puts a' the country down.
Gae tak thy auld cloak about thee.

The Scots were accounted not only proud but boastful. "The Scots will aye be boasting and cracking," wrote an unfriendly English chronicler. "They have liever be esteemed all nobles," declared Bishop Leslie, "or at least bold men of war," than husbandmen or honest men of craft, no matter how rich they are. "Of this comes their haughtiness and boasting of their nobility." Leslie further declared that not only the nobility but every class, indeed the whole people, enjoyed great freedom and liberty, "whereof comes that undiscreet consuetude, undiscreet manners, that pride and boasting of their nobility, which . . . all objects to us." It had been a jest at the University of Paris, where during the Middle Ages many Scots were in attendance, that each was by his own account a cousin of the king of Scots. There was no doubt truth in what the boasting Scot said. The Highlanders were related to their chiefs, whom they counted as their kings, and the Lowlanders often bore the same family name as their laird and were likely to be related to him in one way or another, if they took pains to look back a few generations. The Scot who went abroad with little money and great confidence in himself might easily have compensated for his want of cash by talking about his ancestry. It would have been families with little money and good connections that would have sent their sons abroad for study or to engage in business and such boys might overplay their hands.

But boasting was not confined to Scottish youngsters in Paris. In an anonymous satire in the *Maitland Quarto MS.* the boaster is well described:

> Wheneas thay talk of onye thing
> All tendis to thair awin loving
> Wald ye esteme thame be thair crakis   *boasts*
> Thay were Caesar in weirlie actis.   *warlike*
>
> . . .
>
> Thair riches, as thame seilfis dois count,
> King Cresus thresour will surmount.
> Unto thair taillis wha list attend
> Thay knaw all to the warldlis end.
> Gif ye will trow all that thay tell   *believe*
> In everie thing thay doe excell.

A good deal of Scottish poetry of the early sixteenth century could be quoted to show that the boastful type was common. Arbuthnot praised the simple life and went on to condemn boasters:

Traits Induced

And haittis all schaimles gloriosite,
And me delyt in modest schamfastnes.
Yit sall I not be countit worth ane flie
Without I speik of al mater be ges   *by guess*
Gloir and brag out and tak ane face of bress.   *brass*
Na thing misknawe under the firmament.   *be ignorant of*

Now of course these writers were not indicting all Scots by any means but they were talking about two types that were common enough, the frankly boastful type and the type that was so very sure of itself and was always able to pronounce on any subject. Sir Walter Scott knew the boasting type and put him into *A Legend of Montrose* in the person of the laird Allan McAulay.

The sensitiveness of the Scots to what was said about them was not unrelated to their habit of boasting about themselves. The chronicles furnish abundant proof that the Scots were peculiarly sensitive to what the English thought about them and any criticism of their courage or military prowess met with instant notice and reply.

That the Scot had an uneasy foot is an old story. The Highlander until the eighteenth century usually stayed at home, but the Lowlander went from one end of Europe to the other. It is not surprising. The Anglians, the Normans, and the Flemings, who made up an overlay of the population in the Lowlands, had all been migratory peoples. Whatever their background the Scots were wanderers on the earth. The English proverb that in every port one might find a Scot, a rat, and a Newcastle grindstone is worth remembering. "Quha [who] standis weill, he sulde noucht sterre [stir]," said the rhyming historian Wyntoun. The Scots stood none too well so far as wealth and opportunity were concerned, and they had to stir forth. Bishop Leslie explained the economic urge as due to younger sons. "So many of our countrymen have so good success among strange nations, some in the wars, some in professing of sciences, and some in merchandise." The Scot took to the career of mercenary soldier

95

as naturally as the Swiss. Lindsay of Pitscottie tells how fifteen hundred Scots at one time passed in ships over to Sweden to help the king of that nation against the Muscovites, and the chances are that some Scots were in the armies of the Muscovites. Now and again the Scot rose to great place in the armies of this and that prince. Hardly less often he became a factor working for an English or Scottish company and selling or buying goods for the export and import market. Other Scots, scores of them, went to the continental universities, and particularly to that of Paris, to study, and, when they won degrees, sometimes stayed on the Continent to become priests or teachers. Long before the Middle Ages were over, stray Scots had become members of urban communities in every corner of Europe, from Spain and Italy to far Russia.

Why did the Scots leave home in such large numbers? It has been pointed out that their ancesters had been of roving stock. One might add that in many cases the Scot had to make a living by fishing and that he knew the ways of the sea and was not afraid to venture far from shore till he set himself down on other shores. But the chief reason why the Scot went away from home was because his own country had so few resources and he had imagination enough to guess that he might better his chances by seeking out richer countries.

Humor is a quality that comes late. We do not find much of it among the early Scots. The Highlanders were merry and gay and outgoing but seldom humorous. The Lowlanders were more sophisticated and, as might have been expected, more humorous. We have told the story of the Scot who made off with the English crown. It will be remembered that it was the English lords who laughed at his story, they and Pitscottie, the narrator, who was a Lowland man. The thief himself came from Blair-Athol in the Highlands and was in deadly earnest in what he said. In Barbour's *The Brus* the story is told of how the English were lacking food and could not provision themselves from the sea, and their leader,

Earl de Warenne, sent troops on a foray all over Lothian to find cattle. They brought in one cow, and when De Warenne saw the cow he said

"This is the derrest beiff that I
Saw evir yeit; for sekirly
It cost ane thousand pound and mar."

Humor somewhat more subtle and in the Chaucerian manner we find in Sir David Lyndsay's narrative about Squire Meldrum. When the squire rejoins his mistress the poet tells us that there was mirth and joy, and the chamber door was closed.

They did but kiss, as I suppose it,
If other thing was them between
Let those discover that lovers been,
For I am not in love expert,
And never studied in that art.

In another poem Sir David tells of a promise to pay back a thousand pounds or two of gold, and says payment will be made,

When the Bass and the Isle of May
Be set upon the Mount Senay,
When the low mound beside Falkland
Is lifted to Northumberland,
When kirkmen yearn no dignity,
Nor wives no sovereignty,
Winter bot frost, snow, wind, or rain,   *without*
Then shall I give thy gold again.
                    . . .
After the day of judgment,
Within a month at the least.

All of which reminds us of "Nora's Vow" by Sir Walter Scott, who knew his Sir David well. Nora declared that she would not marry the earlie's son even if Ben Cruachan should fall, and the Awe's fierce stream turn back. Ben Cruachan stands as ever, Sir Walter noted, but the lady had wed the earlie's son.

In Dunbar's "Kynd Kyttock" there was a story full of humor. Kyttock was the alewife of Falkland fells and on her death she was picked up by a newt riding on a snail, and carried to an inn just outside the gate of heaven. She managed to quench her thirst and slipped into heaven where she became the hen wife for our Lady. All went well for seven years and then one day she looked out of the gate and saw an alehouse and her old thirst revived. Out she went through the high gate to get a fresh drink. The ale of heaven had proved sour.

In an anonymous poem equally fantastic there is a description of the way the first Highland man was created.

> God and Saint Peter was gangand be the way   *going*
> Heich up in Argyll where their gait lay.   *way*
> Saint Peter said to God in ane sport word—
> 'Can ye nocht mak a Hielandman of this horse turd?'
> God turned owre the horse turd with his pykit staff,
> And up start a Hielandman black as ony draff.   *malt refuse*
> Quod God to the Hielandman, 'Where wilt thou now?'
> 'I will doun in the Lawland, Lord, and there steal a cow!'
> 'And thou steal a cow, carle, there they will hang thee.'
> 'What reck, Lord, of that, for anis mon I die.'   *once, must*
> God then he leuch and owre the dyke lap,   *laughed, lept*
> And out of his sheath his gully outgat.   *large knife*
> Saint Peter socht the gully fast up and doun,
> Yet could not find it in all that braid roun.
> 'Now,' quod God, 'here a marvell, how can this be,
> That I suld want my gully, and we here bot three.'
> 'Humf,' quod the Hielandman, and turned him about,
> And at his plaid neuk the gully fell out.
> 'Fy,' quod Saint Peter, 'thou will never do weill:
> And thou bot new made and sa soon gais to steal.'   *goes*
> 'Humf,' quod the Hielandman, and sware by yon kirk,
> 'Sa lang as I may gear get to steal, I will never wirk.'

Traits Induced

It has to be admitted that poems with so much humor are hard to find in premodern Scottish writing. Yet the truth is that when we come to the Scottish Reformation, to men such as George Buchanan and Andrew Melville, we find comments upon what is going on around them that are full of a special Scottish humor.

All that I have said about Scottish characteristics before modern times, except for their urge to travel and their humor, enforces the point that they were a provincial people, a still somewhat unsophisticated and unpracticed people, a little remote from the currents of civilization. That was the impression of Ralph Sadleir, Elizabeth's ambassador at the Scottish court. He observed that the nobility and gentry were "well given to the verity of Christ's word and doctrine," by which he meant that they were good Protestants. But he confessed himself disappointed with them, especially with the members of the Privy Council with whom he had most to do. "I see none amongst them that hath any such agility of wit, gravity, learning, or experience, to set forth the same or to take in hand the direction of things." In other words Sadleir felt that the statesman type was wanting. The leaders of Scotland lacked something in gravity and poise. He may have been right. The government of Scotland did not give men political experience. There was no body of civil servants, no men trained in conducting royal affairs. Now one group of nobility surrounded the king and now another, but their experience was chiefly in intrigue. Neither in local communities nor in Edinburgh were they old hands at carrying matters on.

PART II

THE TIDES AND STORMS
OF RELIGIOUS CHANGE

X

THE SCOTTISH WAY OF REFORMATION

WHAT differentiated the modern Scot in character from other peoples more than anything else was the Reformation. He may be an Episcopalian or a Glasgow Marxist, but he is in some degree a product of the Presbyterian movement. He is the descendant of earlier Scots and resembles them in many ways but he is different from them and that difference is connected with the Presbyterian Revolution.

The Reformation concerns us then perhaps more than anything else in Scottish history. It was a hundred and fifty years before Scotland was thoroughly Presbyterianized, and yet the change-over to advanced Protestantism was carried through quickly.

That was because the Roman Church had been losing ground for a long while. James I [1424–37] went about the country visiting the monasteries. In 1425 he addressed letters under the privy seal to the Benedictines and the Augustinians, regretting the fallen state of the monastic establishments in Scotland and "hinting that as sincere religion would bring continued bounty, so a failure to improve might mean a revocation of royal endowments." He had already warned the bishops to look out for Lollards and to punish them. By the middle of the fifteenth century Lollardry had won a foothold in Scotland. The poet Walter Kennedy had written:

> The ship of fate, tempestuous wind and rain
> Drives in the sea of Lollardry that blows.

In the early 1520's Lutheran tracts were coming over in the ships from the Low Countries. The burning of Patrick Hamilton at St. Andrews in 1528 for heresy did what the burning of heretics usually did, spread the heresy. When the Archbishop of St. Andrews came to execute Henry Forrest for having in his possession an English edition of the New Testament and for having declared that Hamilton died as a martyr, John Lindsay urged him to burn him in some hollow cellar, "for the smoke of Mr. Patrick Hamilton hath infected all those on whom it blew."

That there was reason for dissatisfaction is evidenced by contemporary writers. John Major, a perceptive man, and one who remained a conservative in a changing world, had written early in the sixteenth century: "But now for many years we have seen shepherds whose only care it is to find pasture for themselves, men neglectful of the duties of religion. . . . Behold then here what may happen to religion from the possession of great wealth! By open flattery do the worthless sons of our nobility get the governance of convents *in commendam* . . . and they covet these ample revenues, not for the good help that they thence might render to their brethren, but solely for the high position that these places offer, that they may have the direction of them, and out of them may have the chance to fill their own pockets."

Ninian Winzet, who was to do service to the Roman Church and to wage a pamphlet war against Protestantism, testified to the ignorance and ill character of the priesthood and condemned the parish clergy as dumb dogs. "Awake, awake," he wrote, "and put to your hand stoutly to save Peter's ship."

In *Ane Satyre of the Thrie Estattis*, presented in the presence of James V, Sir David Lyndsay makes the priest say:

> My paramours is both as fat and fair
> As any wench in the town of Ayr.
> I send my sons to Paris to the schools;
> I trust in God that they shall be no fools.
> And all my daughters I have well provided.
> Now judge if my office be well guided.

It must be remembered in defense of the clergy that clerical celibacy had been breaking down. The priest in the satire has a large family and possibly by one woman with whom he lived in what amounted to marriage. Even if the priest had several paramours and children by each one, his conduct was not worse than that of many of his generation. Nothing is clearer than that in the late fifteenth and early sixteenth centuries morals in Scotland, as in some other nations, were in a low state. Even marriage was less than sacrosanct. Men could easily procure the sanction of the Church to gain divorce on the ground that in some way or other they were within the prohibited degrees of relationship.

The implication that priests did rather well by themselves is perhaps as much the gravamen of the charge against them as their proneness to increase the population. It was believed that the Church was not unacquisitive. A large part of the revenues of the country, one half, in the judgment of Hume Brown, was probably in the hands of the Church. He believed that the Scottish clergy were in proportion to the wealth of the country perhaps the richest in Europe.

Riches indeed have seldom been a spiritualizing influence upon the clergy. Certainly affluence did not make them popular. To most Scots the struggle for existence was a sharp one and occupied all their energies. They took no pleasure in gazing at a clergy that had grown fat in what seemed an easy institutional life. The clergy themselves may well have lost the force and initiative that come from having to scratch for a living.

Their general conduct was disliked. In 1540 an act of Parliament declared that the "unhonesty and misrule of Kirkmen both in wit, knowledge and manners is the matter and cause that the kirk and kirkmen are lightlied [lightly regarded] and condemned." A provincial council of the Church in 1549 stated that the cause of the troubles of the Church was "corrupt manners and profane lewdness of ecclesiastical persons of almost all ranks, together with their crass ignorance of letters and of all culture."

If the priests were out of touch with letters and culture, they were not wholly to be blamed. Remember that Scotland had been going through a long period of near-anarchy. Moreover the higher clergy were, as Lyndsay had implied, to a considerable degree the relatives of the nobility, the younger sons and brothers, and did not inherit from that preying class many traditions of culture or a disinterested and philanthropic view of life. Disinterestedness is a flower that blooms in a soil that has long been cultivated and enriched by humanistic traditions. The soil of Scotland was still rocky, metaphorically as well as literally. The priests might have found an ideal in the New Testament but many of them had never looked into it; its whole philosophy was one that would hardly have appealed to them. There were lives of saints and records of godly men, but less in Scotland, so far as I can make out, than in England or France; that type of literature does not seem to have had any vogue in the north of Britain. The medieval Scot did not choose his heroes from among saints. The medieval Scottish priest did not live in an atmosphere that would have promoted his spiritual life.

Yet the events of the early sixteenth century should have given him a chance for influence had he been ready for it. The disaster at Flodden destroyed a considerable part of the Scottish nobility and should have left power and prestige in Scotland largely in the hands of the clergy. They were not equal to their opportunity. They could not command the respect of the people whom they should have led. In the towns, among the trading and handicraft classes, there was growing up a body of intelligent opinion, intelligent enough to expect much of the clergy and to realize that an acquisitive Church was failing to do its part, was falling down in its spiritual and social mission.

The Church had been falling down too in its economic mission. The monks and the nuns had been early leaders in handicrafts and working skills. But industry was growing beyond the competence of the monks and nuns, was coming to be a complicated matter to be dealt with by expert men in borough towns. As the Church lost its hold on business, it lost some of its influence with the rising burgher class.

It was losing its influence on country people. They had been neglected. In "The Lamentation of the Lady Scotland" we are told:

> For upland they have not due service.
> The rooms appointed . . .
> To hear God's work, where they should pray together,
> Are now converted into sheep cots and folds,
> Or else are fallen . . .
> . . . they do disdain to hear God's word.
>
> . . .
>
> They go to labor, drinking or to play,
> And not to you [the church] upon the sabbath day.

As against all this, it must be said that there remained many good men in the old Church and that they continued to warn the Church against the evident abuses. Some of them were at length to go over to the Protestant side, some remained Catholic.

Not all the discontent of the time was due to faults of the Church. The times were bad. Moral conditions in both England and Scotland were low; either that, or people were beginning to demand a higher quality of virtue and were more impressed by evil lives than in an earlier time. Sir David Lyndsay wrote:

> Our gentlemen are all degenerate,
> Liberality and loyalty both are lost,
> And cowardice with Lords is laureate,
> And knightly courage turned in brag and boast.
>
> . . .
>
> There is nought else but ilk man for himself.

It is common to harp upon how bad things are, as if they had been better in a former time. But Lyndsay's complaint probably had some basis.

It was the Treaty of Edinburgh in 1560 that finally put the Protestants in the saddle. It was a treaty between French and

English commissioners, and it settled the long rivalry between France and England over Scotland in favor of the neighbor to the south. Cecil exulted to Elizabeth that they had gained the hearts and good will of the nobility and people, "which surely was better for England than the revenue of the crown." In these words, says Mathieson, the stronger nation acknowledges "to the weaker its baffled ambition after two centuries and a half of not ungenerous warfare." But the treaty did more than that. It left in power the Protestant leaders, who had been backed by English military force. Hume Brown calls the treaty the central point of Scottish history. A group of nobles who had decided to go along with the English and who were supporting the Protestant cause formed themselves into the Lords of the Congregation. They were the real victors, quite as much as the English, in the Treaty of Edinburgh, and were not slow to profit from it. There was a thanksgiving service in St. Giles, the great church on High Street; Knox became at once the principal minister in Edinburgh and the religious leader of Protestant Scotland; such Protestant ministers as could be found were set up in various parts of the country. A meeting of the Estates followed. Hume Brown observes that in that meeting the smaller barons from all over the nation, who had not hitherto been attending the Estates, came up in force. The Estates instructed the ministers to draw up a statement of Protestant doctrine and a Confession of Faith was approved and ratified. That Confession dealt explicitly with the "elect" and was thoroughly Calvinist in tone. But it had one wise and moderate qualification: "Not that we think one policy and one order in ceremonies can be appointed for all ages, times and places." The Estates went on to abolish the jurisdiction of the Pope and to ratify the Confession of Faith. The celebration of the mass was forbidden.

Scotland had become Protestant almost overnight.

I have suggested some of the reasons why Catholicism broke down in Scotland. It cannot have escaped the reader that the Roman Church had been falling apart by reason of its own inefficiency and corruption. Indeed the collapse of the old Church had really preceded the establishment of the new Kirk. Even when we realize that, we find ourselves a little surprised that the Reformation was accomplished so quickly and with so little violence. Violent the Scots were before the Reformation, as in the assassination of Cardinal Beaton, and violent they were to be many times after the Reformation, as in the Ruthven Raid. But the actual change-over from Catholicism to Protestantism was less like a storm than a tide. The storms were to come later.

The tidal character of the change is the more amazing when we remember that the Reformation was accomplished by a group of minorities.

A minority of churchmen, a minority of nobles, a minority of burghs were involved in the extraordinary events that put Protestantism on top. Those minorities were well led and were no doubt the aggressive members of their classes. It was as if the supporters of the old Roman Church had little will to resist the innovators. Mary of Lorraine had appealed to them to amend their ways, but most of them had no mind or plan to do so.

The nobility that helped to bring about the change was a small but active group. That class was recovering in some part from the losses of Flodden. There seems to have been among them a considerable body of intelligent and thinking men. Archibald Bell-the-Cat, Earl of Angus, is said to have boasted in his day that only one of his sons could read—that was Gavin Douglas, the poet—but there were now other types of nobles who were educated and cultivated men, aware of the new ideas that were being imported from the Continent and inclined to accept them. Men in sympathy with the new ideas were precisely the kind who were likely to take a lead.

That the nobles were expected to lead is evident from the literature of the time. The people in the country looked to them. In the ballads of the Reformation, nearly all of them excessively bad as poetry but full of stuff for the historian,

109

the writers call on the nobles to bring peace and happiness
to the realm. If a king should betray his people and bring
them into servitude,

> He should in this reformit be, I say,
> Namely by nobles and by men of good.

The ballad maker goes on to execrate the abuses of Scottish
government. Where, he asks, are the men of talent ["wittis"]
"wont to rule Scotland"?

That the lesser classes regarded the nobility as responsible
for government was known to the nobles. The nobles were
on the whole patriotic, much more so than in the early days,
when they had lands in both England and Scotland. Some
of them were possibly as interested in the welfare of Scotland
as in the position of their own class, or as in their own
religion. Two disasters to Scottish arms, Flodden Field, and
Solway Moss a generation later, must have impressed upon a
nobility that had suffered terribly from the first battle, and
not a little from the second, that the royal policy of alliance
with France was too expensive in Scottish lives and in national prestige. "If we can't lick 'em, let's jine 'em" is a modern phrase for a thought that must have come into many
minds. They were considering the future of their country
and the more thoughtful were becoming convinced that good
relations with Protestant England were more desirable than
to be tied up with France. The Protestant cause seemed to
be becoming the national cause and many of the nobles were
already embracing it.

More mercenary thoughts were of course in the minds of
many nobles. These men could not fail to have seen how the
English gentry and nobility had profited from the distribution
of the monastic lands of England. Why should they not do
equally well in plundering the Church lands of Scotland?
Good valley lands were worth the renunciation of the mass.
They were already accustomed to seeing their sons provided

with Church offices and the livings attached to them. They felt a presumptive right to Church property.

If the nobles were still the most important element in Scotland they were beginning to have rivals in influence. The English representative in Scotland in the early 1570's noted that the nobles were becoming less important and that the men in boroughs were having more to say. Many of those men in boroughs had become Protestant. Such towns as Dundee, Ayr, St. Andrews, Montrose, Stirling, and Glasgow led the way toward Protestantism. The trading classes in England found in Puritanism a religion that seemed to suit them, and the trading and industrial classes in Scotland found in Presbyterianism a religion that fitted their needs and aspirations.

The common people turned toward Protestantism slowly and steadily during the long period of the reign of James VI. No doubt they were following their leaders in country and town, but their own situation had much to do with their shift. The ballads of the sixteenth century show that there was great suffering in Scotland due to the unsettled state of affairs. The country was disorganized and the people unhappy. In such a time a new religion has great appeal. One of the ballads, the "Lamentation of the Commons," has described the situation in words that must be quoted from a free translation:

We poor men asked no better life than to go to Edinburgh on our nags with peats and turves and bundles of heather, to make a good sale and then go home merrily under the light of the moon without fear or danger. We colliers, hucksters and carters lose our horses and are put down. We chapmen and basket folk mourn for those simple men that brought their butter and eggs to Edinburgh Cross, and we would again buy a basket of figs and pins and needles and sell them to country lasses. So could we travel where we would. But now we have to stay at home. What man will not pity us that used to bring the wool, the skin and hide to Edinburgh town in peace and charity, from Selkirk, Ha-

111

wick and the parts of Clyde, while now we have to abide in a
corner and like weary wretches pour out our bitter wail. We
tinkers, tailors and craftsmen out of number that had an honest
life have now nothing but care. All our gay garments of sundry
fashions we have to pawn to sustain our bodies. We have nothing
to do but beg, and our wives and children as well. We merchants that with our merchant packs did travel from town to
town to fairs, we now sit at home.

There was discouragement about the state of Scotland.

> In place of peace now murder war upraises
> In place of love envy among us springs
> In place of faith, his friend falsehood betrays
>
> . . .
>
> In place of one we have so many kings.

The Scots, another ballad maker predicted, would be
ashamed of their nationality and would wander far from
their country and mourn.

> Alas that ever they were born
> That dwelt in Scotland us before,
> And lost us such a land
> Which our forbears once thought ours,
> With pleasant castles, towns and towers.

In such a time the common people readily embraced a religion that promised change.

Nobles, burghers, and common people were all moving
in the same direction. There was much discussion. It would
appear that Scotland was beginning to have something like
a public opinion, I had almost said a soul. There was a body
of intelligent men and their minds had been directed, as
never before, to the ills of their country and to questions of
national policy. A feeling for their land that was a broader
thing than it had been in the early days of the long wars with
the English was developing. What was the best thing to

do and on what terms should it be done was the problem that faced the patriotic and astute Maitland of Lethington and his class, and other classes. The answers were various, and the problem had new aspects every little while. But there was beginning to be a certain thread to policy. It was best to go along with England; it was to be hoped that the new religion might cure some of the ills of the nation.

The hopes from the new religion were not wholly justified. Old wrongs and abuses were not all eliminated. What act proved all its thought had been? Scotland had been suffering from defeat and disorder for so long a time that better conditions could not be expected at once. Too much had been hoped from Protestantism.

> Now is the Protestants risen us amang,
> Saying they will make reformation.
> But yet as now more vices never rang,   *reigned*
> As pride, envy, false dissimulation,
> Deceit, adultery, and fornication,
> Theft, rapine, slaughter, oppression of the poor.

It was always thus. A change of religion made no great change in the lives of people, at least at first. Things went on much the same.

The situation in Scotland was not to be better for a long time; a century and a half of struggle was ahead. The Treaty of Edinburgh had seemed to settle matters in favor of the Presbyterians, but it was not long before it looked as if Mary might have her way and carry Scotland back to the old Church. Even after she was a fugitive the issue remained in the balance; she gained as many friends in adversity as in prosperity. The ups and downs of the next century must be told later. Here they concern us only in so far as they offer a comparison with the Reformation in England. Just as Presbyterianism was ceasing to be a minority religion and was winning the Scots, the first two Stuarts proceeded to modify it in an Episcopal direction as much as they could. The National Covenant restored the Kirk of Knox and Melville.

The later Stuarts continued the policy of the earlier Stuarts, but the Revolution of 1689 made the Kirk of Scotland Presbyterian for good.

There was little resemblance and much difference between the progress of the Reformation in England and that in Scotland. England had her breach with Rome brought about by an agreeing king and Parliament, and after a five years' setback settled down to a compromise form of Protestantism that did not seem to the common man too different from what he had known. Anglicanism was born out of the desire of the English to stick together, to find a compromise solution, and Anglicanism in turn developed a social cohesiveness that remained with it. Throughout the first two thirds of Elizabeth's reign there was still danger from Catholicism; there were troubles with the extreme Protestants, that is, the Puritans, and those troubles did not diminish during the reigns of the first two Stuarts. Nevertheless there was a settlement that carried the country in the main with it until the two middle decades of the century, when the Civil Wars and the Puritan regime that followed turned everything upside down. With the Restoration the moderate Church of England was firmly established, even if the Nonconformist sects were active. The toleration those sects received at the Revolution did not really weaken the hold of the Anglican Church.

It was otherwise in the north. The Scots were occupied with one long series of struggles about their Kirk from 1560 to 1689. The English gained a Church that fitted into their tradition of compromise and conservative institutional development. The Scots acquired a fighting faith in which there was no least touch of compromise, a faith that was to be reinforced with memories of fanatics and martyrs. It was a faith that seldom had the great majority of Scots behind it. Instead of a Church that made for national unity and strengthened the hands of the State, the Scots gained a Church that stood apart from the State and from which dissident groups with odd variations of Calvinism were always to separate themselves.

It was also the misfortune of the Scottish Reformation that it was almost untouched by the revival of classical learning. It is true that George Buchanan could write some of the best Latin prose of the sixteenth century; it is true that the Scottish poets, Henryson, Gavin Douglas, and Sir David Lyndsay could use classical models and make classical allusions. But the knowledge of the classics was confined to a few well-read men. There was no kindling enthusiasm for the ancients north of the Cheviots. The Scots had other things to think about. They were occupied with religious struggles from the middle of the sixteenth century on. There were not those conditions of strong and orderly government under which men could occupy themselves with bringing in, translating, and disseminating the literature of Greece and Rome.

The English were more fortunate. The Tudors furnished the kind of government where scholars might flourish and where religious troubles, although important, did not keep the center of attention. The English Renaissance affected every aspect of life. By the late years of Elizabeth's reign and the early ones of James's the country gentlemen and the whole body of reading men became familiar with the Roman writers, absorbed the outlook of those writers into their thinking, and took note of the ideals found in them. From the Romans in part the English learned the virtue of moderation; they came to distrust asceticism and extremes of all kinds. They considered their English problems from the wide view of a great ancient civilization. The Revival of Letters gave to English Protestantism an orderliness and catholic breadth that remained with it and must in some degree have affected English character. Hooker's conception of ecclesiastical polity owed something to the impression of classical ideals upon English Protestantism. That Protestantism managed to preserve some of the enchantments of the medieval Church, managed to keep faith not too far away from what had been the main line, and to avoid in some degree the weakness of dissent and of dissent from dissent. Thus the English people made themselves through the Church and through the classics the inheritors of Rome. The Scots had little religious inheritance.

From that want Scotland suffered. She missed the traditions and beauty of old Church, she missed the humanism of the Renaissance, she missed the moderation. Scotland learned her manners and her codes of behavior not from the Roman Church nor from the Roman writers but from Calvin and the Old Testament. She adopted a serious and sober religion with little beauty in it and much harshness.

XI

MARY QUEEN OF SCOTS, JOHN KNOX

THE story of the Reformation is important in explaining the Scotland that was to emerge and the Scottish character that was to be hammered out by the new religious forces. The personalities of the movement are almost as significant. One cannot deal with the religious revolution without pausing to comment briefly upon the character of Mary because she became the symbol of the old religion; without mentioning Elizabeth's policy, because that illustrated English interference once more in Scottish affairs, with permanent effect. Above all one has to discuss John Knox, the hero of the revolution, and possibly the most important man in Scottish history. Scottish himself to the core, he imposed his character and his beliefs upon Scotland from his day almost to ours. He left his stamp upon Scotland as William of Normandy left his upon England. He did more, he left a stamp upon Scots everywhere. To leave him out would be to omit the greatest individual force in making the Presbyterian Scot.

The fair Mary, Queen of Scots, could hardly have stemmed the tide Protestantward had she been the most virtuous of women. That she can hardly be called even by her loyal admirers, who sometimes go far out on a limb in extenuation of her frailties. It would not be fair to say that her want of restraint by affronting Scottish consciences made the Reformation successful. But it could be safely asserted that she lost whatever chance the Roman Church had to retain its hold on Scotland. She was of course lovely to look upon and a woman of spirit and she must have had a way with her. But she thought of everything in terms of personalities and especially in terms of herself. She needed some man as a master and her needs in that respect were subject to change.

117

Her progress was a play in many acts and scenes. There were action, suspense, and final tragedy. She furnished one of the great dramas to people who loved the dramatic. She was beauty and majesty in distress. She has no place in the history of what has given Scotland a certain character. She is part of the folklore of Scotland, and her vogue is in itself a comment upon Scottish character.

If Mary's influence was a negative one in favor of the Protestant cause, that of Elizabeth of England was positive. This is no place to deal with the character of Elizabeth, but her relation to the Scottish Reformation cannot be overlooked. It is not to be supposed that Elizabeth was interested in making Scotland Protestant through any religious idealism. If Mary had not proved herself a constant threat to Elizabeth's position, Elizabeth would not have been so concerned to support the Scottish Protestants against their sovereign. She had no liking for John Knox, who had written harsh words about female rulers, but she had to have dealings with him. Without her help, without the money and troops which she sent to Scotland, it would hardly have been possible for the Protestant nobles to keep the upper hand. English influence was effectual in other ways. England was a neighbor and the winds blowing Protestantward from England touched Scotland quickly. The Scottish people, nobles, lairds, burghers, farmers, and workers were all of them affected by what happened to the south. They hated the "Englishes" but beneath that hatred was an admiration that often betrayed itself.

It was John Knox that gave the Scottish Reformation its particular twist. He himself was a product of Scottish history. "Only a nation," says Mathieson, "which had been hammered for centuries on the anvil of unequal and almost continuous warfare could have produced such a man; and only in such a nation could he have found followers as strong and unbending as himself." He was moreover an embodiment of some of those qualities that we expect to find in the Scot. "As the exaggerated type of his own countrymen," says Hume

Brown, "Knox, like Voltaire and Dr. Johnson, necessarily repels men of other nations, while his own people, even those who differ most widely from his religious and political teachings, regard even his asperities with the kindly allowance that is made for family idiosyncrasies." That is only partly true. The Catholic and the high Anglican Scots and the Glasgow Reds have little good to say of the great reformer. The literary Scots who live in London and write about their own country have few kind words for him. An American who has come to think of Knox as the greatest of all Scots in his final influence, and certainly as one of the most typical, is a little disappointed when in Scotland to see so little visual evidence that Knox is held in memory. Has Scotland enthroned in its heart the queenly beguiler and forgotten the stern old denouncer of sin?

Knox was a man with wide European experience. Few of the many Scots who studied abroad from medieval times on had gained as much working knowledge of the religious world on the Continent as he. He had been in close touch with the Marian exiles from England and had come to know not only them but the Protestant reformers in south Germany and Switzerland. From the Polish nobleman John à Lasco he had received important ideas and from John Calvin a whole philosophy. In Geneva he had been invited to serve as pastor and was constantly recalled there by his parishoners who begrudged his absence in England and Scotland. He had preached in France and drawn men there to the Protestant faith. In England he had lived and worked and made himself a dynamic figure in the development of Puritanism. It is not too much to say that the whole Protestant movement in western Europe had been under his observation, and he was familiar with its ins and outs. Yet he was not so cosmopolitan as to have lost any of his Scottish quality and he was in demand by the reforming party in Scotland.

With all his continental experience he had been untouched by the Renaissance. He had studied Latin but he never evinced any profound knowledge of it, nor had he any feel-

119

ing for Latin literature. He had learned nothing of Roman moderation or Roman orderliness. He had no Greek sense of beauty. There was not a spark of poetry in his outlook. He had no tears for human affairs. The death of Mary of Lorraine, who like himself had fought for the things she believed in, left him unmoved. There was no pity but much vindictiveness. He was a Hebraized Scot and he did much to perpetuate a Hebraized outlook in Scotland.

Like most reformers and like many of his countrymen, he was a man of intensity of conviction and of expression. His sermons were a combination of passionate feeling and shrewd, subtle appeal. "In the opening of the text," wrote his secretary, "he was moderate; but when he entered on application, he made me so grew [shudder] and tremble that I could not hold a pen to write." Even in his old age when he had had a stroke and had to be helped into the pulpit, he would become so stirred that "he was like to ding [beat] the pulpit in blads [fragments] and fly out of it." There was a certain terrifying majesty and severity about his presence in the pulpit. The vials of God's wrath he could pour forth with a passion that made him the most powerful preacher in Scotland. He was "able," wrote Randolph, the English agent in Scotland, "to put more life in us than five hundred trumpets continually blustering in our ears."

The trumpets were continually denouncing. Mary of Lorraine, the Queen, Moray, Maitland of Lethington, the Protestant nobles, indeed all who disagreed with him all along the line or in any point, suffered from his public castigation. He could call down all the fearful threats of the Old Testament, as if he were "of God's Privy Council." He had God's words at his fingertips. With extraordinary relevance he could quote scripture. His arguments in favor of a certain policy or principle he could marshal at a moment's notice, and they were based upon premises drawn from the Bible. There is no evidence that he was ever swayed by considerations of patriotism, considerations that affected many with whom he had to deal. God was greater than Scotland.

He was right out of the Middle Ages, a leftover from the scholastics, one who reasoned from isolated texts in the Old and New Testaments. His carefully wrought arguments take no hold on us today. He would have denied that his religion was of the Old Testament but he loved its denunciatory passages and he was a wonder at finding them out. He could find them in the New Testament too, and the Christ he talked most about was a militant character.

He was ever a fighter unafraid. Neither power nor pomp nor beauty moved him from his firm base. Mary Queen of Scots he could reduce to tears. He could speak up to the Regent Morton and he could send off lecturing letters to the Queen of England. At his grave, Morton, who had reason to know, declared that Knox "neither feared nor flattered any flesh."

It is no wonder that his life was a series of ups and downs, of victories over the powers of evil and of discouragements and defeats. He took defeats badly, and poured out biblical threats and prophecies upon those who had got the better of him. Victories he took in his stride and thought of what came next. He did not live to see the full accomplishment of his aims and toward the end he grew weary of the strife. He had been preaching some sermons on St. John and wrote Mrs. Locke that he was now finishing the last one and with that would be glad to end his miseries. "For now, sister, I seek for rest."

With all his passion for serving God, he was in some ways a practical man, seldom deceiving himself about the immediate situation and considering carefully the next move. If he had little compromise in his make-up and less tolerance for those who sought the advancement of Protestantism by more cautious and canny methods, he had nevertheless a skilled eye to estimate forces and to look into the future and guess what would happen. It has been suggested by Hume Brown that his thoroughgoing, uncompromising methods were better from the point of view of success than those of the men more willing to go halfway with Mary of Lorraine and later with Mary Queen of Scots. Yet he was sometimes ruthless when a little compromise seemed in order. At a time when the Scottish reformers owed much to England and just at the point when there seemed a chance that Elizabeth might persuade Mary to become an Anglican in hope of the succession to the English crown, a consummation that would have secured Protestantism in Scotland, Knox spoke out against the Anglican service as having some "dregs of Papistry." He would have no truck with a dilute Protestantism and he could be very ungracious about it.

He was not a destroyer, as were many reformers. He was a builder, one of "devout imaginations," an architect of a heavenly kingdom on this earth, nothing less indeed than a theocracy. It was built upon narrow foundations and it could not hope to command that wide support which a national Church needs. Yet if Knox's new Kirk never wholly won Scotland it had enormous influence upon Scottish history and character.

He was not one of those who looked out for himself. He had no eye for the main chance. He had refused to be tempted by an English bishopric. He left little money. At the end of his life he could assert that he had corrupted none and defrauded none. "Merchandise have I not made," he declared, not without a certain pride in his integrity. He was so unself-seeking that he assumed the disinterestedness of others and failed to see through men whose aspirations for themselves were quaintly covered up with a mantle of godliness.

Yet he thought of himself as the center of the Scottish Reformation and his history of that movement in five books is a narrative of John Knox and of those who worked with him and those arrayed against him. He was only concerned for the glory of God, but he knew better than others what

122

would bring it about. He strove so earnestly for it that he could not forbear taking control; he knew what ought to be done. He was qualified by nature to be the leader of revolution.

This uncompromising figure had some touch of Scottish warmth in his make-up. He felt and enjoyed all the loyalties that belong to a Scot. Bothwell had done everything he regarded as wicked, but Knox's ancestors had been retainers of the Bothwells and he felt a natural friendliness to the earl which he did not attempt to conceal. Old friends who had differed with him and turned against him he found it hard to denounce, though in the end he generally succeeded, for the cause of his God was greater than that of friendship. But friends he had, and he liked to gather them about him at dinner and talk the evening out. Good stories he enjoyed telling and would often intersperse them in his writing. His narrative of the Reformation was marked by irony, raciness, and even humor. His humor was at its best when he gloated over the discomfitures of the enemies of God.

That he came from obscure origins seems to have made little difference to him or to others. There was a natural greatness in him, the kind of greatness that his countrymen could quickly recognize. It was not the greatness of vision and insight but of vehemence and passion, yes and of courage when the cause seemed hopeless. Even the Scots nobles, who reserved most greatness to themselves, listened to him, many of them followed him and would have admitted his right to speak first.

He must be reckoned great by any estimate based upon influence. He imposed upon the Scots a religion that was harsh and exacting but curiously fitted to the needs of a small and poor people. It was in many ways as suitable to the Scots as that of the wealthy prelates had been unsuitable. The experience of the Scots was such that they could do with a religion of austerity; their inclination to dialectic was such that they could understand a religion of Calvinistic logic.

The greatness of Knox rests upon an influence that went far beyond Scotland. His Kirk was carried across the water to Canada and the United States and to far islands. No other Scot, save possibly Sir Walter, has so affected the world. Knox could hardly have foreseen that. His influence upon his country he was assured of. "What I have been to my country, albeit this unthankful age will not know, yet the ages to come will be compelled to bear witness to the truth."

XII

THE TWO BOOKS OF DISCIPLINE

TWO chapters have been given to explaining how the Scottish Reformation came about and to sketching its personalities. It will be necessary to devote two more to its further development, so much did that movement transform Scotland and turn the Scots into the people they have since become. In this chapter I will analyze the two Books of Discipline, because in those documents we shall learn the program of the new Kirk. At its end I will tell of Andrew Melville, who had much to do with the Second Book of Discipline, and who, next to Knox, was the begetter and hero of Scottish Presbyterianism. Heroes are almost as important for our purposes as their policies.

The reader will recall the Treaty of Edinburgh in 1560 which left the Lords of the Congregation in power and established Protestantism as the State religion. In the same year the Privy Council was induced by the Reforming ministers to set up a commission of five men to frame a standard of ecclesiastical government. That group, of whom John Knox was the leader, submitted to the General Assembly in 1561 the First Book of Discipline. It was ratified by the General Assembly of the Church but was never formally adopted by the civil authorities.

No other document in Scottish history is more significant. It has to be examined closely if we are to understand those forms of organization and rules of conduct that were to impress Scottish character in the centuries to follow.

The First Book of Discipline set up a heavenly kingdom on earth. That kingdom was to be republican in form. The members of the kirk were to elect their own minister, who could not leave at pleasure or be forced out at the pleasure of his flock. They were to elect elders whose terms were to be for one year but who might be re-elected. They were also to elect deacons who looked after the financial affairs of the parish. "They may also assist in judgment with the ministers and elders and may be admitted to read in the assembly if they be required and be found able thereto." No presbytery and no synod were mentioned, but there was a council or what became known later as the General Assembly. The details of this assembly were not prescribed, but it was evidently intended that ministers and elders were to be sent to it as representatives, and that it should deal with general questions of doctrine and with problems referred to it.

The Reformers were evidently puzzled as to what officials they should use in place of bishops. They had suffered from bishops, and the very word "bishop" had a Roman sound to them. Yet some official was needed between the General Assembly and the separate congregations, and particularly in a time when the organization was still in the making. They set up an official who was to travel round his "province," and they arranged for ten provinces in Scotland. He was to look after vacant churches and to co-operate with them in providing pastors, and he was to serve in establishing new churches. He was to be called a superintendent, but was to remain a minister in a principal town within the province, leaving that town to preach in vacant churches, to examine the diligence and behavior of ministers and the manners of the people, to observe how the poor were cared for and the youth taught.

The immediate need of the new national Church was for trained ministers, and there was no way of providing enough competent men quickly. In that situation "readers" were to be put in charge, "the most apt men that distinctly can read the Common Prayers and the Scriptures." The readers could exhort and explain the Scriptures but were not to administer the sacraments. It was hoped that in time many of them would qualify as ministers.

The churches were to take to themselves large judicial

authority. Blasphemy, adultery, murder, perjury, and other crimes capital, worthy of death, were assigned to the "civil sword." But drunkenness, excess in apparel or in eating and drinking, fornication, oppression of the poor by exactions, deceiving of them in buying and selling, wanton words, and licentious living, all such sins appertained to the Church to punish. If the sinner's offence was known to few, he was to be privately admonished; if it were generally known, he was to be called before the minister, the elders, and the deacons, and, if he confessed his sin before the congregation, expressed deep penitence, and changed his ways, he was to be forgiven. If he refused, he was to be excommunicated. With one excommunicated no one was allowed to have any "conversation," his family excepted, "be it in eating and drinking, buying or selling, yea, in saluting or talking with him."

The Book of Discipline dealt also with those "that commit horrible crimes, as murderers, man-slayers and adulterers," which the civil sword should punish with death. "But in case they be permitted to live," then the Church was to summon them and, if they were impenitent, excommunicate them. But if they offered themselves to the ministers and elders asking for prayers and requesting them to be intercessors to the Church that they be admitted to public repentance, the minister announced the fact to the Kirk, asking them to pray that God would work in the heart of the offenders unfeigned repentance of their grievous crimes. Then if a sinner confessed his crime before the Church and showed in an examination by the minister that he had contempt of his crime, the minister would exhort the Church to receive the penitent brother. In other words even murderers, if sufficiently penitent, were to be forgiven. It was a time when murder as a result of quarrels was a common sin, and the Church not only recognized that the civil authorities might fail to punish the murderer but provided for his possible return into the membership of the Kirk.

The inquisition of behavior and moral conduct was carefully provided for. "To discipline must all estates within this realm be subject, if they offend, as well the rulers as they that are ruled, yea and the preachers themselves as well as the poorest within the church." It was the duty of the elders in every kirk to take heed to the life, manners, diligence, and study of their minister and, if necessary, to admonish him and correct him if he did not preach "fruitful doctrine," or even if he showed lightness of conversation or negligence in his study. His wife and children were to come under censure as well. It might be that the family lived riotously or avariciously. How they spent the minister's salary was to be watched. Moreover the minister was not to frequent alehouses or taverns; he was not to "haunt the Court," nor accept any office in civil affairs.

The minister was not the only target of criticism. "The elders and deacons . . . must be under the same censure that is prescribed for the ministers." It was the duty of the minister and of the neighboring ministers to admonish and reprove elders and deacons whose manners and conversation were deemed worthy of blame.

The penalties for sin were not all invented by Knox and his Calvinistic associates. For centuries the Roman Catholic Church had set up penalties for wrongdoing upon the part of parishioners. But that Church had been wise enough to make allowance for human frailties. It was believed by the Reformers that the penitential discipline of the old Church had failed. "Neither was virtue rightly praised neither vice severely punished." The Scottish Reformers took over earlier theories and attempted to make them into a reality. They made the minister subject to oversight by his parishioners, something that the Roman Church had never done. They organized the censorship of behavior so that even trivial faults were a matter for criticism. They put a premium upon spying. They arranged for continuous moral judgments, such as human beings are only too prone to indulge themselves in. They raised the scrutiny of one's fellows to a public virtue. They set up a system of moral over-

128

sight which was to affect the manners and character of Scotsmen from that day on.

The Book of Discipline provided for a system of national education that in some respects followed fairly closely the educational system used earlier in the Roman Catholic Church. Each kirk in every town of "any reputation" was to provide a schoolmaster who was to teach grammar and Latin. In smaller places the minister or reader was to instruct the children in "their first rudiments" and in the catechism. In larger towns there were to be secondary schools, "colleges" in which logic and rhetoric and the languages should be taught by "sufficient masters." At the head of the system were the three universities, St. Andrews, Aberdeen, and Glasgow, where students should finish their professional work by the age of twenty-four. Great pains were taken to set forth the advanced work to be given in divinity, law, and medicine. The object of the whole scheme was to turn out men "to serve the Church or Commonwealth," although those who finished their education at one of the earlier stages might go into "handicrafts or to some other profitable exercise." It was provided that the expenses of poor boys should be taken care of by the kirks and that the rich man should be compelled to send his boys to school and could not "use his children at his own fantasie." It was furthermore provided that those found "apt to letters and learning," i.e., the best students, "must be charged to continue their study, so that the Commonwealth may have some comfort by them." That is, the best scholars from the elementary schools were to be sent on to the secondary schools and the best scholars in them on to the universities, the poor at the expense of the kirks and the rich at their fathers' expense.

It was a considered system of education based upon the needs of the Church and State for able men and so planned as to command such talent. The difficulty with it was that the "heritors" in the separate parishes (the proprietors of houses and lands subject to public charges) would be loath to pay the expenses of a schoolmaster and the expenses of the poor boys. It was an ideal that was set up, an ideal reinforced again and again, as in the act of legislation of 1696. But the money was seldom forthcoming.

The Scots have always been praised for their emphasis upon education. Much of that praise is deserved, but we shall find as we later observe the workings of Scottish education that the systems planned were always far ahead of what was carried out.

The Book of Discipline was no less concerned with religious instruction. Sermons and prayers with some exercise in the reading of the Scriptures were to be offered daily in larger towns, and in "notable" towns one day a week besides Sunday was appointed for a sermon. In every town where "schools and repair of learned men are" there was to be one weekly service known as an "exercise." At that service a passage of Scripture was to be read upon which someone was to comment, and his comment was then to be followed by that of others, never however by more than three altogether, "for avoiding of confusion." Such exercises were deemed necessary so that the Kirk might "have judgment and knowledge of the graces, gifts and utterances of every man within their own body." In this way the "simple and such as have somewhat profited shall be encouraged daily to study and proceed in knowledge . . . and every man shall have liberty to utter and declare his mind and knowledge." Children were to be examined upon the catechism publicly. The heads of families had the duty of imparting religious instruction to their children and servants. At least once a year the minister and the elders were to examine publicly every member of the Church about the chief points of religion.

These were elaborate provisions. They meant that every boy and girl was in matters of religion given an intellectual discipline, and that all members of the Church were continuously trained in the knowledge of their faith. The effect upon the religious and intellectual character of the Scottish people must have been considerable. Those who have observed the Scottish peasantry have remarked again and again that their ability to argue points of religion was extraordinary. Their knowledge of the Bible and their ability to quote it never failed to amaze travelers. The Scots were trained from youth up in their religion, as probably no other people in Europe.

The Book of Discipline bears close reading for its implications. Preachers were enjoined not to have respect to persons in their preaching and not to pay too much attention to the funerals of the rich and honorable, "seeing that before God there is no respect of persons." This was an early indication of the fiercely democratic feeling that was to spring from Calvinism and that was to manifest itself eventually in Scottish character.

In the matter of divorce the Book declared that in the case of adultery, proved before the civil magistrate, the offender ought to be executed and the innocent one go free. Yet if the life of the guilty one were spared, "as it ought not to be," and if he showed long penitence, he was to be admitted again to the sacrament. As to the offender marrying again, "we answer that if they cannot live continent and if the necessity be such as that they fear farther offence of God, we cannot forbid them to use the remedy ordained of God." In other words marriage was a remedy to prevent sin. But what is more worth observation is that not only murderers, as already observed, but adulterers, if not executed by the State, might be readmitted to the Church after sufficient penance. Calvinism was a harsh religion but it held out hope to the worst sinners.

The Book of Discipline imposed a theocratic republic upon Scotland, a republic with a certain absolute control over the individual. "For no man may be permitted to live as best pleaseth him within the Church of God; but every man must be constrained by fraternal admonition and correction to bestow his labors when of the Church they are required, to the edification of others." If men were unwilling

131

so to do, "discipline must proceed against them, provided that the civil magistrate concur with the judgment and election of the Church."

This was interference with the individual with a vengeance. Not only was he to be watched over by the elders and the minister but he was to be told what religious duties he should perform, and, if he showed any laxity in such performance, was to be disciplined by the State. It is true that the State might refuse to follow the injunctions of the Kirk as to discipline. That saving clause about the civil magistrate was worth a good deal.

One thinks of the Reformation as laying emphasis upon the individual. The individual read and interpreted the Bible. He looked to God directly and not through the priest. And yet in Scotland the Kirk was to dictate to the individual.

The Second Book of Discipline was prepared by commissioners set up by the General Assembly, worked over by that assembly, and passed in 1578. It had no other ratification. It was a much shorter statement than the First Book of Discipline and dealt more vaguely with most matters. The Kirk had just won a victory over the king and the bishops, and was enunciating its platform as to government. The Second Book emphasized the separateness of the jurisdiction of Kirk and State, a principle already predicated but now brought into sharp relief. "As ministers are subject to the judgment and punishment of the magistrate in external things, if they offend, so ought the magistrates to submit themselves to the discipline of the Kirk if they transgress in matters of conscience and religion." The power of the Kirk, it was asserted, flowed directly from God and "is spiritual, not having a temporal head on earth." The Kirk indeed had the best of it as compared with the secular power, for while the ministers looked only to God for their power, it was their duty to "teach the magistrates how it [the civil authority] should be exercised according to the Word." But on the other hand the ministers were forbidden to interfere with the civil jurisdiction.

The question of bishops was much to the fore in Scotland at this time. The Second Book made it clear that bishops had no authority over ministers and were not superior to them, and said nothing about those superintendents of provinces which had been provided for in the First Book of Discipline. The Second Book made provision for groups of elders of several small churches close to one another to meet together and consult especially in regard to matters of discipline, and this group of elders from several churches may be called the beginning of what was later to be known as a presbytery. The Second Book declared that the ministers and elders of a province might meet together to consult and deal with matters in the province and to act as a kind of higher court or court of appeal above the separate kirks. Above this body, to be known later as the Synod, was the General Assembly, the national body of the Kirk, which was attended by select ministers and elders. How they were to be selected is not stated but later they were to be elected as representatives of the smaller bodies. It will be observed that although these several bodies one above the other were set up, the main power rested still in the individual kirk, in its congregation, and in its body of elders and its minister.

The matter of patrons, i.e., of great men in the community who claimed the right to name ministers to kirks, was dealt with and the right was declared to be a Popish custom and to have no ground in the word of God. Upon this point many ecclesiastical struggles were to take place throughout Scottish history.

Both the First and Second Books of Discipline stressed the needs of the poor. The property of the old Church, which those programs demanded for the Reformed Church, was to be appropriated to pay for the ministers, for education, and for the poor. That the poor should profit from the wealth of the Church had been demanded in a curious placard put up on abbey and cathedral doors in 1559. There can be little doubt that the distress in Scotland had a good deal to do with strengthening the hands of the Reformers, and no doubt that

133

the Reformers had a genuine interest in ameliorating the conditions of poverty. The First Book of Discipline had urged that "ye have respect to your poor brethren, the laborers and manurers of the ground, who by these cruel beasts, the Papists, have been so oppressed that their life to them have been dolorous and bitter. . . . Ye must have compassion upon your brethren, appointing them to pay so reasonable teinds [tithes] that they may feel some benefit of Christ Jesus now preached unto them." The poor were to be cared for out of parish funds. "Every several kirk must provide for the poor within the self; for fearful and horrible it is, that the poor whom not only God the Father in his law . . . hath so earnestly commended to our care, are universally so condemned and despised." The Book goes on to make an exception of stubborn and idle beggars but includes the widow and fatherless, the aged, the impotent and lame.

The Second Book of Discipline was equally considerate of the poor "who so greatly increase and multiply among us." They were no longer to be defrauded of that part of the patrimony of the Kirk "which justly belongs unto them." "And by this order, if it be duly put to execution, the burden of them shall be taken off us to our great comfort, the streets shall be cleansed of their cryings and murmurings; so as we shall no more be a scandal to other nations, as we have hitherto been."

In framing the Second Book of Discipline and in making the fight for the separate jurisdiction of the Kirk as against the State, the most important person was Andrew Melville, who was to a considerable degree the successor of Knox in the leadership of the Kirk of Scotland and who stands next to him among Scottish heroes of the Reformation. He was almost as typical a Scot as Knox and deserves our attention. The youngest of nine boys brought up by their mother, he was "a sickly tender boy and took pleasure in na thing sa mikle as his buik." At New College, St. Andrews, the provost used to take the boy on his knees before the fire and, with a blessing on him, say, "My silly [frail] fatherless and motherless child, its ill to wit [to know] what God may make of thee yet." Melville became a Greek and Latin scholar, spent much time on the Continent, and returned to become principal at the University of Glasgow and then at St. Mary's College, St. Andrews. He soon became a leader in the Kirk and in writing the Second Book of Discipline.

Melville was as fearless a fighter as Knox. When Regent Morton told him there would be no quiet in the country "till half a dozen of you be hanged or banished," Melville answered him: "Tush, Sir, threaten your courtiers in that fashion. It's all one to me whether I rot on the earth or in the air." In 1583 Melville was summoned before the council for using treasonable language in his sermons. "Mr. Andro, never jarging [swerving] nor dashed a whit . . . plainly told the King and Council that they presumed overboldly . . . to take upon them to judge the doctrine, and control the ambassadors and messengers of a King and Council greater nor [than] they and far above them." Then unclasping his little Hebrew Bible from his girdle and clanking it down before the king and the chancellor he said: "There is my instructions and warrant." The story of how Melville told James there were two kings and two kingdoms is generally known. There was Christ Jesus, and his kingdom, the Kirk, whose subject King James VI was. Melville could awe the king, who was "fain to take it up betwixt them with gentle terms and merry talk."

Most of Melville's work was undone, as we shall see. James had no patience with a Kirk that had separate powers from the State of which he was the head, and he knew perfectly well that the republican institutions which Knox and Melville had set up agreed not at all with monarchy. James won, and Melville was sent into exile on the Continent and died there. Yet in the long run Melville's conceptions of the power and separateness of the Kirk were to prevail and were to affect the outlook of Scots and their character. When in 1843 Thomas Chalmers and four hundred members of the General Assembly walked out of that body on the question of patronage, they were accompanied by the ghost of "Mr. Andro."

XIII

SEVENTEENTH-CENTURY STRUGGLES AND
THE COVENANTERS

ONE more chapter will be given to the Reformation, this one to the ups and downs of Presbyterianism in the seventeenth century. The Reformation which is often dated from the Treaty of Edinburgh in 1560 cannot be said to have been concluded until the Revolution of 1689 saw the Church of Scotland established for good. Not until then could John Knox and Andrew Melville sleep peacefully.

The seventeenth century was a decisive one for both England and Scotland.

In England the question of the relation of Parliament and the king was fought over at Westminster and between the hedges of the Midlands and over the walls of the north, and determined at length in 1689. The two parties that were to divide England and that were to form the basis of her politics up to the Great War were becoming distinguishable. The cabinet system was in germ. Classical literature had been absorbed into English thought and ways of behavior. Superstition was beginning in the last part of the century to be laughed out of court and out of courts. A great nation was shaking off its medievalism and setting out to realize its destiny.

What a different century Scotland went through! There struggles over religion followed one another in endless variety. Classical influences hardly touched thinking or manners. Not until the eighteenth century did philosophers appear. Thinking was almost exclusively in fixed theological terms. There was no Milton in Scotland to define the theory of Puritanism and to put its case on a high level; there was no tinker of Bedford to trace the progress of Mr. Christian. No great political leaders such as John Pym and Oliver Cromwell gave a program to Puritan ideals and breadth and some tolerance to Puritan rule.

English Puritanism was establishing itself as a philosophy of conduct within and without the Church and was outside the Church to become at length the Nonconformist Conscience. The Puritans of England were interested in the development of science. Natural phenomena were being observed and catalogued and the reign of law was foreseen. But the Puritans of Scotland, the Presbyterians, were unaware of the methods of observation and not even interested in the possible laws of nature. One imaginative Scot, to be sure, Napier of Merchistoun, had invented logarithms. But in general the Presbyterians saw in what happened not the operation of natural laws but the interposition of the Deity. The time was to come when the Scots were to show themselves more alert to the possibilities of science than the English.

The English Puritans were defining earlier vague notions of the powers of Parliament and expanding them. In consequence of immediate political needs they were developing the theory that the king ruled through Parliament. It has been seen that the Scots failed to make much of their Parliament. The legislative powers of that body had been sluiced off into a committee called the Lords of the Articles, who initiated legislation and did pretty much what they were told to do by the king and the Privy Council. In 1640 after the National Covenant the Scottish Estates had determined that Parliament might choose or might not choose a Committee of the Articles, but in 1661 the Lords of the Articles had been restored to their former powers with the important exception that others than the committee could introduce legislation. From that time on there was a certain amount of life in the Scottish Parliament. With the Revolution of 1689 the Lords of the Articles were done away with, and from that day to the Union in 1707 the Scottish Parliament was a going concern. There is some evidence indeed that English parliamentary methods were being observed in Edinburgh. Up

137

to the Revolution members of the Scottish Parliament had gained little experience in government, and the body to which they belonged had exercised little restraining power. The king of Scots had been really limited only by the possibility of revolt.

The Scottish Presbyterians developed little political theory. It is true that in the late sixteenth century George Buchanan had written forcefully to prove that monarchs were limited, citing Greek and Roman writers as well as Scripture. In 1641 Samuel Rutherford published a book to show that the king was not omnipotent. In a letter written to Drummond of Hawthornden, probably by Montrose, it was asserted that kings were limited by the "laws of God and nature and some laws of the country . . . which secure to the good subject his honor, his life and the property of his goods."

The Scots had little mind to look southward for theory or practice. When they were riding high with their National Covenant they were so unaware of English institutions rooted in the past that they sought to impose their Covenant upon England. They would co-operate with the English only upon the preposterous condition that the English adopted the Scottish system of religion. In a Puritanized Church or in the system of Independency they had no interest. England must become Presbyterian as well as Scotland. There was only one God and he was a rigid Calvinist.

In such comparisons one can easily be too hard on the Scots. Theirs was a small country with no lively center as yet where talent gathered and exchanged ideas. One would not think of making comparisons were it not that Scotland later became so important to Britain, contributing ideas and men of parts. When the Scots gained wealth and the leisure that went with it, they were to make a wonderful showing. It must be said further that the narrow Presbyterianism to which they were so attached in the seventeenth century was eventually to affect the world profoundly.

Nor can it be forgotten that Scotland, for all her smallness, played a decisive part in molding the destinies of England. The uprising in Scotland in 1638 forced Charles I to call the Long Parliament which was to set off the Civil Wars. Scottish support of the parliamentary party in those wars had much to do with the outcome, with the overthrow of Charles I. It is true that Charles II was to come into his own, but the results of the 1640's were made permanent in 1689 and the Scots may fairly claim a part in that consummation.

To come back again to England, we may observe that the stage for the seventeenth century had been set by the Tudors. Those rulers had so managed it that the old nobility, who had been the country outposts of government, had less to do with looking after the districts adjacent to their seats. No longer did they live in fortified strongholds, like so many of the Scots nobility, no longer did they have retainers on a large scale. The Tudors, by means of the monastic lands they grabbed and gave away, created a new nobility that was dependent upon the crown. By the same means they brought up a new gentry to whom they gave continuous jobs as justices of the peace and deputy lieutenants, hard jobs that took up much of their time and gave those officials a sense of being useful to the government and of being responsible for local conditions. To the smaller folk the Tudors assigned jobs as churchwardens, surveyors of the highway, and overseers of the poor. The government developed an elaborate system of unpaid local officials. That system gave all but the humblest classes work to do and experience in government. It was kept in motion by the Privy Council, who prodded local officials into performing their functions.

Any such system the Scottish kings could not have hoped to set up. They had a people utterly unused to local government. To be sure many of the nobles, especially in the Highlands, still administered judicial powers over their tenants, powers which they had inherited from feudal days. Those lords had the power of life and death, but each one acted on his own. The lairds, who were the Scottish equivalent of the

139

English country gentlemen, enjoyed no political functions whatever and consequently none of that social prestige that went with political duty and responsibility.

James VI was the first king who really succeeded, after he got his hand in, in building up the royal power methodically and in keeping the nobles in due subjection. Four years after he became king of England he could say to the Parliament of that country: "This I must say for Scotland, and I may truly vaunt it: here I sit and govern it with my pen: I write and it is done, and by a clerk of the Council I govern Scotland now—which others could not do by the sword."

His departure in 1603 to become James I of Britain left Scotland with a king four hundred miles away. But in Edinburgh there was a Privy Council experienced in the ways of the king and ready to carry out his will. There was still much to do in strengthening the central power. The Western Islands and the restless Border districts were brought under control. Yet even in the Lowlands and in the country close to the capital there was much crime, and murder was frequent among all classes. James provided that justices ayre which had ceased to be held regularly should be held twice a year in every shire, and appointed justices of the peace on the model of the English justices. It was a long time before those justices could win the influence and sway they had in England.

With the Kirk James made progress more slowly and yet surely. He wished not only to bring it under control but to make it as much as possible like the English Church. Resistance he met, as was to be expected, but he was skilful in biding his time and in getting what he wanted. In 1618 he gained the approval of a packed General Assembly for the Five Articles of Perth, and later had them passed by the Estates. The most important of these articles required that members should kneel at the communion, which meant to Presbyterians a recognition of the Roman Catholic theory that a supernatural change took place in the elements. No more welcome to the Presbyterians was the provision for the

140

observance of Christmas, Good Friday, Easter, Ascension Day, and Trinity Sunday. Even before he set up the Five Articles James had established a Court of High Commission modeled on the English court of that name, to enforce ecclesiastical discipline and to punish those who failed to obey the decrees of the Church. James had made the rules and set up the new machinery but he could not induce the people to obey. Everywhere there was resistance to the Five Articles.

He had gone too far. Some of his own Scottish bishops had warned him that he ought to go slow in anglicizing the Kirk of Scotland. Archbishop Spottiswoode and William Cowper, Bishop of Galloway, were emphatic in urging a moderate policy. "Brethren, I beseech you in Christ," declared the Bishop of Galloway to some of the zealous Episcopalians, "Remember these things are not so essential points as to rend the bowels of the Kirk for them." Spottiswoode strove with the king for a milder policy. Smaller men there were, several of them, who, while they leaned in an Episcopal direction, sought peace and wished to gain it by a moderate policy. They hoped that the Kirk of Scotland might include men of all groups and that the numerous Presbyterian group might not be pushed too far. But these hopes came to nothing. The moderates were not listened to. That there was such a group as early as James VI is indicative of something promising in a land of extremes. The authoritarian James was not swayed from his purposes and took the path of most resistance.

Charles learned nothing from the opposition to his father. He went beyond him. His first policies, however, had something to be said for them. The Act of Revocation of 1625 took back into the hands of the crown all the Church and crown lands which had been alienated since the beginning of Mary's reign, but promised those who would surrender them a reasonable compensation. It is impossible to explain this act, and the question of "teinds" or tithes involved, in a few words; it would be hard enough to explain in many words. Suffice it to say that by the new arrangements the

141

ministry was permanently the gainer. Not so the nobility, who stood to lose heavily in respect to properties they had held for a good while. Having done what he could to rouse a powerful class against him, Charles proceeded to look for further trouble. He set out to impose upon a Scottish Church a Prayer Book denounced by the Scots as more Popish than the English Book. The graphic Robert Baillie described the situation resulting: "Presbyteries, sessions, assemblies must down; the bishop and his official, the warden and the clerk and the priest of the parish must up; the new forms of baptism, eucharist, marriage, burial, prayers, psalms, preaching must be received, under the pains of deposition, excommunication and horning [outlawing]; who will not yield, he is a seditious factious rebel, not only against the kirk and king, but God and his fifth command."

Charles had no sense of the possible, nor any understanding of the Scots. When the new Prayer Book was read in St. Giles Kirk some women started a riot. The Scots broke into rebellion, broke more easily and naturally than the English. Rising against the king was an old story and meant little more than an effort to correct his policy. Rebellion in Scotland corresponded to parliamentary resistance in England. The rebels wished merely to force the king to give up his innovations.

"What shall be the event, God knows," wrote Baillie. "There was in our land never such an appearance of a stir. The whole people thinks Popery at the doors . . . I think our people possessed with a bloody devil. . . . For myself I think, God, to revenge the crying sins of all estates and professions . . . is going to execute his long denounced threatnings, and to give us over unto madness, that we may everyone shoot our swords in our neighbors' hearts . . . The barricades of Paris, the Catholic League of France is much before my eyes." It was the *praefervidum ingenium Scotorum* all over again. The Scots were more deeply incensed against their king than the English could ever be. They would cry Popery all over the streets of Edinburgh.

But they would be much more ready to come to an accommodation with him than would the English.*

Charles played a poor game but he had a bad hand. A National Covenant was drawn up by three of the most astute men in Scotland; it sounded very reasonable. It was based upon the negative Confession of Faith signed by the king and his household in 1581, condemning the tenets of Rome. The Covenant enumerated the acts of Parliament passed in confirmation of the Confession and finally put forth an oath in support of the crown and true religion. It was so cleverly drawn that little could be said against it and yet it was a call to resistance. It was no time before it was being signed by most of the nobility and by every class of Scottish people.

The heather was on fire. All the bishops save four fled to England. A General Assembly was called in Scotland, and there were efforts to find a means of accommodation. But Charles was steadily preparing for war and the signers of the Covenant were doing the same. Charles moved north with an army and General Leslie with a Scottish army moved toward the Border.

There is no space here to deal with the First and Second Bishops Wars. Eventually the Scots found themselves allied with the parliamentary party in England in the Great Rebellion. Presbyterianism was wholly restored in Scotland and all the Anglican ceremonies done away with. In a few short years the Scots had gone back with a rush to John Knox and Andrew Melville. They had had an English army almost at their mercy.

The Civil Wars were a bad time in Scotland, a good deal worse than in England. In England there were two parties arrayed against each other. The supporters of Parliament and those of a Puritan inclination were on one side, and the adherents of the royal prerogative and of high Anglicanism

---

* The Scots were less given to compromise than the English. But disturbance and rebellion were with them substitutes for constitutional resistance and might be called off when the king yielded. The English drew the sword and sheathed it less lightly.

were on the other. One can think of exceptions, of men who plumped for the king out of sheer loyalty, while believing in parliamentary government and disliking bishops. One can think too of families who followed the parliamentary cause because they had failed to gain what they asked from the crown. But the issue was sharper than such issues generally are.

The picture was more confused in Scotland. Now the head of a great family, with his many retainers, was fighting for the National Covenant, and perhaps presently for the king, as the great Marquis of Montrose.

In England the war was carried on with a great deal of consideration for noncombatants and prisoners as well as for women and children. The leaders on both sides were nobles and country gentlemen and they knew the gentlemen on the other side and treated them as such. Women and children were often allowed to go through the lines and prisoners were usually treated with decency and sometimes permitted to go off on their own paroles.

It was not a gentlemanly war in Scotland. Too many zealous ministers with influence were close to the military. When men surrendered on promise of their lives, those promises were sometimes forgotten. After Mercat Cross, Sir Philip Nesbit, a boy of eighteen who had been captured, was executed, and the Reverend Mr. Dixon is said to have exulted, "The work goes bonnily on." When Leslie defeated Montrose near Selkirk, he promised quarter to a large body of men, but the ministers gathered round him and persuaded him against his own better judgment that only the head officers should be saved and that the rest of the prisoners should be killed. At another time when the same thing happened, General Leslie, who was walking over the field with one of the ministers, Mr. Nevoy, turned and said to him: "Now, Mr. John, have you not once gotten your fill of blood?"

It will be recalled that after Charles I was executed the Presbyterians negotiated with Charles II, drew him from the Continent to Scotland, and persuaded him to accept the

National Covenant. They sermonized him drearily and at great length, they pointed out his failures in Sabbath observance, they did their level best to make a Presbyterian out of one who was not gifted in spiritual matters and who loved his ease and pleasure. There is nothing funnier in Scottish history than Charles II in the hands of the Presbyterians. The battle of Worcester changed all that, Charles II went on his travels, and Cromwell took over Scotland and ruled it.

Scotland enjoyed firm and good government. One can learn about it from the Scottish diarist, John Nicoll, who wrote: "Yet there was courts holden in Leith, by the English commanders, wherein justice was ministered summarily to all parties complaining, without partiality or favor; their carriages and ways in that behalf condemning ours in Scotland, as was alleged by many, who having actions and complaints given in before them, returned from them with great contentment." Nicoll went on to say that the English commanders punished one of their own soldiers for robbing a Scot. In another passage he remarked: "And, to speak truth, the Englishes were more indulgent and merciful to the Scots nor [than] was the Scots to their own countrymen and neighbors, as was too evident, and their justice exceeded the Scots in many things, as was reported. They also filled up the rooms of justice courts with very honest clerks and members of that judicatory."

Their honesty and fairness availed the English little. Were they not the ancient invaders come back again? Cromwell was in Scottish eyes almost another Edward I. He was a Puritan and a worthy one, but he was the wrong kind of Puritan, an Independent. The Scots, who had never approved of the execution of Charles I, began to exhibit that singular loyalty to the Stuarts which was to become a feature of their history and tradition.

The Restoration was welcomed by the people of Scotland. The Presbyterians, both the "Resolutioners," who in 1650 had accepted Charles II, and the "Remonstrants" or "Protesters," who had refused to accept him at that time, hoped for the best from the restored monarchy. Very soon they were disillusioned. Charles made it clear that he intended to restore Episcopacy. Some of the Protesters were at once imprisoned. Bishops were set up and given large powers, the General Assembly was done away with, and all that was left of the Presbyterian system was synods, presbyteries, and sessions. Ministers were required to seek presentation from a patron and collation from their bishops, and if they failed to do so were to be dismissed. Many did so fail and then young, inexperienced men were put in their places.

In general the Resolutioners made the best of the situation with as good grace as possible. But in the counties mainly of the southwest, where the Protesters had been strong, there was trouble at once. The people refused to go to the kirk, refused to listen to the new youngsters put in the pulpits, and assembled in secret places to hear their old preachers. The Estates, as the Scottish Parliament was usually called, passed an act which forbade these conventicles, and provided fines for those who did not attend the church. Troops were sent into the country and quartered on the people at their expense. John Welch of Irongray and Gabriel Semple of Kirkpatrick began preaching in the open fields, believing, as Terry tells us, that "if the Lord could be tied to any place, it is to the mosses and muirs of Scotland." It was not long before conventicles were being widely arranged all over the southwest.

The government set out ruthlessly to put them down. Out of that effort sprang the Pentland Rising of November, 1666, which looked for the moment formidable but was put down at Rullion Green and some of the instigators tortured and executed. It was long remembered that Hugh McKail, who had been tortured with the "boot," died in a rapture of joy, crying, "Farewell, sun, moon and stars. Farewell, kindred and friends, farewell, world and time, farewell, weak and frail body. Welcome eternity, welcome angels and saints."

Conventicles went on, men and women in hundreds and

146

occasionally in thousands gathered at appointed places in glens of the mountains or in "mosses" to listen to sermons, to sing psalms, and to take the communion together. More and more the men were armed and outposts were put out to keep watch for the soldiers who might be sent against them. Simple men they were, fanatics, who, had they been in power, would have persecuted those who did not accept their special forms of religion. Few of the gentry attached themselves to the cause but many ministers, who unhappily differed from one another in respect to theology and in respect to immediate policy. In 1679 John Graham of Claverhouse was sent against them and was defeated at Drumclog. Later a large force under the Duke of Monmouth was sent out, with Claverhouse as one of the subordinates. The Covenanters were now in strong force and, had they been able to agree with one another, might have defeated the forces sent against them. But they were so divided among themselves, some of their preachers urging that they should accept the Letter of Indulgence recently offered to the Presbyterians by the crown and some of them refusing to accept anything that came from Charles Stuart, that they ceased to be a compact body of fighting men. At Bothwell Brig they were beaten and many of them captured. The prisoners were some of them executed, some imprisoned out of doors in Greyfriars churchyard at Edinburgh, and some shipped to the Barbados. Frenzied men they were, who knew well enough they could not hope to succeed in rebellion but went ahead, and died "unconcernedly." A few of the fanatics had murdered Archbishop Sharp on the highway at Magus Moor near St. Andrews and believed that they were serving God in doing so, for the bishop had sent many of their fellows to death and was planning to send more.

At the moment the abortive risings rather strengthened the hands of the king than aided the cause of Presbyterianism. The great body of Scots at the time had no doubt a certain pity for the misguided Covenanters but were unwilling to assist them. When James VII, known in English history

147

ıs James II, attempted by one quick move after another to put Roman Catholics into the government of Scotland and was preparing the way for bringing Scotland back into the Roman fold, Scottish opinion against the sovereign hardened in the towns and among the nobility. But had it not been for the English nobility who attached themselves to William of Orange and furthered the movement for him in England, had it not been for the success of the English Revolution, it is hard to say what might have happened in Scotland. James VII might have had his way and might have restored Catholicism. The nobility did not have the habit of acting together; there was no tradition of parliamentary opposition; and the Duke of Lauderdale, that renegade Presbyterian, had managed in the reign of Charles II to bring all power into the hands of the king and of his obedient Privy Council. But one cannot say for sure what would have happened. In an emergency—the Scots were a violent people.

The Revolution settlement of 1689 was more of a revolution in Scotland even than in England. For a hundred years Stuart kings had been trying to impose Episcopacy upon an unwilling people of Presbyterian inclination. The Revolution put the Presbyterians back in charge of the Kirk. The General Assembly, which had not met for a generation, gathered together every year from this time on and assumed its place as the voice of the Kirk of Scotland. The Scottish Parliament became a proper parliament with debates that had significance.

The Covenanters had suffered untimely deaths for ideals but dimly understood by their countrymen. From the long point of view they were fortunate creatures. What they could not accomplish was done for them by the Revolution. With the success of the Presbyterian Church, the writers of Presbyterian history, and notably that lively storyteller, Robert Wodrow, came to think of the fanatics of the west as the martyrs of the Presbyterian Kirk. Their dying words were cherished; their skirmishes, Rullion Green, Drumclog, and Bothwell Brig, became part of the lore of their land; and

Greyfriars churchyard in Edinburgh came to be a hallowed spot. Their field conventicles are famous in story and painting. Unimportant peasants who were transported or executed, and simple ministers, who with their wives and children were driven out of their homes and hunted through the glens and over the moors, have become names in the martyrology of the country. They all made up another lost cause. The Patrick Hamiltons and the George Wisharts, the martyrs of the beginning of the Reformation, men of considerable caliber, have been obscured in favor of the narrow sectarians of the Covenanting days.

It was characteristic of the Scots to accept the Covenanters as heroes, of the Presbyterian struggles. The Covenanters were in a true Scottish tradition. They were as loyal to their causes as the clansmen of earlier days had been to their chiefs; they were men of zeal, of courage beyond estimate, and of some capacity for action. Usually they acted before they considered. They were partisans of their special brands of Christianity. How much affected they were by the lovelier and deeper aspects of Christianity it is hard to say. They could threaten their enemies and murder an archbishop, and yet withal they may have had some notion of eternal lovingkindness. It was not easy to throw aside their ancient instinct for violence when grievous wrongs were to be righted. To find the right in some odd offshoot of a creed was Presbyterian, Scottish Presbyterian. The whole history of Presbyterianism in the eighteenth and early nineteenth centuries was to follow that pattern.

XIV

THE PRESBYTERIAN INFLUENCE:
ITS STRENGTH

IN explaining Scottish character nothing is more important than religion. I have been tracing the story of
the Reformation and following the rise of Presbyterianism in detail because it is fundamental to my subject.
How Presbyterianism affected the Scot is a long story to be
told in 'the chapters that follow. In this chapter I shall con-
fine myself to the more obvious effects in the seventeenth
century up to the time of Charles II. These were of two
kinds, through the organization of the Church and through
the ideas of the Church.

The Calvinistic form of organization had eventually wide
effects throughout the world. Its influence in Scotland was
almost immediate.

The election of the elders and ministers by the membership of the kirk and the election of representatives to a national General Assembly gave the Scots experience in making
their own choices as to who should govern them. As presbyteries and synods, intermediate bodies between the kirks and
the General Assembly, developed, that experience became
wider and more significant. The Scots gained practice in
governing themselves, even if only in Church matters, that
the English had long known in matters of State, if not
in matters of Church. Representative government became
a custom among the Scots in one all-important department
of their lives. Wherever they went in the world during the
time to follow they carried with them the idea of representation.

How far political experience and representative institutions made for social democracy in Scotland it is hard to
estimate. It will be recalled that the First Book of Discipline

declared that the minister should devote no more attention to the funerals of the rich and great than to those of the poor. Yet from the beginnings of the Presbyterian system in Scotland the nobles and the lairds were more likely to be elected to the session, that is, the body of elders, and to the General Assembly, than men respected merely for godliness. When we come to examine the writings and the attitudes of the ministers we find that they often asserted that all men were equal before God and sometimes lived up to that ideal with considerable courage. Yet they were human beings too, living in an everyday world which recognized differences in class as part of an appointed order, and they were likely to show a certain deference to the nobles, the lairds, and the heritors of the parish. When the minister entered the pulpit he bowed to the heritors of the parish. That was a formality of course but one with significance. It was not to be expected that in a country still feudal the minister should ignore the gradations of rank and wealth.

The ministers were not unaware of the existence of poverty. The First Book of Discipline had provided, it will be recalled, that part of the Church property should be allocated for the benefit of the poor. We have seen that the property left over from the old Church did not materialize. Hence it remained the duty of the elders to press for contributions for the poor of the parish, and the poor box was brought round to those who refused to pay. In at least one instance it was provided that the poor who had fallen sick were to be listed and the list shown to the surgeons who were to give them free medical assistance. The matter of parish assistance I shall deal with in a later chapter.

The elders had another duty: to keep everyone in the parish under surveillance. It was their function, according to the First Book of Discipline, to keep tab on the life of the minister and of his whole family. Furthermore the elders and the minister were to have an inquisitorial function about every member of the parish. All questions of morals and of personal behavior came within their purview. The elders learned to ask questions and to encourage those who could tell tales. The result was that everyone assumed an inquisitorial capacity and the whole parish spied upon one another's conduct. That everyone should be his brother's keeper had been the principle implicit in the First Book of Discipline. It is no wonder that the Scots became sensitive to public opinion and that sobriety of conduct became the norm expected of people.

It was expected in particular of ministers. The First Book of Discipline, it will be remembered, had emphasized the necessity of sobriety and dignity upon the part of the ministry. They were not to enter alehouses, they were not to haunt the court, they were to carry themselves becomingly. So important was their dignity that the Book of Discipline insisted that the ministers should have good salaries. The Presbyterians had it in their minds that their ministers should be looked up to in their communities. The evidence goes to show that the ministers satisfied the expectations set forth in the Book of Discipline. Serious-minded men they were, sober in every respect, who regarded themselves as the spokesmen of the Lord. They were not carried away with light things. They believed in a certain high decorum, an austere dignity. It can hardly be doubted that the serious-mindedness enjoined upon the ministry and practised by them left its mark upon Scottish character. The elder and the man who hoped to become an elder conducted themselves with some of the same gravity and austerity as the minister. The carefree liveliness of the earlier Scot in "Peblis to the Play" or "Christis Kirk on the Green" was not for them.

I come now to the ideas of the Presbyterians. Naturally we deal first with foreordination. Foreordination sprang out of Presbyterian logic. The Presbyterian preachers had learned from their teachers in the universities the uses of logic and of reasoning from premises. Dialectic was deep in Scottish custom and character, as we have already seen. The doctrine of foreordination or predestination was logic in

152

religion carried to the utmost degree. One could put no limits to the power and knowledge of God. Hence He, knowing all things, knew in advance the decision that every individual would make, whether he would accept the redemption of his sins by Christ's atonement and so take the path toward heaven or whether he would reject it and move in another direction. There were the happy "elect" and the unfortunate "reprobate." The good Presbyterians were able to reconcile foreknowledge and free will. God knew, they said, what choice a man was going to make, but the man was nevertheless free to choose as he pleased and was responsible for his choice. There were those who declared that foreknowledge by God could not be distinguished from determinism, that predestination meant that God had from all eternity predestined some to heaven and some to hell. The good Bishop Leighton, a mystic, spoke of predestination as "a great abyss into which I choose to sink rather than attempt to sound it."

In Scotland today we hear little about election, and not much about it in Presbyterian churches outside of Scotland. It is a subject that no longer interests the Presbyterians of the north and it has ceased within the last two or three generations to interest Presbyterians elsewhere. But in the seventeenth century it did interest them profoundly.

The suggestion is sometimes made that belief in foreordination made the Scot into something of a fatalist, that he came as a result of his doctrine to expect a certain inevitability of events. I cannot disprove this suggestion but I certainly cannot say that I have seen the evidence for it.

It is true rather that if one goes back to medieval times and to the sixteenth century one can find some notion of Fortune and her ways and even some fatalism. The notion of Fortune, however, a kind of mystic deity that controls us all, is to be found everywhere in medieval literature as well as in Scottish writing. In *The Kingis Quair* written probably by James I, the question of free will is considered.

153

Some clerks, the poets wrote, hold that all chances are caused by the high heavens and that the diversity of the working of Fortune should cause necessity, but other clerks hold that

> the man himself
> Has in himself the choice and liberty
> To cause his fortune, how or when.

A good deal of fatalism was to be found in the old ballads and in other poetry. The poor lovers in the ballads were fated to be joined only in the grave. The Scots of pre-Presbyterian days were fond of believing that a certain man was "fey," that is, doomed to follow a certain course to his own undoing. They believed, like many other peoples, in prophecies as to when they should die. When the Douglas was wounded at Otterburn in 1388 he told the men gathered round the brackenbush where he lay:

> I have dreamed a dreary dream,
> Beyond the Isle of Skye,
> I saw a dead man win a fight,
> And I think that man was I.

That is not precisely fatalism but it comes close to it. Closer indeed are the lines of Sir William Alexander, later Earl of Stirling (1580–1640), lines that remind us of Shakespeare's words in *The Tempest* and that were published several years before *The Tempest* was played.

> Those golden palaces, those gorgeous halls,
> With furniture superfluously fair;
> Those stately courts, those sky-encountering walls,
> Evanish all—like vapors in the air.
>
> Our painted pleasures but apparel pain;
> We spend our days in dread, our lives in dangers,
> Balls to the stars and thralls to Fortune's reign,
> Known unto all, yet to ourselves but strangers.

The Presbyterian Influence: Its Strength

It is possible that the belief in predestination made the Scots more fatalistic, but I find less fatalism after Presbyterianism became established than before. Certainly that belief did not release them from their fears of doing wrong or from their censure of those who broke the regulations of the Kirk. Nor did any such belief weaken the initiative of the Scot or cause him to struggle less to control the future.

On the contrary. The belief in election proved an incentive. Lord Eustace Percy in his brilliant life of John Knox shows that Calvinism was a creed of hope, of incitement to action. It was nothing less than a philosophy of history. God had a slowly unfolding purpose to achieve on earth through his elect. The elect, always a few, had a job to do, to work through and with God to bring about his kingdom on earth by doing away with evil and injustice. They were enlisted in the eternal war between God and Satan. They made up an organic and organized communion, with a corporate discipline. "Not suddenly, not by sporadic enthusiasms, will God work out his purpose. His too are the settled disciplines of the world. *Omnis potestas a Deo,* the secular powers are also ordained by him—and his new revelations tend always to a new order, not less settled and effective than the old."

This philosophy, Lord Eustace believes, was the parent of the liberal movements of the last three hundred years, at least in Britain, Holland, and North America. He says that it held out to the sober minded a prospect of ordered liberty. That is to give Calvinism a great deal of credit. We shall see in future chapters that the Presbyterians in Scotland were not always to be the protagonists of liberalism. It may be remarked that Knox was the disciple of Calvin who strove most zealously for a theocratic state. The Presbyterians who succeeded him saw God's plans still revealing themselves in new ways, as we shall see in their sabbatarianism and in their rising opposition to the theater. Knox had been disappointed in his aims, but the men who set up the National Covenant came near to erecting a theocracy after his own heart.

Sabbatarianism can hardly be called an idea of the Presbyterians any more than of the Puritans in general, save that eventually it was carried farther in Presbyterian Scotland than anywhere else. It did not begin to show itself until the latter part of the sixteenth century. It was a new idea in both England and Scotland. John Knox and Andrew Melville had not insisted on any such observance of the Sabbath as the Presbyterians were later to demand. At the end of the sixteenth century it was provided that during preaching time taverns should be closed and that children were not to play. But the notion that the whole of the Sabbath day was to be taken up with religious exercises and meditation, while it was gaining ground all through the seventeenth century, was hardly characteristic of the first part. It is true that in many boroughs rather severe regulations were enforced. In some places elders were authorized to go round during church time and see who were absenting themselves from church or who were engaged in unnecessary occupations. That the Sabbath lasted from Saturday at six or eight o'clock to Sunday at the same hour was the usual conception, and unnecessary work during that period was frowned upon. But it was during church time that the Sabbath was utterly sacred.

The Presbyterian attitude toward the theater went through somewhat the same history as that toward the Sabbath. In the late sixteenth century the Presbyterians opposed "clerk plays," that is, religious plays based upon the Bible and upon the Apocrypha. But it is to be noted that ordinary plays, if not performed on Sunday, were as late as the reign of James VI still not under Presbyterian proscription. It was later that the Presbyterians set themselves so relentlessly against all theatrical productions.

That education for the young was supremely important may be called an idea that the Presbyterians took to heart. I have already mentioned the demand in the First Book of Discipline for a system of national education. In that system it was intended that the best lads in the elementary schools be sent to the secondary schools and the best boys there to the universities, at public expense, if necessary. But the difficulty was that the money to pay for the teaching and for scholars' stipends was to come largely from the funds that had once belonged to the Roman Church and that were now to be annexed to the Reformed Kirk. In addition the heritors of the parishes were to provide funds. Now the Kirk was never able, as we have seen, to get for itself the lands it expected. Most of them were kept by the nobility, and the heritors were singularly slow to vote the taxes upon themselves to pay for schools. Hence the system of education laid down was long a blueprint.

Yet the Presbyterians did accomplish something. Their leaders reformed the universities, put in more and better professors, and developed new teaching methods. In 1616 the Privy Council, not at that time, to be sure, under Presbyterian influence, provided that schools should be set up in every parish where convenient means might be found, and teachers appointed at the expense of the parishioners. In 1646, in the heyday of the Presbyterians, it was enacted by statute that wherever there was no school the heritors of the parish were to provide a schoolhouse and pay for the schoolmaster, and appropriate salaries for the schoolmasters were to be fixed. Unhappily that legislation was repealed shortly after the Restoration. But in 1696, when Presbyterianism had again come into its own, it was declared by law that schools should be established in every parish. Such legislation was of course a good sign, but it was not easily enforced. It was a long while before remoter districts, especially in the Highlands, were provided with schools.

Scottish education was different from the English. In the secondary schools Latin was the main subject. Indeed the secondary schools were jealous of the teaching of Latin in the universities. Nevertheless Latin was studied at the universities and of course the lectures were given in Latin. But the Scottish universities laid their emphasis upon Greek, rhetoric, moral philosophy, logic, metaphysics, natural philosophy, and theology. The results of such an education

157

should be evident in the writings of the graduates. Ministers of course made up a considerable share of those graduates and it is noticeable that they rarely quoted classical authors or showed any sympathetic understanding of classical thought. How far other graduates were affected by the Romans and the Greeks I do not know but I suspect not a great deal. Was the Scot so disciplined in grammar that he failed to catch any notion of the literature and ideas?

It is probable that the everyday Scot up to the nineteenth century gained no little part of his intellectual training from the Shorter Catechism and from hearing the interpretation of the Bible. Many kirk sessions required of communicants that they should satisfy the minister of their knowledge of the Ten Commandments, the Confession of Faith, and the Lord's Prayer. The same knowledge was usually required of those who wished to be married and of parents who presented children for baptism. But this was a minimum of knowledge. The records of the sessions show that often there were two meetings a week in the late afternoon in which not only were the doctrines of the Kirk examined but scriptural texts were dealt with. The diaries of the ministers indicate that their writers were largely occupied with training their flocks in the reasons of belief and in showing them what they ought to do and to leave undone. So well were the people brought up on the Scripture that the minister's interpretation of it in his sermons interested them and gave them the blessed chance to agree or disagree. Robert Stirling told Wodrow how a group of harvesters had taken time off in the midst of the day to listen to his father's preaching "with great eagerness." The soldiers in the Covenanting army that resisted Charles I listened to "good sermons morning and even under the roof of heaven." The historian Burnet tells about the intellectual curiosity and intelligence of the common people in the western counties. He was dealing with the early reign of Charles II but we may fairly assume that conditions were not essentially different from a few years before. He says: "We were indeed amazed to see a poor commonalty so capable to argue upon points of government, and on the bounds to be set to the power of princes in matters of religion; upon all these topics they had texts of scripture at hand; and were ready with their answers to anything that was said to them. This measure of knowledge was spread even amongst the meanest of them, their cottagers and their servants. They were indeed vain of their knowledge, much conceited of themselves, and were full of a most entangled scrupulosity."

The Presbyterian influence upon education extended to the Anglicization of the language. The Scottish Reformers brought north Tyndale's translation into English of the New Testament and part of the Old Testament and Coverdale's translation of the whole Bible. The Genevan Bible appeared in 1560. "Then might have been seen," wrote Knox, "the Bible lying almost upon every gentleman's table. The New Testament was borne about in many man's hands." There was as yet no translation of the Bible into the Scottish dialect and men had to read the English translations. Those must have done a great deal to further the use of English in Scotland. The controversial literature about religion in England was quickly conveyed north. Knox and his fellow Reformers were back and forth between England and Scotland and tended to write and speak a Scottish tongue that approached English. Their successors in the next century, the Presbyterian preachers, were so much in touch with the Puritan divines in England and so familiar with their works that they could not fail to show the effect in their own writing and speaking. It was not only the ministers but the whole reading public in Scotland that were compelled to read English if they were to keep abreast of the main interest of the times, religion.

Presbyterian and other influences were driving out the Gaelic. "The Scots tongue is now forget with me, specially in writing," declared Henry Scrimger in 1572. Sir Thomas Craig, who flourished in the reign of James VI, could recall a time within his memory when the people of Stirling and Dumbarton spoke pure Gaelic. By his old age they were talking English. Gaelic had been relegated to Argyllshire and the Islands. Not many generations earlier Sir Thomas' ancestors

159

might have heard Gaelic over most of south Scotland, except in the Anglian country of the east shore. Sir Thomas observed that English was making progress in the Highlands and even in the Orkneys and the Shetlands where Norse had been the prevalent tongue. Now, he said, the ministers were using English in churches and were "well enough understood," and he predicted that with the development of schools the people of the Highlands would come to speak English. His predictions were to be slowly fulfilled. Gaelic continued to be spoken in the remote parts of the Highlands, is still spoken in the Western Isles and in out-of-the-way glens, but for more than two centuries English has been the language of the country. The pronunciation is of course different from that in the south of England although not so utterly removed from that in the north.

The popularization of the English language, which would have come no doubt without the help of the Presbyterians, but which was aided by them, did more perhaps than statesmen had ever been able to do for the unification of England and Scotland. Two neighboring nations that spoke the same language could not in a time of the spread of the printed word escape interchange of ideas and community of thought. As the Scots came to talk and write like the English, political union with the nation south of the Border became more conceivable.

The dominance of the English language was a victory too for the Anglians of the east coast. Those people, who were most closely related to the English, had won in the old days the political battle against the prevailing Gaels. Now they were winning the battle of the language.

It may be thought that I have given the Presbyterians too large a share in the making of Scottish character, I do not believe that I have exaggerated their effect. It must, however, be always remembered that people to some degree make a religion that suits them. If Presbyterianism affected the Scottish people a great deal, it was because it was a religion that met their needs and aspirations.

XV

THE PRESBYTERIAN INFLUENCE:
ITS DEFICIENCIES

WHEN I come to the matter of what the Presbyterians lacked that the English had, I have to speak relatively, comparing them constantly with the English. The Presbyterians of the seventeenth century were singularly wanting in any sense of beauty and what goes with it, proportion, orderliness, and restraint.

The want of a feeling for beauty is perhaps best evidenced by the absence of poetry, drama, and effective prose. The poets of the late fifteenth and early sixteenth centuries had been an element in the greatness of Scotland. Scotland ought at all times to have produced poets, for the language lends itself to poetry. The ballad makers, whose names we do not know, had left a heritage of the greatest ballads known to any country, ballads that sprang out of the life of common people on an exciting Border. There had also been a beginning of play writing. Sir David Lyndsay had shown the possibilities of what might have become a Scottish dramatic movement. There were poets in the seventeenth century but with the exception of Drummond of Hawthornden they are mostly forgotten today and were of slight importance in their own time. New ballads there were, but they were only imitations of the old ones. Play writing disappeared and the theater failed to materialize. The sudden decline in the forms of art was not due alone to the fact that Presbyterians were not interested in the beautiful—they had a suspicion that beauty was pagan and of the evil one—but to their entire preoccupation with theology and with the politics that supported theology. That reflectiveness out of which great poetry might have come was wasted on immediate problems of policy; those emotions that might have abetted the creative spirit were given to prayers and exhortations.

161

It is unnecessary to point to the contrast with England, unnecessary even to name the poets and dramatists of England during the same period. The long and bitter struggle over Parliament and Puritanism did not silence the poets or the prose writers. Even the closing of the theaters during the Puritan regime was only an episode. It cannot be said that the short period of wars and Puritan government in mid-century seriously arrested the natural current of creativeness.

The want of feeling for beauty in Presbyterian Scotland was shown by the outward and inward appearance of the kirks as well as by the services within them. No doubt the unlovely exteriors and interiors were due in part to the poverty of the people. But the Scots did not, like the English, spend time and thought from generation to generation in improving the buildings and in making them fair to look upon. There seemed in Scotland to be no pride in the ecclesiastical fabric. Even today the country churches of Scotland are a disappointment to the traveler who has looked on many English churches. If the churches were ugly, the services were impressive but hardly beautiful. There was no prayer book, no pealing organ, no practised choir. Such things the Scots would have regarded as excrescences upon an austere religion, as relics of Romanism. In England even the least churchly of men look back upon the village church which they attended in youth with affection; they know the words of the Prayer Book and revere them, even when they have given up belief. The Englishman about to be killed by an Afghan tribe recalls

> the gray little church across the park,
> The mounds that hid the loved and honour'd dead;
> The Norman arch, the chancel softly dark,
> The brasses black and red.

The literature of England is full of allusions to the village church. I do not recall a single Scottish poem that deals lovingly with the village kirk. The Scottish poets think rather

162

of their auld Kirk as a whole and of its sufferings in the past. It was Robert Louis Stevenson who asked that when dying he might

> Hear about the graves of the martyrs the peewees crying,
>   And hear no more at all.

The Scot could do without the loveliness in his church and its services that the Englishman required. Dignity and order, pomp and circumstance were not for him. Such things were vanities. Yet the Scot was often at heart a poet, and a dying Cameronian might express himself in rhythmic words that haunted the memory. Moreover the Scots have known how to catch the poetry in the stories of their martyrs. To them beauty has come slowly out of long reflection and often out of suffering; they did not cherish her for every day.

The seventeenth-century minister showed little of that restraint that is the beginning of beauty. The minister was often a man whose outward dignity was all that could be desired but whose outlook was narrow and whose language was marked by little moderation. The reader has seen something of the intolerance of the Presbyterian ministers, but to realize the degree and extent of that intolerance he would have to follow the wearisome details of politics from the signing of the Covenant on. The ministers were intent upon putting down all who disagreed with them even in details; they were willing to send their opponents to the block or the scaffold. Loving-kindness was not in them, nor feeling for the fellowship of all Christians. The beauty of holiness was beyond their ken. The true-blue Presbyterian was concerned to force all others including the English into his mold.

He preached long sermons; it was deemed not right that he should read them. It was natural for him to belabor a point. Often he played round it with much use of quotation from the Scripture and with many illustrations and figures of speech. The Reverend Samuel Rutherford, one of the great figures of seventeenth-century Presbyterianism, sometimes called the "saint of the Covenant," but a bigoted one, left a large body of letters from which we can guess something as to his style of preaching. To Lady Kenmure he wrote on the death of her husband: "I trust your Lord will remember . . . that ye may be a free woman for Christ, who is now suiting for the marriage love of you; and therefore, since you lie alone in your bed, let Christ be as a bundle of myrrh to sleep and lie all the night betwixt your breasts." Rutherford's letters were full of such metaphorical language, the result perhaps of familiarity with the Song of Solomon. He was not alone in the richness of his verbiage. Other Presbyterian divines were addicted to the same overrich and fanciful metaphors. While the Puritan preachers in England, some of them, indulged in figurative language, I do not recall any such luxuriance as was common in Scotland.

There were indeed occasional ministers whose words and deeds were marked by restraint. Two of the most noteworthy were Robert Leighton and Henry Scougal, both of whom were scholars and leaned in an Episcopal direction. Leighton was a saintly man who "seemed to be in perpetual meditation"; Doctrinal principles failed to interest him and he besought men to be "meek and gentle, lovers and exhorters of peace, private and public, among all ranks of men." The debates and contentions of the country seemed to worry him, and he tried to avoid the bishopric and archbishopric thrust upon him, and used his authority to obtain as much toleration as possible. Scougal "loved goodness wherever he found it, and entertained no harsh thoughts of men merely upon their differing from him in this or that opinion." Such men—there were a few others—were in the tradition of Spottiswoode and and William Cowper of the early part of the century and they proved that not all Scots were zealots.

The emotionalism that was beginning to appear in the seventeenth century was another indication of the want of restraint. Presbyterianism, as much as any religion, was an intellectual faith, based upon premises and developed from them, and its founders may be called intellectual men, even

164

if often passionate. But already by the middle of the seventeenth century there was becoming evident an emotionalism in preaching that was to be more pronounced toward the end of the century and early in the next. The ministers were moved by the plight of sinners and sometimes the minister would have his audience in tears. It was written of the Reverend John Welsh that "no man could hardly hear him and forbear weeping, his conveyance was so affecting." The Reverend John Livingstone noted how the spirit of God moved his people: "I have seen above a thousand persons all at once lifting up their hands, and the tears dropping from their eyes." But this was unusual and Mr. Livingstone recognized as much.

It has to be said that emotional preaching was practised also by Nonconformist ministers in England. Anyone who will read the daybooks of Oliver Heywood of the West Riding and Lancashire at the end of the seventeenth century will find the type of weeping preacher. Others could have been found among the Nonconformist brethren of the north of England.

It was part of the lack of a sense of proportion in the Presbyterians that they addressed the Deity in familiar terms, though it had been done in Scotland before the Presbyterians came upon the scene. But the Presbyterians talked so much about their God and his immediate personal relation with each one of them that they tended to personalize him as near at hand. When William Guthry, one of the leaders of the Scottish ministry, was dying, Johnston of Waristoun, an important Presbyterian layman, was in the room. "All that prayed before Waristoun were conditional in their petitions for his life. When he [Waristoun] came to pray, he was mighty peremptory and would not at all take a refusal, and said, 'Lord, Thou knowest this Church cannot want him.'" Johnston of Waristoun was so given to prayer that he may have thought he could take liberties. But when the unhappy Covenanters knew that their rebellion was about to be crushed and that they themselves were on the verge of capture and execution, Mr. Robinson asked a blessing before a meal. "He summoned God very imperiously to be their secondary. 'And if,' said he, 'Thou wilt not be our secondary, we will not fight for Thee at all, for it is not our cause but Thy cause; and if Thou wilt not fight for our cause and Thy own cause, we are not obliged to fight for it." Poor Mr. Robinson was no doubt a desperate man when he addressed the Deity in that summary fashion, but his words were not out of character. Passages of a somewhat similar kind could be found in the prayers and sermons of the old Scottish ministers. They sometimes kept God too near at hand for reverence.

The want of a sense of proportion was evident throughout Scottish writings of the seventeenth century. The Presbyterian Scot was too intent upon his salvation and that of his neighbor to see the men about him in comic relief. He was too serious minded to laugh at the incongruities of life. It is an effort to think of writings that betray humor of any kind. Sir Thomas Urquhart wrote his *Discovery of a Most Exquisite Jewel* to vindicate the "honor of Scotland from the infamy whereinto the rigid Presbyterian party of the nation . . . hath involved it"—a not unworthy aim—and his book is said to have nice touches of humor. It is possible to think of a few poems that have a certain rollicking fun in them. But those in search of humor would turn naturally to the *Letters and Journals* of Robert Baillie, covering the years 1637–1662. Baillie has been called the Scottish Pepys. He watched the Long Parliament at its work, was with the Scottish army in the north, took part in the Westminster Assembly, and of course wrote many of his letters from Scotland. Those letters are pungent and vivid. Baillie had much entertainment at the scene; he took pleasure in probing to the inwardness of a situation and revealing the knavery of the opposition; he had a gift of sharp characterization. But he was really less humorous than satirical. One looks hopefully into *The Staggering State of Scotland* by Sir John Scot of Scotstarvet, expecting to find humor. Sir John gathered the gossip of moral and financial delinquency among the great of his country. Had he been a little more light handed, he might have given us many a good laugh at his highborn sinners.

The conditions of Scottish villages of the time can hardly be laid to the Presbyterians and yet those conditions were an aspect of the lack of orderliness and restraint that then characterized the Scots. Scottish villages may not have been different from villages in other countries. The old saying goes that God made the country and man made the town and a variant reading has it that the devil made the small town. To judge from what some of the ministers said of life in Scottish villages, it was not all it might have been. Not only the sins of unchastity and murder abounded, but the meaner little sins of pettiness, quarreling, and re-crimination flourished. Women indulged in backbiting and got into one another's hair. Men used knives in dark wynds on those they disliked. Some of the pictures that we derive from the sessions records and from the statements of ministers remind us of the sordid villages of a later day pictured in George Douglas Brown's *House with the Green Shutters*. Of course as the ministers tell the story, they were able to better conditions and some of the evil-living villagers became humble worshipers at the kirk. We may believe them, and we may believe too that Scottish villages appear the worse because the sessions records happen to survive and offer so vivid a picture of evil. Yet one is inclined to suspect that English villages, at least in the south of England, were pleasanter places to live in.

To improve the state of the villages the Scottish ministers did what they could, but some of them were small and self-important men. A university training did not always induce the graces of the spirit. Neither the ministers nor the lairds were a generally humanizing influence. The examples of gentle manners and breeding were possibly as important in civilizing men as sermons and prayers, and that was something the Presbyterians did not realize and could not have done much about. They were not to blame for the sordidness of village life, but they were probably able to do less than the English clergy to ameliorate conditions.

But having said so much about the sordidness of Scottish villages I must remark that the West Riding villages which Oliver Heywood tells us about at the end of the seventeenth century were little better. Drunkenness and rough play flourished and sex sins were common. It was a country of few gentlemen and scattered churches. It was also the north of England, a part of the country still almost as unsoftened in manners as Scotland.

The Presbyterian faith was not beautiful in its spiritual design. It put discipline into men, but it did not tend to make them more gentle. It was still to a considerable degree a religion of the Old Testament and that was not a religion of kindness to one's fellows or of gentle manners, but a religion filled with descriptions of sin and denunciations of it. Not only the chosen people but their Deity was given to revenge. But such a religion made its appeal to the seventeenth-century Scots, as it had done to John Knox and his contemporaries.

Yet there is evidence, I think, that the Presbyterians were becoming more interested in the New Testament. From an utterly inadequate knowledge of Presbyterian sermons of the seventeenth century, I will venture the opinion that more stress was laid than earlier on the virtues preached by the unconventional Christ, the virtues of charitableness and active kindness to one's neighbors. I may add that an occasional Presbyterian preacher proved himself to have some of the graces of the spirit. I am thinking, for example, of Mr. John Livingstone, in whose autobiography I recognize the lineaments of a high-minded character. But in a general way the Presbyterians were still concerned with the thou-shalt-nots of the Old Testament. Their religion was not one that resembled that of St. Francis.

Even the thou-shalts in Presbyterianism, were not of a kind to make it a faith of beauty. Their preachers insisted upon the duty of hard work and decried idleness. They frowned upon worldly pleasures and so encouraged thrift, a thrift already natural to a poor people. As they read the Old Testament they could see for themselves that God prospered those who were humble before Him by increasing their flocks and herds. It was easy to draw the conclusion that those who prospered might be regarded as having behaved worthily in the sight of God, and from that conclusion the Presbyterians did not shrink. They had respect for success. This is not the place to discuss Puritanism and capitalism, a large and controversial subject. It is enough to say that the Presbyterians encouraged success in this world.

The Church of England taught men to be satisfied with that state to which God had called them. The Anglican parson was not concerned with the worldly future of his parishioners; on the whole he sided with the squire in supporting a static society. But he made the spiritual life something fair and restrained and proportioned.

If one should ask why the Presbyterians had so little feeling for beauty, order, and restraint, as compared with the Anglicans, it might be answered that they had no old ecclesiastical heritage upon which to build their Church. They had broken entirely with Rome and had to build up a new ecclesiastical organization and faith. Their Church was a made-to-order structure, based upon logic. It was not a growth. It was a new building, unweathered, unimproved by the slow accretions and repairs of time.

Allow me a reservation. I have indicated that the Presbyterians lacked a feeling for beauty. Let us not lay all the blame upon the Presbyterians. The Scots had had few chances to think of the beautiful or the restrained. They had been too poor, too busy fighting hunger and cold, too close to elementary needs, to cherish the goddess whose worship requires ease and leisure.

169

PART III

THE MODERN SCOTS

XVI

SCOTS IN THE PRESBYTERIAN IMAGE

THE Rule of the Presbyterian Kirk at the end of the seventeenth century and during the first part of the eighteenth century must have left a marked impression upon Scottish character. Presbyterianism had the upper hand as never before, and it was unmodified as yet by multiplicity of sects or by any liberal outlook upon life.

The elders of the kirks were in the saddle, and their inquisitorial functions enhanced their prestige in their communities. They inquired into the moral conduct of every member of the parish—they set those guilty of moral dereliction upon the stool of penitence. The stool was not a new thing in Scottish history but it was becoming in the early eighteenth century more common than ever before. Indeed it gave a piquancy to attendance upon the kirk. One could view the sinners fronting the congregation, one could listen to the titillating details of their shortcomings. To judge from the poets it was the young women who stood most often on the stool, young women whose misstep was often evident in any case. At the "Blythesome Bridal" we are told who will be at the party, and among them were

> snivelling Lily, and Tibbie,
> The lass that stands aft on the stool.

Allan Ramsay describes Jenny Nettles singing to her bairn:

> Robin Rattle's bastard;
> To flee the dool upon the stool
> And ilka ane that mocks her,
> She round about seeks Robin out.

The same poet deals with the female condemned to the stool:

Better to marry than miscarry
. . .

To thole the dule, to mount the stool,	*endure, grief*
I downa bide to think o't	*dare not*

Had Eppy's apron bidden down	*bided*
The kirk had ne'er a kend it,	
But when the word's gane thro' the town,	
Alake! how can she mend it?	
Now Tom man face the minister,	*must*
And she man mount the pillar,	
And that's the way they man gae,	
For poor folk has na siller.	*silver*

The last line tells a story that was common enough. The well to do could contribute to the funds of the kirk and buy themselves out of standing on the stool. The elders, who were often tenants of the laird, were afraid to punish one who had some power over them, and were willing to allow him to ransom himself from public disgrace. The poor could not pay, and hence had to stand sometimes week after week and occasionally in one kirk after another. A fearful humiliation it was, that bore harder on the decent girl who had made a single misstep than on the old sinner.

The Kirk fought ceaselessly for morality, but there was little sign that it was winning the battle. The evidence seems to indicate that sexual laxity was widely prevalent and that the influence of the Kirk and all its penalties had slight effect in bettering conditions.

The Kirk had ways of bearing down on the community that must have been repellent. The role of the sinner, i.e., of anyone who did not give himself wholly over to religious thought and exercise, must have been a hard one. Whatever he did was wrong. At communion seasons the audience was warned that to partake of the communion when in a state of sin was to incur everlasting damnation. "Oh, sirs," shouted

Mr. Spalding as he presided at the "fencing of the table," "will ye seal this damnation to yourselves and, as it were, make it sure, ye shall be damned, and so drive the last nail in your damnation. Rather put a knife to your throat than approach. What, man! will ye kill and be guilty of His body and blood? The worst morsel that ever ye tasted is to eat and drink eternal vengeance." The same minister denounced those who refused to partake: "Dare ye bide away and take His anger upon ye, and give that affront to do what in you lies to spite His Supper and frustrate the grace of God?"

The ministers were skilful in making their parishioners uncomfortable. They were mighty men at quoting the Scripture and could find out texts for every situation. They were versed in theology and acquainted with all the subtleties of Calvinism. The Reverend Mr. Livistoun, after a visit to England, told a west country group of ministers that the English sermons were like their knives, very beautiful to look at, but "there are some of your Kilmarnock whittles, that though they look not so fair on it as your English knives, yet have a better edge and will cut as well and much longer than they do." No doubt Mr. Livistoun had a certain natural prejudice in favor of his fellow Scottish divines and thought that, though they were less smooth in performance, they made sharper distinctions. This was precisely what they had been trained to do at the universities, where they were taught logic and dialectic. They had to practice their skill if they were to please their exacting audiences. The country people had been brought up of old by their leaders to exercise their wits upon religious problems, as we have seen, and the hearing of sermons was an opportunity for them to test their skill, the best opportunity they had in the week.

We have seen that even in the early seventeenth century the ministers were prone to stir the emotions of their hearers. With the late seventeenth century and early eighteenth the tendency upon the part of the preachers to play upon the feelings of their audience was increasing. James Alexander, Wodrow tells us, "used to weep much in prayer and preaching, he was every way most savory." Mr. Francis Aird was "a great weeper, both in prayer and preaching. . . . When he was very heartily weeping he would have been complaining much of the hardness of his heart; he would have said, 'We need not take out a napkin to wipe the tears off our eyes, for we cannot weep'—when he was weeping as fast as he could." Mr. John Carstares was "an excellent and brave orator, and of a most tender and melting disposition, for he used to weep much in prayer." The Duke of Hamilton said of him: "I never heard such a prayer as this since your father died," and then Wodrow continues: "He made them all, generally, weep who were in the Chancellor's chamber; he had such a strange and ravishing way of prayer." Wodrow tells us that Mr. Peter Kid was a choice, godly man, "a most serious and affectionate preacher." It is said that there is an epitaph of him in Carluke churchyard that goes:

A faithful, holy minister here lies hid,
One of a thousand, Mr. Peter Kid,
Firm as a stone, but of a heart contrite,
A wrestling, praying, weeping Israelite.

This heart-stirring type of preaching was relished by many congregations. The field services which developed out of the Covenanting tradition were likely to be conducted by "affectionate" preachers, and the excitement among the crowds was often intense. That excitement contributed not only to spiritual edification. The Reverend Mr. Hutcheson made a comment upon the preaching of Robert Stirling that is quoted by Wodrow: "And when the gospel was doing most good in his parish, then the devil of uncleanness was made to rage greatly against him; for in a very little time five adulteries brake out, all one after another, and one of them fell to be a mighty great professor of religion, Jean Whithill." Her slip was not so surprising as it seemed to Hutcheson and Wodrow. The strange relation

between religious emotion and outbreaks of sexual irregularity has been observed in revivals of our time and was
observed by Robert Burns in "The Holy Fair."*

One had to be on one's guard about the devil. The pleasures of this world were always to be scanned with mis-
giving, lest they interfere with work and duty and a serious
walk with God. The laird of Brodie in the late seventeenth
century recreated his body with the pastime of golf but
noted in his diary: "Lord, let this be no snare to me." On
the day following he resolved that he must not bestow so
much time in recreation. When he walked out in the fields
and found his heart rising with "carnal delight in fields,
grass, woods, etc." he was distressed. He prayed the Lord
to guard him against such decaying, corruptible, poor com-
forts. What a change had come over the Scot who in the
Middle Ages had rejoiced in fields and woods and brooks!
From the seventeenth century to the last part of the eighteenth century he was afraid to enjoy anything, even the
out-of-doors.

A people that feared pleasure was afraid of a Sunday
of rest and holiday amusements. Never was there a time
when Sabbatarianism flourished more in Scotland than in
the first part of the eighteenth century. It will be remembered that the Sabbath was a new thing in Scotland. But
the seventeenth century, when Presbyterianism was fighting
for its life there, saw the growing insistence upon the strictly
religious use of the first day. With the Presbyterians well
in the ascendant after the Revolution, the observance of the
Sabbath became part of the creed. Indeed feeling for the

---

* Take the last stanza of "The Holy Fair."

> How monie hearts this day converts
>   O' sinners and o' lasses!
> Their hearts o' stane, gin night, are gane
>   As saft as onie flesh is:
> There's some are fou o' love divine;
>   There's some are fou o' brandy:
> An' monie jobs that day begin
>   May end in houghmagandie   *fornication*
>   Some ither day.

177

entire devotion of the Sabbath to religious observances lasted longer in Scotland than anywhere else.

The sacred use of the Sabbath became widespread and an absolute duty. Men were expected to close the blinds of their houses, to refrain from walking or "vaguing" in the street, to spend the day in going to the kirk, a two-hour service in the morning and another long one in the afternoon, and to use what was left of the day in prayers, religious observances, and meditations. The Reverend John Wilson declared that God "hath appointed graciously a variety of exercises on the Sabbath day that when we are weary of one, another may be our recreation. Are you weary of hearing? Then recreate yourself with prayer. If of that, recreate yourself with singing God's praises. If of that, recreate yourself with meditating. If you weary of that, recreate yourself with Christian conference, repeating sermons, instructing your families . . . If you weary of public duties, then go to private." He was afraid of spiritual weariness. "How think you to spend a whole eternity in spiritual exercises when you weary so much of one day?" To many an independent mind the promise of another world must have seemed a doubtful blessing.

In Presbyterian homes a cold lunch was the custom but a warm dinner in the evening was tolerated. No work must be done. The ministers found themselves subject to criticism for crossing a ferry in order to arrive at the kirk where they were to conduct services. They should have taken the ferry the day before. On the farms the most limited work in connection with feeding the stock in the barn was permitted. Elders constituted themselves committees to walk round the village, peer into windows, open doors, and even go through houses in order to see that the Sabbath was being kept in the strictest degree. Sometimes they delegated their duties to men known as "seizers."

How the Scots stood for such observation is hard to understand. An Englishman knew that his house was his castle, but a Scotsman's house was no such thing. The Scot had no inner fortress of his own, nor privacy. Indoors and out he was subject to the discipline of the Kirk and he could do nothing about it. The verdicts of the elders were backed up by local authorities, and failure to conform was punished by fines and humiliation and if necessary by excommunication. The pious Scot had allowed himself to become a slave of the Kirk. He had no day of rest and gladness.

Edward Burt in his *Letters from the North* declared that the people would startle more at the humming or whistling of a tune on a Sunday than if anybody should tell you that you had ruined a family. The whistling of a tune would have been especially objectionable because it would have implied pleasure on the Sabbath. An observer at a later period in Scottish history noted that to sail on the Sabbath was a more serious offence than to row, because sailing was more fun. When Jeanie Deans in *The Heart of Midlothian* found herself in the hands of the gypsies and heard them singing, she cried in natural alarm: "But ye shuldna sing upon the Sabbath." In 1672 that pious laird of Brodie, who sought grace to be faithful in reproving, rebuked his guest, the minister: "I spoke sharply to him for his travelling on the Lord's day."

It was not merely the Brodies and pious Presbyterians who insisted upon Sabbath observance. Henry Grey Graham, from whose *Social Life of Scotland in the Eighteenth Century* I have been drawing many details, says that the Episcopalians were not far behind the Presbyterians in their emphasis upon the solemnity of the Sabbath, though they were not so rigorous about it. It would seem that the keeping of the Sabbath became a national habit of the Scots. It is so easy for people to make fetishes of the externals of religion.

The effect of rigid Sabbatarianism was no doubt considerable. Stendhal remarked neatly that the Scots lost one day in seven. Yet there was something to be said for the quietness and meditation that the Sabbath made necessary. If men thought too much about one subject, their spiritual welfare,

179

they did at least indulge in reflection. If they thought about their past records and the sins they had committed, they gained some perspective upon their own careers and upon the conduct of life. What a bad time it must have been for the mothers who had to keep their children as sober and quiet as their parents! What a bad time for the children! We cannot but pity them. They may have gained indeed a certain austerity of outlook which they carried with them throughout life. Even those who, when they grew up, accepted philosophies other than the Calvinistic still retained scruples about the Sabbath and would confess as much. What is more, they revered a certain high seriousness and expected it in those to whom they looked up. Witness Lord Cockburn in his books about the Scots he knew in the early nineteenth century. Witness Robert Louis Stevenson. Whatever he came to believe in later days, the Scot was likely to retain something of the character the Calvinists expected, or else to "go bad" and revolt utterly and perhaps unhappily against all his upbringing.

The Presbyterians could not impose their strictness upon all the people all the time. In the eighteenth century there was a considerable revolt against their hard rules of behavior. Sabbatarianism was being considerably modified in certain quarters, especially in cities such as Edinburgh where "Moderate" ministers ventured to dine with their friends on Sunday evening. What was worse, there were those to make fun of the Presbyterian Sabbath.

> There was a Cameronian cat was hunting for his prey,
> And in the house she catched a mouse upon the Sabbath day.
>
> The Whig being offended at such an act profane
> Laid by his book, his cat he took, and bound it with a chain.
>   . . .
> And straight to execution poor baudrons he was drawn,
> And high hanged upon a tree—Mess John he sung a
>   psalm.   *the minister*

Scots in the Presbyterian Image

The godly were disturbed at the way things were going. It is evident from Robert Wodrow's comments upon conditions in Scotland in the 1740's that there were many who disappointed him religiously. He thought that young men had been affected by the want of religion in England and especially in London. The English influences upon Scottish life were, in the estimation of many of the old Scottish ministers, of a worldly kind. People were playing golf upon the Sabbath, going off on pleasure jaunts, filling up the streets; they were attending the theater. Plays were coming into Scotland from England, and theatrical companies were trying their luck in Edinburgh and Glasgow. All that was true. As Scots grew richer the pull of pleasure increased. The rule of the Presbyterians had been the harder to bear because the Scots had always had a bent for gaiety.

The enjoyment of life at the moment had been, it will be remembered, a theme of medieval poets. Dunbar had written:

> Now all this time let us be merry
> And set not by this world a cherry,
> Now while there is good wine to sell;
> He that does on dry bread wirry   *worry*
> I give him to the Devil of Hell

The Scottish poets of the eighteenth century were beginning to take up the old Scottish idea:

> Let neist day come as it thinks fit,   *next day*
> The present minute's only ours;
> On pleasure let's employ our wit
> And laugh at fortune's feckless powers.

> Be sure ye dinna quat the grip
> Of ilka joy when ye are young,
> Before auld age your vitals nip
> And lay ye twafald o'er a rung.

Or again:

> See that shining glass of claret,
>   How invitingly it looks!
> Take it aff, and let's have mair o't.
>   Pox on fighting, trade, and books,
> Let's have pleasure while we're able,
>   Bring us in the meikle bowl,
> Place't on the middle of the table,
>   And let the wind and weather gowl. *howl*

Burns was to carry on the theme that Allan Ramsay set forth. To grasp at pleasure while it was to be had was an old philosophy, older than Presbyterianism, older indeed than Scotland, but one that fitted into the inclinations of many Scots. The Scots were not alone in their eagerness for immediate enjoyment. The French and the Welsh had the same eagerness. It hás been said that the English were different, that they took their pleasures sadly. Rather they took their pleasures quietly. The Scot took his gladly, sometimes even with a certain abandon.

XVII

THE DARIEN EPISODE, THE UNION, JACOBITE RISINGS

THE Darien episode is important in the history of Scotland because it is connected with the Union and because it offered a comment on Scottish character. A people later to be famous in Britain, the United States, and Canada for business acumen proved themselves at that time singularly unpractised in large-scale business enterprise. They rushed eagerly into a project that was destined from the beginning to be a failure.

Since the two countries had been united in one crown, Scotland had been getting the worst of it. She was denied that free trade with England which she had expected to gain. Furthermore the Navigation Act of Charles II treated Scotland as a foreign nation and cut off much Scottish trade. The Dutch wars of Charles II had cut Scotland off from her hitherto lucrative trade with the Low Countries. The French wars of William III put a stop to her trade with France. It is true that Scotland was developing some manufacturing industry at home, but her trade in the other countries was almost destroyed, and that at a time when the great nations were pushing their foreign trade and when her great rival was multiplying her profits from India. The result was poverty in Scotland. Glasgow had whole streets of vacant houses and other seaports were equally hard hit.

The Scots were unhappy about the situation, and the more unhappy as they watched the progress of the East India Company. Could they not establish something in Scotland like the East India Company? In 1693 an act was passed by the Scottish Parliament to permit the establishment of trading companies and in 1695 another act was passed setting up a great company for trade in Asia and Africa and in

America. The act was approved in London in King William's absence. But business interests in England immediately smelled danger to themselves and brought pressure upon the English Parliament which petitioned the king against the new company. When William returned home, he showed himself at once unfriendly and proceeded to order the English plantations to refuse to help the new company. The action of the king was deeply resented in Scotland and there was increasing talk there that the two nations should be entirely separated and that Scotland should have its own king. What the Scots failed to realize was that with English opposition it would be impossible for them to go ahead. They gave up the plan for trading to Asia and Africa and made another scheme. William Patterson devised it, and his name carried weight, for he was himself a Scot by birth and had been one of the first directors of the Bank of England and more nearly than anyone else its founder. When he suggested that the Scots send out an expedition to Darien on the Isthmus of Panama, an isthmus that seemed to have great possibilities, the Scots were taken in. That Darien was close to Spanish possessions on all sides and that William would not wish to become involved with Spain when he was at war with France seem not to have occurred to the Scottish people. They put over £200,000 of their own savings into the undertaking. It became a national enterprise in which every class save the peasants was involved. The ministers prayed for the success of the expedition. "There is such an earnestness and disposition towards that matter," wrote Lord Marchmont, "without any sparing either of their persons or purses that every observer must think it wonderful." One expedition after another was sent out with goods and colonists. But the selection of goods was not well considered; such items as periwigs were included, and heavy woolen cloth of little use in the tropics. The expeditions were a failure, many of the colonists died, and others surrendered to the Spanish fleet. Nearly all the ready capital of Scotland was dissipated at a time when the country could ill afford losses. The English were blamed, and feeling against England increased. But the Scots were to blame themselves. They had been extraordinarily simple minded when they put their money into such a project, and especially the Lowlanders who were supposed to be hardheaded businessmen. Colonial enterprises were a "tickle matter" at best; the English had made failures of their first adventures in the New World. The Scots were inexperienced in such matters and should have known better than attempt such an undertaking until they had learned more about the history of such affairs and the methods by which they might be rendered successful.

The national pride was hurt. Lord Melville, Mathieson tells us, wrote that there was no more speaking to people now than to a man in a fever. Melville was grieved to "see this poor nation grow still madder and madder."

The Union of 1707 was in some ways the most important single event in the long annals of Scotland. This is not the place to deal with the confused and complex details that led up to it. At few times in history had Scotland been so unfriendly to England. The Darien fiasco was fresh in mind. Something had to be done, and many Scots would have been glad to break completely with England. But both nations needed the Union, England to guard herself against Jacobite plots, Scotland to save herself from even more economic discrimination than she had endured, and to preserve herself as well from the possibility of Catholic rule. Had she said good-by to England and attempted to go her own way, she could hardly have stopped the fierce onslaught of the Jacobites. At that point the Protestant interest, so Hume Brown has asserted in his history, would have had to call on England for help, as it had done in the time of Elizabeth. By every rule of logic those who hoped to keep Scotland within the Presbyterian fold had to support the Union. Scotland had "to drink the potion to prevent greater evils."

It was a plunge for Scotland to give up the Parliament that had recently begun to function actively and to surrender her political nationality. That nationality went a long way back and had been maintained with fearful and continuous effort. Scottish patriotism was becoming something much more thoughtful than in earlier days and was profoundly felt. For the last hundred and fifty years it had guided the policies of her ablest leaders It had been the motive force behind the devious movemer ts of Maitland of Lethington in the days of Mary and it was at this time the fierce inspiration of Fletcher of Saltoun, who fought the Union tooth and nail. The people were as patriotic as their leaders, although they did not understand what was best to do. No wonder that, when it came to a pinch, when Scotland was about to be merged with the old enemy, they could not follow their leaders. From parishes, from shires, and from presbyteries came petitions against the Union. Fiery ministers devoted their sermons to denouncing it.

The Union was finally accepted by the Scots only because a considerable body of thinking men believed it to be necessary to the long interest of Scotland, and because the country was to a considerable degree still led by her nobility, many of whom, though there was a bitter minority, had come reluctantly to believe that Union was the best policy. The nobility was at this time a fairly intelligent lot of men, not ill fitted to guide national destinies, more fitted indeed than it had been to guide them in medieval times. The aristocratic leadership of Scotland had not always proved a benefit but in this instance it served the country well.

It took courage upon the part of the nobles. Those who attended the meetings of the commissioners and were believed to be favorable to the Union knew perfectly well, as they walked to and from the sessions, that they were in danger of their lives from angry groups in the streets. They were resisting what seemed to be public opinion. They were putting their trust in the wiser judgment of men who looked ahead and considered matters coolly. Among those men were at length most of the leaders of the Kirk. The Scots might be a passionate people, but there was now a national will that refused to be guided by feeling and sentiment, even by memories and traditions. They weighed the pros and cons and made a deliberate decision. Scotland was about to lose her political nationality but she had now a national mind and purpose.

The end of the Scottish Parliament was a trying occasion. As Chancellor Seafield handed the Act of Union to the Clerk of the House, he is said to have exclaimed: "Now there's ane end of ane auld sang." The church bells of St. Giles in Edinburgh rang out but it was noted that the first tune played was "Why Should I Be Sad on My Wedding Day?"

The Union made a great difference.

The Scottish nobility began moving on London, realizing that there were favors to be had for themselves and their sons. As slowly they became accustomed to spending part of the year in London, they took on English manners and English ways. Their Anglicization was to prove a misfortune for Scotland. The people were to be separated from what had been their ruling class. That class was to be marked off in ideals and outlook from others.

The Union had other results more agreeable to the people. It made it possible for Scots to take part in the building of the British Empire, a significant part for which they were fitted by experience. From early times the Scots had been travelers in far countries. Travelers they continued to be, and as the years went on found their way into every British possession. They were to become explorers, even more than the English, explorers who discovered and opened up new parts of Canada, Australia, New Zealand, and Africa to the white man. Highland troops, as we shall later see, helped to extend the British Empire and maintained it when threatened. As the empire spread out over the seven seas, the Scots enjoyed the glory of being citizens of a great country. They came to think of the empire as their inheritance, as well as that of the English, and with reason.

Today the extreme Scottish nationalists would assert that, in spite of the advantages that accrued to Scotland and to the Scots from the Union, it was a bitter misfortune. Political amalgamation with England meant in the long run, they would say, the end of Scottish nationality and eventually the assimilation of Scottish character to English. Yet that assimilation has shown itself chiefly among the upper classes. Scotland may have lost her political nationality, but the Scottish people retain their special traits. Scottish character is a hard metal not easily fused with any other. The Scots have carried with them to every part of the Empire Scottish ways and Scottish outlooks. Thus through partnership with England in an empire the influence of Scottish ways has been felt all over the world. Many small nations have been marked off by strong qualities of their own. Few have had the fortune of the Scots in making their national impress evident in every part of the globe.

The Scots had believed that in order to save Scottish trade and the Presbyterian Church it was necessary to join in the Union. They were disappointed in English policy afterward. The Union was followed by one move after another to humiliate Scotland in unnecessary ways, to handicap Scottish business and to weaken the hold of the Presbyterian Church. For the next forty years after the Union the Scots who had supported it wondered if they had been mistaken and the rest of the Scots said we told you so. But the dominant element in Scotland, which was after all Presbyterian, could not forget that the Union had afforded the best hope of preventing the return of the Stuarts and a Catholic monarchy. That remained a paramount consideration. By the end of forty years Scotland was beginning to profit from the connection with England, and Scottish businessmen were buying and selling in the markets of the East and of the New World. Glasgow was becoming a flourishing city. Measured in business terms the establishment of the Union at length wholly justified itself.

Meanwhile The 'Fifteen and The 'Forty-five took place, two attempts by the Stuarts from the Highlands to retake their lost throne. Those two risings of the Highlands may be called the last expiring kicks of Scottish feudalism. They depended upon great chiefs in the Highlands who could arm their feudatories and take them with them into war. Save for some few small districts in south Scotland the risings drew their support from the more unregenerate Highlanders. Those Highlanders were so accustomed to cattle raids upon the Lowlands that they lightly followed their chiefs in movements southward that seemed little different. Cockburn tells a story of a Highlander who had gone all the way to Derby with the Pretender in 1745. When asked whether he did not regard the dethroning of the House of Hanover as absurd, he replied: "No, sir, I ne'er thocht about it. I just ay' thocht hoo pleesant it wad be to see Donald riflin' London."

There was really no strong support in Scotland for the Jacobites. The Lowlands stood aloof. Many Lowland women were sentimentally affected by the Chevalier, but their men folk were not risking their lands and heads, and now and then a woman held a husband from going "out" for the cause. The average Lowlander knew that the success of the Jacobites meant nothing less than the end of Presbyterianism. The refusal of the Lowlands to embrace the Jacobite cause showed how far Scotland had progressed. The steady part of Scotland proved steady in a pinch. They were no longer merely Scottish, they were indeed becoming British. Dissatisfied in many ways with the policy of their government, they remained true to it as their best choice. They refused to be carried away by sentimental considerations. The modern, hardheaded, realistic Scotsman was beginning to make himself felt. The burghers of Edinburgh and Glasgow; of Aberdeen and Perth and Dundee, and the money-minded lairds of the Lowlands were having more to say, and they were not going to go off after old gods. In their reasoned loyalty to the Hanoverian throne they were supported by some of the great nobles, by men such as that Duke of Argyll who in Scott's novel had befriended Jeanie Deans, men who had not wholly lost their influence in Scotland even if they did spend too much time in London.

As for the Jacobites, they deserved their defeat. In the

best old Scottish feudal tradition they fell out among themselves. Indeed the Jacobite movements were in many ways a reversion to the fifteenth or early sixteenth century. Personal jealousies and the desire for individual glory ruined whatever chances the Jacobites had of success.

When the Jacobite movement was put down, it became at once one of the lost causes for which the Scots have a predilection. That cause enlisted the support of song writers and sentimentalists. It has been said that the Stuarts were men whom it was easier to adore and die for when they were exiles than to trust at home as kings. But singing and romanticizing about them, after their final defeat, cost no blood. There must be a hundred songs about the Jacobite cause, songs such as "Charlie Is My Darling," "Hey, Johnnie Cope, Are Ye Waukin Yet?" "The Wee, Wee German Lairdie," "Wae's Me for Prince Charlie," "Over the Sea to Skye," "Will Ye No Come Back Again?" Those songs have become almost the expression of Scottish nationality, and a cause to which most of Scotland had never adhered has become identified with Scotland. Flora Macdonald who accompanied the escaping prince, representing him as her female servant, has become one of the heroines of Scotland.

For all the romancing about them, The 'Fifteen and The 'Forty-five did not seem to contemporaries as important as they have seemed to novelists and a certain school of writers since. Episodes they were in Scottish history, episodes that have been overplayed and given more significance than they deserved. It was a couplet that really hit the matter off:

> Ilka thing hath its time,
> And so had kings of the Stewart line.*

It has to be said that in the development of the Jacobite cult the English did their part. The executions that followed

---

* In 1521 John Major quoted a Scottish saying which compared the Stuarts to the horses of Mar, which were good in youth but bad in old age. Major said he did not share the view. He was writing long before the Stuarts had shown themselves at their worst.

the putting down of the uprisings were probably unnecessary and gave the Jacobites the inestimable advantage of having martyrs. But the English have their peculiar wisdom too. At a turn in the road along the Scottish side of the Border can be seen a monument to the two Earls of Derwentwater executed on Tower Hill after The 'Fifteen and The 'Forty-five, "in defence of their rightful king." The British government allows such monuments to stand and thus proves how long buried is the Jacobite cause.

The English at the time feared more rebellions from the Highlands and believed that a harsh policy was the best preventive, as it seldom is. They were wiser in putting down the old feudal jurisdictions and in placing all judicial processes in the hands of the government. Thus they took away some of the power of the Highland chiefs. What was left to them was the influence that resulted from clan loyalty, and that loyalty was to fade out in a modern world.

XVIII

THE HIGHLANDERS

BRITAIN has a way of forgiving those who fight her and even those who rebel against her. She punished a few leaders, and she might have put the whole race of Highlanders on a proscribed list. But she wakened to the fact that the Highlanders were brave men and could be used to advantage in her far-flung wars. It was William Pitt, later Lord Chatham, who followed the advice given by President Forbes, and urged the recruiting of soldiers from the Highlands. "I sought for merit wherever it could be found . . . I was the first minister who looked for it in the mountains of the north. I called it forth, and drew it into your service, a hardy and intrepid race of men—men who, when left by your jealousy, became a prey to the artifice of your enemies, and had gone nigh to have overturned the state in the war before the last. These men in the last war were brought to combat on your side, they served with fidelity, as they fought with valor, and conquered for you in every quarter of the world."

They were indeed some of the best fighters in the Old World. As in medieval days, they won by impetuosity. They went straight to the enemy; they fought best when they had to face cold steel. At the battle of Fontenoy the French wrote that "the Highland furies rushed in upon them with more violence than ever did a sea driven by a tempest." In complicated operations they were less skilful; they did not know how to retreat. They could be taught to retire if everything was explained to them so that they thoroughly understood what they were about. When they were actually in contact with the enemy the officers lost control and each Highlander fought more or less on his own. Whether it is the best way I

192

do not know, but it is an established fact that the Highlanders swept things before them on many a field until their name became a synonym for bravery, and Britain delighted to honor her Highland regiments.

When the Highlanders were enrolled in the British army their worth and courage became famous; their part in defending and extending the British Empire gave them standing throughout that empire. The Lowlanders in Scotland, who had despised and feared the cattle thieves from the mountains, began to feel a touch of pride in the Highlanders and to realize that the men from the hills were Scots too and had a share in the old glory of Caledonia.

The virtues and the medievalism of the Highlanders were made known to the English world at the end of the eighteenth century and in the early nineteenth by many travelers. Samuel Johnson had gone to the Hebrides in the middle of the eighteenth century and had seen something as well of the Highlands. He was followed by a series of travelers, most of them English but occasionally some French, who reported on what they saw and picked up. They had much to say about the courtesy of the Highlanders, their generosity, their hospitality and politeness, "which often flows from the meanest when least expected." Many of my readers will remember the picture in *Rob Roy* of the reception of Bailie Jarvie and the young Englishman, Osbaldistone, by Rob Roy. The visitors were treated with dignity and kindliness by the Highland chief and his wife. It is a little hard to understand just how it was that wild mountaineers who for hundreds of years had been raiding the Lowlands had so much courtesy and dignity. But the testimony seems adequate. It has been suggested that the ordinary Highlander learned his good manners and courtesy from close association in daily routine with his chief. We must remember moreover that the Highlander was a highly self-respecting person who assumed the respect of others and gave respect in turn. He might be compared to a very different person, the Arab, whose dignity and politeness have long been commented upon. But one need not go so far afield. The medieval Scot had that natural friendliness which is the beginning of good manners.

In many ways the Highlanders retained the qualities we have observed in the medieval Scots.

They took a keen and inquiring interest in people, as the Scots had done in the old days. They did not see strangers too often. Villages and houses in the Highlands were far apart and a stranger was an object of suspicion, or, if properly certified, of pleasure. There can be no doubt that the Highlanders were almost infinitely curious about outsiders and about their neighbors. That curiosity was observed by Pennant who wrote: "Exceptionally inquisitive after your business, your name, and other particulars of little consequence to them—most curious after the politics of the world, and, when they procure an old newspaper, will listen to it with all the avidity of Shakespeare's blacksmith."

Pennant would have us believe that their curiosity was more than personal, that it was the curiosity of a people of natural endowments, eager to learn about the great world from which they were remote. The geologist, Macculloch, writing of the Highlands about 1824, tells of a curiosity that seems personal indeed. He describes his attempt to find out how far it was to the town of Killin. When he put the question to the Highlander he received the answer, "It's a fine day."

"Aye, it's a fine day for your hay."
"Ah! there's no muckle hay; this is an unco cauld glen."
"I suppose this is the road to Killin," said the traveler, trying him on another tack.
"That's an unco fat beast of yours."
"Yes, she is much too fat; she is just from grass."
"Ah, it's a mere, I see; it's a gude beast to gang, I'se warn you."
"Yes, yes, it's a very good pony."
"I selled just sic another at Doune fair, five years by-past; I warn ye, she's a Highland bred beast."
"I don't know; I bought her in Edinburgh."

"A weel a weel, mony sic-like gangs to the Edinburgh market frae the Highlands."

"Very likely; she seems to have Highland blood in her."

"Aye, aye, would you be selling her?"

"No, I don't want to sell her; do you want to buy her?"

"Na! I was na thinking of that; has she had na a foal?"

"Not that I know of."

"I had a gude colt out of ours when I selled her. Ye're na ganging to Doune the year?"

"No, I am going to Killin, and want to know how far it is."

"Aye, ye'll be gaing to the sacraments there the morn."

"No, I don't belong to your kirk."

"Ye'll be an Episcopalian than? Or a Roman Catholic? Na, na, ye're nae Roman."

"And so it is twelve miles to Killin?" (putting a leading question).

"Na, it's na just that."

"It's ten, then, I suppose."

"Ye'll be for cattle than, for the Falkirk tryst."

"No, I know nothing about cattle."

"I thocht ye'd ha been just ane of thae English drovers. Ye have nae siccan hills as this in your country."

"No; not so high."

"But ye'll hae bonny farms."

"Yes, yes, very good lands."

.   .   .   .   .

"Ye'll be for a farm hereawa."

"No, I am just looking at the country."

"And ye have nae business."

"No."

"Well, that's the easiest way."

"And this is the road to Killin."

And so the conversation continued until the traveler found out finally that it was ten miles to Killin, but not before he had to admit that he was a single man and had been told he should marry.

The Highland man concluded. "O, aye, ye'll excuse me, but we countra folk speers muckle questions."

The same unremitting curiosity may be found in nearly all the accounts of the Highlanders by travelers. Moreover the Scots who have set down autobiographies or left letters that have been published are very likely to include stories illustrative of the Scottish desire to find out, and especially upon the part of cottars in the glens of the Highlands.*

The Highlanders were medieval in their remembrance of old wrongs. A Highlander might insinuate himself into the friendship of a man whose ancestor had wronged one of his forebears and bide his time and kill him. Or he might turn against a friend who, he fancied, had misused him. For the Highlander was impulsive and did not always wait to find out the other side of the story. Sir Walter thought that quality Scottish. In *The Abbot* he makes an Englishman say:

"What now, Master Roland, do you, who are half an Englishman, think that I, who am a whole one, would keep up anger against you, and you in distress? That were like one of the Scots . . . who can be fair and false and wait their time, and keep their mind, as they say, to themselves, and touch pot and flagon with you, and hunt and hawk with you, and after all, when time serves, pay off some old feud with the point of the dagger."

This is no isolated passage in Scott's novels. In his other works and in his letters he often said the same thing about his countrymen and especially about the Highlanders. It was certainly true of many Highlanders and of some Lowlanders in days not too far back. The Scot nursed his injuries somewhat as his fellow Gael, the Irishman. As prosperity has increased and with it civilization, the Scot has had fewer injuries to nurse; he has learned that revenge is not quite

---

* Robert Fergusson, writing in the middle of the eighteenth century about Auld Reekie, tells how the people gather in Luckenbooths:

wi' glowering eye,
Their neighbours sma'est faults descry;
If any loun shou'd dander there,   *wander*
O' aukward gate and foreign air,
They trace his steps, till they can tell
His pedigree as weel's himsell.

good manners and is not reckoned as becoming to the godly. But the Highlanders were remote; they took on new codes slowly and gained little of the prosperity that the Lowlanders won by their industry. To a late date they continued to betray characteristics usually ascribed to the medieval Scots.

The Highlanders remained a poor people; the wealth that was coming to Scotland during the eighteenth century seldom reached the Highlands. Travelers in the north were still impressed with the poverty of the people and with their laziness. The Reverend James Hall, who wrote one of the best travel books on Scotland (London, 1807), declared the laziness of the Highlanders was second nature. "Brought up from their infancy in tending sheep and cattle, and seeing no other object to rouse their attention, they grow callous and indifferent and . . . delight to drone on doing nothing. . . . Yet, rouse their 'attention, and shew them any prospect that promises success, and they become active, enterprising, and persevering." This theory that the Highlanders were lazy because they had no opportunity, and that they would be enterprising if given a proper chance, was to be borne out by later events.

The old clan loyalty of the Highlander that had been characteristic of his race from medieval times had not yet disappeared. The chiefs remained great figures in the' eyes of their tenants and clansmen. A hundred stories could be told of that amazing loyalty. Mr. James Hall, when traveling along the Spey, picked up one story of the period before 1748 that may well be true, and that is illustrative of the attitude of the tenants toward their chief. The proprietor of Ballindoch on the Spey condemned a tenant to death and put him in the "pit" till the gallows was prepared. In some way the condemned man procured a sword and declared that he would kill the first man that laid hands on him. But his wife spoke to him: "Come up quietly and be hanged and do not anger the laird." The man submitted.

It was probably somewhat later, about the middle of the eighteenth century, that McFarlane of Glentartan brought his four sons to the Earl of Mar. "My lord," said he, "I and mine have been warmly attached for ages to the family of Mar. Now I am old and infirm, unable to serve your lordship any longer. But here are my four sons, hale of lith and limb, whom I present in my stead. If they do not serve you by day and by night, in a good cause and in a bad cause, God's curse light upon them."

That loyalty of Highlanders to their chief, when transmuted into loyalty to officers in British armies, proved a wonderful support of the empire. It remained a quality of the Highlanders in all the ill days ahead of them.

They were almost as superstitious as in the early days. There was still a great deal of primitive animism left. It is probable that their beliefs in specters, in fairies and brownies, affected their everyday life quite as much as a Christianity which had only slowly been imposed upon them. There were witches in many glens and terrible stories of how the Devil had come at length for his own. There were brownies who helped farmers with their work. Fairies were known and seen.

> For there, and several other places,
> About mill-dams and green brae faces,
> Both elrich elfs and brownies stayed,   *eldritch,* i.e. *weird*
> And green-gowned fairies daunc'd and played.

The poet said that when John Knox came in,

> They suddenly took to their heels,
> And did no more frequent these fields.

The fairies may have largely left the Lowlands but they lived long in the Highlands. The specters of the dead played a part in the lives of the Highlanders. Mrs. Grant, the American-born Scotswoman who went from the Hudson to live there, maintained that the Highlanders refrained from murder, when they did, because of their fear of the specter of the slain one.

The Highlanders

The Highlander treated death with familiarity. He would ask you where you meant to be buried. He did not feel death as a wrench, Mrs. Grant said, because he believed that the dead would continue to live "in the songs, the conversation, the dreams and meditations of all whom they loved on earth." She tells a story of a Highland son who did not marry because he was devoted to his mother. On her birthday he would gather his brothers and sisters and their families to a feast and in conclusion he would give a toast in Gaelic, which Mrs. Grant translated as "An easy and decorous departure to our Mother."

Some of the Highlanders retained the Catholicism of their ancestors, others were Episcopalian, but a surprising number had become Presbyterian. When they embraced the Presbyterian faith they sometimes gave it special twists of their own. Some of them became Presbyterian mystics and found texts in the Book of Revelation and in the obscure prophets of the Old Testament that suited their temperaments. Others indulged in religious ecstasies. Their religious tenets were occasionally stricter than their behavior. Sir John Clerk of Penicuik tells of the tenants of a duke who were very poor and not overly honest, though great pretenders to religion. Religion meant to them hearing long sermons and idling their time away on the sides of hills, "reading books of controversy and acts of the General Assemblies."

It has been said that some of the Highlanders stayed by the Episcopalian Church. The story is told of a Highland congregation that was assigned against its will a Presbyterian minister. The Episcopalian clergyman was prepared to leave and encouraged the parishioners to accept the new minister. But when the minister came to conduct the service, the congregation remained outside the kirk while twelve armed men, with the utmost politeness, to be sure, escorted the new minister to the bounds of the parish and warned him never to return. The parishioners continued to listen to their old clergyman as long as he lived.

Why the Highlanders had largely given up the Roman

199

Church remains somewhat of a mystery. It is true that the Society for Propagating the Gospel had sent qualified schoolmasters into the Highlands to teach the people, and those schoolmasters were under the control of the presbyteries. Furthermore a royal bounty had been given by the king to catechists and preachers, who were to go from house to house in the glens far from parish churches and teach the people. Whatever the cause, the fact remains that in the late seventeenth and early eighteenth centuries the Highlanders seem largely to have accepted the religion of the Lowlands.

I have said that Pitt encouraged the Highlanders to become soldiers in British regiments, regiments equipped with Highland dress and accouterments. Those regiments went everywhere; they fought to win India for the British crown, and fought at the time of the Mutiny to retain it. They fought in the Crimea, in Afghanistan, and in the Sudan. They went over the world and now and then came home long enough to spread among their kin and friends the news of the opportunities open across the seas. Their relatives and neighbors took the hint and found their way to the valley of the St. Lawrence and westward. Whole villages settled together in the New World where there was land to be had such as they had never seen.

They went away partly because they were being displaced by the demand for cattle and sheep. The south was calling for beef, and arable land was turned into pasture for the heavier cattle now being raised. Furthermore it was discovered by landlords in the north that sheep raising was more profitable than had been supposed, more profitable even than cattle raising. The change-over from cattle to sheep meant that fewer men were employed. What was worse, the new profits led landlords to raise the rents, which crofters thought themselves unable to pay, and some gave up their holdings. Others were actually forced out because the valleys where they lived were needed for winter shelter for sheep. Many of them went into fishing along the coast or took ship for the new world.* It was a pitiful business. The stewards of the landlords were eager to make a good showing in profits and were not always considerate in their dealings with conservative peasants. The landlords themselves were often away in Edinburgh and London and failed to realize what was happening on their properties, and some of them may well have thought that the crofters were standing in the way of progress, as Highlanders were only too likely to do. Not all of the landlords, however, were out of touch with their people. Some great families in the north looked out for their tenants carefully. Economic change was hard on the poor, as so often in history. The misery of those who left the glens has not been forgotten. At the very time, however, when the crofters were leaving, the population of the Highlands was on the increase.

* See W. L. Mathieson, *Awakening of Scotland*, pp. 290–294.

XIX

THE MODERATES AND THE HIGH-FLYERS

THERE were influences evident in the eighteenth century that would have distressed John Knox and "Mr. Andro" Melville. The rise of the Moderates alarmed Robert Wodrow, the historian of Presbyterianism, and it alarmed all the inheritors of the Covenanting tradition. With uneasiness Wodrow noted the spread of infidelity among the upper classes and among the young people in boroughs; he mentioned groups of young men who mocked at the churches and at the sermons of the time. The young ministers were objects of suspicion to him; some of them, he understood, were preaching morality rather than the gospel. The works and sermons of the great English Deists were finding their way into Scotland. Wodrow could smell Deism blowing across the Border. Skepticism was in the air and seemed to be spreading like a plague. The *Aufklärung* in Germany and the movement in France that centered round Voltaire were symptoms of a shift in thinking over western Europe. The new ideas reached Scotland quite as early as the Continent.

Wodrow might well fear the new conceptions that were coming in at more and more points and penetrating beyond the university class. The Scots were reading English books, especially Addison and Swift. The upper classes and the well to do were spending part of the year in London and coming back filled with the latest English ideas. They were becoming sophisticated and worldly, more concerned with this life than with the next. They were putting religion into one corner of their living and displacing it from the center of consideration. They made fun of the "affectionate" preachers and distrusted the zealous. Some of them indeed went further.

The affectionate preachers, usually men of simple backgrounds, could not hope to maintain their influence over their more knowing and cultivated parishioners. Those parishioners wished religious guidance from men of their own kind, from men in touch with the thinking of the times and capable of taking part in it. It was under these circumstances that the Moderates, often called the "New Lights," gained their hold in Scotland and retained it till nearly the end of the eighteenth century. By their enemies they were dubbed Socinians because they seemed to emphasize works rather than faith. They were accused of neglecting the gospel, an accusation that is not borne out by an examination of their sermons. But they did preach about conduct and behavior; they did analyze the problems of morality from a philosophical point of view. They quoted even the Greek and Roman philosophers. Their religious liberalism went down ill with the Evangelicals. But what seemed even worse was that they believed in the right of patrons to nominate ministers to parishes, a right which would have been an abomination to Knox and Melville. They would have pleased Melville more, however, by their insistence upon the right of the General Assembly to be the final judge of ecclesiastical problems.

The Moderates soon gained wide influence, especially in the General Assembly, where the men naturally fitted by talents and prestige to be leaders happened to be of their persuasion. The General Assembly was able to enforce its authority upon presbyteries and churches in the matter of patronage. Out of that cause of dissension and others came a secession from the Established Kirk of Scotland of a considerable number of the more zealous of the conservative ministers. They and their followers came to be known as "the Seceders" and soon split into two different organizations, the Burghers and the anti-Burghers.

The Moderates were not only touched by the heresy of good works but were less rigid in practice. They attended supper parties on Sunday evening; some of them, especially those far from home parishes, attended the theater; and one of them, a minister at that, produced a play, *Douglas*, while seven other ministers, including "Jupiter" Carlyle (the Reverend Alexander, called "Jupiter" by reason of his handsome appearance), attended the performance. Such laxity called for punishment, but the General Assembly was so much under the influence of the Moderates that the Reverend John Home, the author, saved himself by resigning his pastorate, and Carlyle got off with a mild vote of censure. The truth is that the Moderates did not regard pleasures as wholly from the Evil One. In a sermon Dr. Blair suggested that they were a part of man's due recreation. The leaders of the Moderates were, some of them, members of the well-known dining clubs in Edinburgh and Glasgow, and a few of them were intimate friends of the "atheist," David Hume, of Lord Kames who was almost as much under suspicion as Hume, and of the less-than-devout Adam Smith. "Jupiter" Carlyle was a minister who loved the good things of this world and those who could dispense them, and left lively memoirs because he dined in town and visited in country houses and castles. Yet he was not quite a follower of Mammon but one ready to fight for anything that seemed liberal in custom or theology.

What is surprising is that the Moderates gained the sway they did. It was less than a century after the Covenants and hardly more than half a century after the Covenanting martyrs. Why did the reaction against the High-flyers and the affectionate preachers go so far? I have already alluded to the improving trade in Scotland. But there must have been more to it than that. The Presbyterian ministers who had come in after the Revolution had been a comparatively uneducated lot of men. Charles I and Charles II had so put down the Presbyterian Kirk that it had ceased to command the best talent in Scotland, and the preachers who were available when Presbyterianism came into its own with the Revolution were not by any means fitted to carry the weight of influence entrusted to them. They were men of limited experience, often more zealous than learned or wise.

But the leaders of the Moderates were men of breadth and of experience, of intellectual vigor and of spiritual life as well. They were in touch with the best of the social life of the time. It was Francis Hutcheson (1694–1746), professor of moral philosophy at Glasgow, who prepared the way for the Moderates. Such men as Robert Wallace (1697-1771), Hugh Blair (1718–1800), and especially William Robertson (1721–83) gave the Moderate cause dignity and standing.

Hutcheson has been called the "leader of the Scottish Enlightenment." Born in north Ireland of Scottish ancestry, he had two generations of Presbyterian ministers behind him. Like many Ulstermen he attended Glasgow University and for six years studied mathematics, Greek, natural philosophy, and in particular philosophy and divinity. Back in Ulster as the only teacher in a new academy at Dublin he met young men of ideas and had entrée to the viceregal lodge under Cartaret. As a result of his book, *An Inquiry into the Original of Our Ideas of Beauty and Virtue,* he was called to the University of Glasgow in 1729 and became at once a figure in that center. His influence was exerted less through his writings than through a wide circle of students. Adam Smith studied with him and gained ideas from him. Leechman who became his colleague and supporter in liberal causes was a favorite student. David Hume corresponded with him and learned much from him, though holding a different philosophic position. Hutcheson himself owed much to the philosophy of Shaftesbury and something to Bishop Butler of the famous *Analogy,* but he drew increasingly in his later years from the Roman writers and especially from the Stoics. He stressed the value of benevolence and altruism. He maintained that beauty was a form of virtue at a time when beauty had been nearly forgotten in Puritan Scotland. In his wide tolerance of differing forms of belief he reminds us of those early Scottish moderates of the seventeenth century, Spottiswoode, Leighton, and Scougal. Hutcheson wished, he declared, to put a new face upon theology in Scotland and whenever a professorship fell vacant he sought to fill it with a man of tolerance and breadth. "I hope," he wrote to a friend, "I am contributing to promote the more moderate and charitable sentiments in religious matters in this country; where there yet remains too much warmth and animosity about matters of no great consequence to real religion." What a danger the Presbyterians of the straiter sect must have found him! But he was opposed to patronage, as they were, and his life was so gentle and his active helpfulness to his students so great that he was a hard man to attack. In the classroom he was the preacher of goodness and beauty and of liberty as well. It is hardly too much to say that from his time on the chairs of moral philosophy in the Scottish universities have been pulpits for the development of character and culture. Scotland had enjoyed few humanists save George Buchanan, and Hutcheson may well be called an eighteenth-century humanist. He set the stage for the Moderates, though more moderate than the Moderates proved to be.

Dr. Robert Wallace, "one of the first of our philosophical clergy," was a renowned Edinburgh preacher in the middle of the eighteenth century. His sermons were marked by a "massiveness of matter and a glow of sentiment." He was not afraid to launch out into independent speculations of his own and wrote careful and provocative pamphlets about population and about the economic outlook for England and Scotland. It was said to be his ambition to "make the learned, the rich and the fashionable part of the community pious and devout without foregoing the pursuits of elegance and eloquence." Dr. Wallace would have defended himself in that point of view by saying that the learned and fashionable gave the others their cues and that if the Church did not hold them it would lose the others.

Dr. Hugh Blair, a great-grandson of the persecuted Robert Blair of the seventeenth century, was a less gifted but a more popular preacher than Wallace. He was counted one of the great preachers of Scotland, and when a selection of his sermons was published, it had an immense vogue in Scotland, England, and elsewhere. During much of his life Blair was professor of rhetoric and belles-lettres at Edinburgh, taught the principles of English composition and published

Lectures on Rhetoric, a book not wholly forgotten. His sermons prove what a skilful master of the sentence and paragraph he was. He dealt with the conduct of the Christian life, covering in two volumes almost every aspect of the duties of a God-fearing person. He pronounced solemn truths undisputed by his generation in verbose but mellifluous sentences that remind one vaguely of Addison's prose. His sermons pleased his fashionable audience who were appreciative of his English idiom and who found it easy to agree with him. He never failed to make some appeal, in a well-bred and restrained manner, to the hearts of his listeners, nor to enforce wisdom and kindness upon them. He was a master at extracting the wisdom of the Bible and putting it to use. Yet he was a timid man, afraid of venturing far, chary of seeking out principles, content indeed with received Christian doctrine, stating with firm confidence what was generally accepted. Here is the way he dealt with sympathy: "There are situations, not a few, in human life, where the encouraging reception, the condescending behaviour and the look of sympathy, bring greater relief to the heart than the most beautiful gift. While, on the other side, when the hand of liberality is extended to bestow, the want of gentle·ness is sufficient to frustrate the intention of the benefit."

Wallace and Blair were eminently respectable ministers of a respectable time, appealing to the most respectable and intelligent audiences in Scotland. They had spirituality; there was nothing hypocritical about either of them, though Adam Smith deemed Blair pompous and if we could meet him in our time we would so deem him and many others of his time. There was no touch of the old Presbyterian in either of them. John Calvin and John Knox had been thrown out of the window. Wallace and Blair did not reason with the force of the Deists in England, though Wallace was no mean reasoner, and they did not dilute Christianity as much as did the Deists. They were good representatives of the Moderates.

Robertson was a more striking and significant figure. He

was a man of such force of character and decorum, such cultivation and affability, practical sagacity and skill in persuasion, that he became Moderator of the General Assembly, the leader of the national Church, and leader of it he remained till the 1780's, almost to the time of his death. His dignity was almost overwhelming and his conversation his friends found sometimes wanting in freshness. But he had a strong hold on the men of his generation and worked ceaselessly to carry out the aims of the Moderates.

Those aims became rather clear. The Moderates desired a Church that would appeal to the upper classes; they sought a type of minister who was himself a man of good background and of culture sufficient to exert an influence over his parishioners. The Scots looked up to their ministers as men set apart and it was just as well that they should be men worthy of being looked up to. No doubt the Moderates had observed—Robertson knew his England well—that the English clergyman was usually of a class above that of most of his listeners, and that his culture enhanced the dignity of his position and possibly increased his influence over his flock. The Moderates valued brains as well and hoped to develop a ministry aware of the intellectual life of the time, not dependent merely upon a knowledge of the Scripture and upon an ability to rouse the emotions of their hearers. Enthusiasm was being cried down and the Moderates were inclined to put a damper upon it.

The Moderates represented in Scotland only in part what the Deists represented in England. That conception of a universe governed by law and order with the great Mathematician at the center, which the Deists envisaged, was not in the minds of the Moderates. Nor were they essaying, like the Latitudinarians of the seventeenth century, to frame a religion that would include all Christians. They are sometimes said to have been the inheritors of the tradition of the moderate men of the seventeenth century, but the connection is rather tenuous. Here and there indeed in the country a Moderate minister did preach tolerance of all forms of

Christian belief and looked to the reunion of all Christians. The Moderates professed liberal principles, which meant that they did not insist upon the old orthodoxy, but they were hardly more tolerant of the Evangelicals than the Evangelicals of them. In their pursuit of liberal views they could not escape some Scottish ardor. They represented a kind of liberalism that met skepticism halfway—though they would not have admitted as much—and stressed Christian living rather than faith. They dominated the Scottish Kirk until the French Revolution came along and changed all the currents in Scotland as elsewhere. Their period of dominance has sometimes been called the golden age of the Scottish Church.

It was not so regarded by the conservatives, by the High-flyers or the Wild party or the Popular party (three names for the same thing), who held to saving grace as against works. They called the period the Midnight of the Church. They were ready to prove that during the reign of the Moderates the Church went into eclipse and that the common people ceased to attend the services. Even the Moderates themselves lived to see the failure of their plans. They had believed that patronage would result in a better type of minister. The result was often otherwise. Small, self-seeking men learned how to ingratiate themselves with patrons and to gain preferments. The old Presbyterian system of the election of the minister by the members of the church was probably a better method of ensuring talent and distinction in the pulpit.

The Moderates were no doubt affected by what was going on in England. But the reaction against Deism that swept England in the form of Methodism and the Evangelical movement did not greatly influence the north. Methodism won the humble classes in England but made little headway north of the Cheviots. John Wesley found the road to Scotland but caused little stir there. His was a religion of enthusiasm and saving grace, a gospel with contagion in it but a contagion that did not infect the Scots. The High-flyers were inclined to listen to Whitefield but they were wary of Wesley, whose devotion to the Episcopal form of organization could not have been agreeable to them.

The success of the Moderates over the forty years from about 1740 to 1780 is a comment upon Scottish character. That the most Presbyterian of peoples could in considerable numbers have accepted a gospel of good works and ethical conduct, could have been so far influenced by the tendencies of the times, argues much. That a small people, far in the north, were just as quick as the people of greater nations to catch out of the air the new ideas tells us something of the Scottish mind and character. The rise of the Moderates represented a change in outlook for the Scots almost as sudden and sweeping as the Reformation, if much less lasting. It was no greater a change than the economic change and was no doubt connected with it. It indicated a certain flexibility and readiness to listen to new ideas, a quality the Scots have always displayed. The Scots were a verra releegious folk but they were also a people given to metaphysical speculation, and the speculations of Scottish philosophers, when carried into the pulpit by men of talent and character, could not but make an impression. The Scots were conservative, but that did not prevent them from playing with new ideas. Dealing with abstracts was their métier. Ideas were always worth examination and consideration. One can see that even that stiff-necked Presbyterian, Robert Wodrow was interested in the new opinions, although he feared them. And many a country minister who had preached the gospel of John Knox listened to the notions of the Moderates. Even rigid old John Knox had once had new ideas about religion.

The eventual failure of the Moderates affords us some comment upon Scottish character. It was not in the Scot to be satisfied with good works. He demanded more poetry in his religion and more passion. The Moderates did not offer enough. They did not offer a real liberalism, a breadth of view and comprehension. They were not tolerant of other

views, as we have seen. They did not bring Christians together into one flock; their efforts brought about more divi-
sion. They stressed the importance of patronage which ran
dead against Presbyterian schemes of government. Had their
aims been really comprehensive, they might have maintained
their hold and might possibly have liberalized the Scottish
Kirk, though whether they could have done so at that time
is doubtful. Their failure threw the Kirk back into the hands
of the orthodox and the unco guid.

Yet one of the lasting effects of the Moderates was upon
the High-flyers. The Evangelical Scots took on some of the
good manners and intellectual quality of the Moderates.
They succumbed, too, occasionally to the pleasures of this
world. Dr. Alexander Webster, one of the leaders of the
Popular party and an arch-enemy of the Moderates, was as
much known for his prowess in drinking as for his apt
prayers, and is best remembered as Dr. Bonum Magnum.

Moderates and High-flyers, both influenced the Scottish
people. They accustomed them to great themes, to themes
of life and death, of good and evil; they encouraged them
to do what they enjoyed doing, to think and reflect about
the ways of God and the chief end of man. If they were
unable to stem the prevalence of sexual irregularity and
the avariciousness of lairds and burghers, they taught the
people the virtues of neighborliness and consideration for
others, virtues that had not always been evident in their
warlike ancestors. Even the affectionate preachers played
their part in giving the common people what Sir Walter
Scott called the "education of the heart."

XX

THE FIRST PERICLEAN AGE:
HUME AND ADAM SMITH

THE great age of Scotland extended from about mid-eighteenth century to the death of Sir Walter Scott in 1832. That age may be roughly divided into two periods, which overlap one another. The first extended from say 1750 to nearly the close of the century and the second followed hard upon it. During those eighty years or nearly three generations, Scotland had a series of notable men, all of them leading figures in Scotland and some of them famous wherever people read and thought.

Those men are worth considering as part of a movement. A country cannot be judged only by its great figures, but if there are enough of them, thinking and writing in close relation with one another, they do afford evidence of the character of the people. We judge the Greeks of the Periclean Age to a considerable degree by a few names. In connection with the Elizabethan Age we think of the Queen, the Cecils and Walsingham, Ralegh and Gilbert, Spenser and Shakespeare. The Victorian Age is linked in our minds with Peel and Palmerston, with Gladstone and Disraeli, with Tennyson and Browning. English character expressed itself through those men, even in the case of Disraeli who was of Spanish—Jewish ancestry. Of course a few men never represent all the aspects of character of a nation at a given time, but in their relations to one another they do give clues. They would hardly have gained the hearing they did, had they not been expressing what people were thinking and doing. Thus we may well stop to consider the men who made Scotland famous in the late eighteenth and early nineteenth centuries.

To understand those men we must go back to the universities and to the students who were reared in them. The increasing prosperity of the country was making it possible for more boys of talent than ever before to find their way to St. Andrews, Aberdeen, Glasgow, and Edinburgh. The young men were flocking to those institutions from all parts of the country. A much larger proportion of the population went (and still go) to the universities than in England, a larger proportion, I suspect, than in any other nation of Europe. Many of them were poor boys. The fees at the universities were small, the distances to travel were not great, save for those who lived in the northwest of Scotland or in the islands off the west coast. When the students reached the university they could find quarters in some mean lodging at low rents.' The universities provided as yet few residential facilities for students. The student found himself a cheap room and in many instances lived on the bread, potatoes, and oatmeal that were sent from home. Often he sent his laundry home. Hence it was possible for poor boys of "pairts," when encouraged by their dominies and ministers, to venture from home to the university. Once they enrolled they found ways of staying on till they graduated. Not only the sons of tenant farmers went, but the sons of nobles, of lairds and lawyers, of ministers and country-town merchants. A considerable part of the young talent of the country was drawn to the universities and was bound in a time of peace and increasing leisure to make itself felt in the life of the country.

The boys had been fairly well prepared before they came to the universities. They had attended parish schools, burgh schools, grammar schools, or academies. Even in the parish schools Latin was taught and in the burgh schools and academies a great deal of Latin and some Greek. When the boys came to the university they had to have Latin fairly well in hand to understand and take notes as the professors droned out their lectures—though it is true that Francis Hutcheson, the professor of moral philosophy at Glasgow, had broken away from lecturing in Latin as early as the 1730's, and his example was soon followed by his colleagues.

Education may have been narrow by our standards but it was thorough. A reading and talking knowledge of Latin meant that the students had absorbed a certain orderliness of thought and at an early age, when that training was likely to remain with them. The other subjects they studied at the universities were often Greek, logic, natural philosophy (or science), and moral philosophy.

They had the advantage of a distinguished lot of teachers. There was no such thing as a tutorial system, but some of the faculty took talented boys into their homes as boarders and afforded them advantages of professorial conversation. Otherwise there was not much contact between students and faculty. But all four universities did provide in the professorial chairs some of the outstanding figures of the country, along with many less-known men who were often skilful teachers and "moral influences."

The professors were merely a segment, though a considerable one, of the group of intellectual men of the time. In Glasgow and especially in Edinburgh there was beginning to be an intellectual society that included many men with different outlooks but nearly all of them with a wide range of interests. Adam Smith* was one of the founders of a club to discuss economic and trade questions. It was possibly the first Economics club ever gathered together. In Edinburgh the Select Society was founded in 1754 by Allan Ramsay, the painter and son of the poet, with the co-operation of Adam Smith. Ramsay had been in France and was modeling the Edinburgh dining club on those he had seen in France. The Select Society consisted at first of fifteen members and then of thirty and later of a hundred and thirty. It became the most desirable organization to belong to in Scotland. David Hume, the philosopher and historian; Sir David Dalrymple (later Lord Hailes), who did much to put early

---

* To John Rae's *Life of Adam Smith* (London, 1895) I owe most of my information about Glasgow and Edinburgh clubs, but much is also to be found in Dugald Stewart's *Biographical Memoirs of Adam Smith, William Robertson and Thomas Reid* (Edinburgh, 1811).

Scottish history on a firm foundation of truth; John Adam, the architect; Adam Ferguson, the moral philosopher; William Cullen, the chemist and professor of medicine; William Robertson, the historian and leader of the Moderates—all of them were members. Among the members were Lord Monboddo, a queer body who was laughed at for his opinion that men and monkeys were related; Lord Kames, a noted judge and an amateur interested in intellectual matters of many kinds; Lord Elibank who took all knowledge for his province and constituted himself with Hume and Lord Kames a guardian of literary taste; and many country gentlemen and aristocrats. The society at each meeting proposed questions to be discussed at the next meeting, questions put in the form of active propositions. Its debates became a feature of Scottish life and men made their reputation by speeches before the society, though one of the greatest members, Adam Smith, hardly opened his mouth in the meetings.

As the Select Society lost its first fine impulse, and faded out after about ten years, the Poker Club, established in 1762 to agitate for a Scottish militia, became the rendezvous of the literati and country gentlemen and included much of the best of the Select Society among its members. There was also the Oyster Club that included Cullen; Joseph Black, the chemist and physician; Hutton, the geologist; Robert Adam, the architect; Adam Smith, who was not only the greatest of economic thinkers but a man with a gift for friendship and conviviality; and John Clerk of Eldin who, although he had never been to sea, developed new theories of naval strategy. The Oyster Club had a narrower membership than the other clubs and was distinctly more scientific. It was really based upon the friendship of its three founders, Adam Smith, Joseph Black, and James Hutton.

Lord Brougham, who had known all the best orators of Westminster, declared that for pure intellectual gratification he would like to sit in his old chemistry class again and hear Black. No lad, said Cockburn reminiscing, could ever be irreverent toward a man so pale, so gentle, and so illustrious. Playfair remarked of Black and Hutton that Black hated nothing so much as error and Hutton nothing so much as ignorance. Of the three men he declared: "As all the three possessed great talents, enlarged views, and extensive information, without any of the stateliness and formality which men of letters think it sometimes necessary to affect, as they were all three easily amused, and as the sincerity of their friendship had never been darkened by the least shade of envy, it would be hard to find an example where everything favorable to good society was more perfectly united and everything adverse more entirely excluded."

There was another dining club, this one at Glasgow, that met weekly in the 1780's, known as the Anderston Club because it met for supper every Friday night and went out to a "change-house" [alehouse] in the village of Anderston for dinner on Saturday. Adam Smith, Joseph Black, and James Watt were three important members of this club. Watt tells us that the conversation, besides the subjects usual with young men, turned principally on "literary topics, religion, morality, belles-lettres, etc." Robin Simson, the professor of mathematics, was a leading spirit of this club and used to sing Greek odes set to modern music. Professor Robinson recalled hearing him sing a Latin hymn to the Divine Geometer with the tears coursing down his cheeks.

It will be observed that while the thinkers and writers of the time played a leading part in the clubs, most of the clubs had a decidedly aristocratic coloring, and that was an advantage for their influence. When aristocrats and thinkers met, the aristocrats did not always supply the ideas but they were likely to take them up and give them standing among the general public, which was often inclined to distrust men of thought and listen to men of birth and acres.

The Scots met one another not only in Edinburgh clubs but at dining rooms and taverns in London. Adam Smith would stop at the British Coffee House in Cockspur Street kept by a sister of Bishop Douglas. There he would have been able to dine with Scottish friends, with Dr. William Hunter, with Robert Adam and John Home. In London too he would have seen Sir John Pringle, William Robertson whom he ran into constantly in Edinburgh, and the novelist Tobias Smollett who had taken the road to London from Scotland many years before but kept up to some degree his Scottish connections.

These men seem to have had a good deal of time on their hands to talk with one another. It was possibly because talented men had so much spare time that they were impelled to make use of their talents in ways not hitherto practised in Scotland. The young brains of Scotland turned naturally to the ministry or law. The poor boys from the country, often themselves sons of ministers, tended to prepare for the pulpit while the sons of well-to-do burghers and of lairds and of the nobility were likely to follow the study of law, more of them than could possibly find work to do. Young lawyers without clients used their time to investigate other subjects, to write books upon those subjects, and sometimes to become men of wide learning. As for the ministers, they led a comparatively leisurely life and the best of them mixed in the society of Edinburgh and Glasgow and did more than preach. Robertson, in addition to his parish obligations and his duties as Moderator of the General Assembly, wrote his *History of Scotland during the Reigns of Queen Mary and King James the Sixth,* his *History of Charles V,* and his *History of America.* Those works were so notable in their time that Gibbon joined his name with that of Hume and Adam Smith as among those who had been responsible for the strong ray of philosophic light that had come from Scotland. Robertson was at pains to find out sources, to have manuscripts copied for his examination, and to present a narrative that conformed to the facts then known. His models in writing were Swift and Defoe. His insistence upon the dignity of history was characteristic of the man who had a certain massive dignity of his own that was no doubt an element in his influence upon his fellow countrymen.

Two ministers closely associated with him were Home and Carlyle. John Home, after making a success of his *Douglas,* gave up his ministerial work to write plays. They were produced in Edinburgh and in London, and zealous Scots thought them comparable to those of Shakespeare. Jupiter Carlyle, while holding a country parish, wrote his recollections of the whole circle about whom I have been talking and thereby put many people in his debt.

All these men of talent could turn their hands to various kinds of work. Thomas Reid, the philosopher of common sense, taught almost all the various branches of science. Adam Smith taught English literature and moral philosophy and eventually became Commissioner of Customs. Adam Ferguson, the moral philosopher, had been a chaplain and a brave one at that, and was, before his death, the historian of Rome. None of the great men of late eighteenth-century Scotland stuck to one occupation, and yet some of them were able to leave their mark upon their own times and after.

It was still a period when the bounds of knowledge were so limited that a man could hope to know one field well and yet look over the fence into other fields and have intelligent opinions about them. The beauty of it was that men were constantly considering the relations of each field to every other.

These men were in touch with thinking men in other countries. They were interested in the Continent, in France in particular, but also in the Low Countries. They were aware of what was being thought and written in England.

The influence of France upon the leaders of Scottish thought in the late eighteenth century can be seen in the case of the two greatest figures. That Scottish writers looked to France is one reason why Scottish thinking was so different from English. David Hume spent three years in France between the ages of twenty-three and twenty-six, devoted largely to reading and discussing, and to writing his *Treatise of Human Nature.* Later in his life he accompanied the Earl of Hertford to Paris when the earl went there as ambassador, and, when Hertford went to Ireland, Hume became chargé d'affaires in Paris. It was natural that he should be thrown with the best society in Paris; he met not only royalty and duchesses but the literary and intellectual leaders of France, became lifelong friends with some of them and continued to correspond with them. Adam Smith was hardly less affected by France. In early life he had become familiar with the works of Voltaire and Racine and eventually with most of the French dramatists. When he accompanied the Duke of Buccleuch to France he met, as a result of his friendship with Hume, the literary men, philosophers, and economic thinkers of France and came to know well Turgot and Quesnay. How far his opinions published later were influenced by the French physiocrats has been a matter of dispute, but it seems probable that Adam Smith had developed much of his own theory of wealth before his meetings with the physiocrats. In any case his whole method of presentation was French, as was his approach to economics and philosophy. A much less eminent man, Adam Ferguson, in his teaching of moral philosophy at Edinburgh was to some degree a follower of Montesquieu.

The influence of England and of English thinkers upon the great men of Scotland during the late eighteenth century was considerable. Young Scots who went first to a Scottish university occasionally continued their studies at Oxford. Adam Smith spent six years at Balliol College, deriving a great deal from reading widely in English literature and thought in the Bodleian but gaining little, as he afterward believed, from his teachers. Throughout his life he was in and out of London, meeting in later years many of the English statesmen and influencing them more than they did him. Thomas Reid, the greatest of Scottish philosophers in the eighteenth century save Hume, had a purely Scottish education, but his thinking was affected by the scientific outlook of Bacon and Locke and by Bishop Butler and Shaftesbury. David Hume gained what he learned from the English by reading, but his philosophy owed little to them. His history of England by its breadth of understanding as well as by its prejudices proved how thorough a Britisher he had become. John Home, the playwright, went again and again to London and was in touch with the English theater and with writing men in England. Robertson looked to the south for advice and suggestion and support in his historical work.

The dependence of these men upon France and England was less shown in their ideas—the French and the English indeed gained ideas from them—than in their eagerness for approval in those countries. As Hume and Adam Smith visited in London and Paris they sent back word what this man and that thought of the productions of their fellow Scots; each of them was glad to win the approval of great names in England and France for what was being done in Scotland. Hume wrote to Robertson what the critical verdict was in England concerning Robertson's narratives and what people were saying about the latest work of Ferguson. The Scots were following out their lines of thought with independence but they were glad to win approval in the two great capitals of Paris and London.

The story of the scientific men in Scotland in the late eighteenth century is not very different from that of the other thinkers but is less known to laymen. They were an almost equally distinguished group of men. William Cullen deserves to be mentioned first since he started so many scientists. He developed the medical work at Glasgow and then became professor of chemistry at Edinburgh and later of the practice of physic. Early in life he discovered principles about the evolution of heat in chemical combinations, but he was above all a teacher and a philosopher of science. One of his students was Joseph Black, who lived in daily intercourse with him. Black developed new methods of quantitative analysis and "opened the door to pneumatic chemistry," and later, when professor of anatomy and chemistry at Glasgow, hit upon the principle of latent heat. Another student of Cullen's was William Hunter, whose work after his start in the north was carried on in London. In London he used to foregather with the Scots and give the toast: "May no English nobleman venture out of the world without a Scottish physician, as I am sure there are none who venture in." John Hunter, who never attended a Scottish university, made his way to London where he was influenced by his brother William and lived to be a greater anatomist even than his brother. John Pringle [later Sir John] was not in the Cullen tradition, but a student at Aberdeen and Edinburgh Universities, who became professor of metaphysics and moral philosophy at Edinburgh, while practising medicine, and later moved to London, where he reformed military medicine and sanitation. As important as any of the Scottish scientists was James Hutton, who started in chemistry and medicine at Edinburgh, became interested in agriculture, and from that in geology, and wrote at length the *Theory of the Earth*, which revolutionized geology and settled his status as the first of British geologists.

What a versatile lot these scientific Scots were! Most of them were grounded in philosophy, which a Scottish student of that time could hardly escape, and each of them taught or investigated such a range of scientific subjects that he was compelled to look at science in the large and to consider in a philosophic way the relations of each science to every other. It was an advantage to investigators that the lines between the sciences were not as yet closely drawn.

Along with investigators there was a supremely talented inventor. James Watt, whose name will live with those of Hume and Adam Smith, of Joseph Black and James Hutton, was a practical Scot who took out his curiosity in mechanical contrivances. He developed the steam engine. By the addition of a separate condenser to the engine already in use and by the application of steam alternately on both sides of the piston, he made the steam engine an instrument that could be widely and generally used for power. He was an inventor rather than a scientist, yet his great invention— he made many—depended upon the principle of latent heat, at the truth of which he seems to have arrived himself, although Joseph Black had already discovered it. Watt had been in contact with scientists at the University of Glasgow; indeed that university had given him a place to work, and had asked him to repair a Newcomen steam engine. It was dealing with this steam engine that started him on his career of invention. As his work went on he acquired more and more friends at the university and they put him in touch with men in Scotland and England who could help him, especially on the financial side. One of the most generous of those friends was Joseph Black.

Watt had begun as a handicraftsman, but one who was constantly experimenting, and in his experiments reaching out for principles. He applied knowledge and ingenuity, or imagination, to his problems and after many bad starts found the solutions.

> Nor pass the tentie curious lad,
> Who o'er the ingle hangs his head,
> And begs of neighbors books to read,
>   For hence arise
> Thy country's sons who far are spread,
>   Baith bold and wise.

Watt was almost pathological in his want of confidence in his own abilities to meet and deal with people. He did not have too much confidence in his own inventions. The English manufacturer, Boulton, who had much to do with keeping Watt on his job and developing the improvements and manufacture of his steam engine, once wrote him:

"I cannot help recommending it to you to pray, morning and evening, after the manner of your countrymen, 'the Lord grant us a gude conceit of ourselves,' for you want nothing but a good opinion and confidence in yourself, and good health."

Watt did much for his fellow Scots of a mechanical turn. Hitherto engines had to be set up and built in the place where they were to be used. Watt's new engine could be sold and moved from place to place. As it transformed industry by virtue of its power it set large numbers of wheels going and those wheels had to be looked after by men who had a talent for machinery and who enjoyed the ways of wheels. For some reason there were many Scots with that talent, and the steam engine gave them their opportunity.

That Watt's engine speeded the Industrial Revolution and so added to the wealth of Scotland is an obvious fact, as obvious as the fact that it also drew thousands of families out of the pleasant country into crowded city streets.

Watt was a disinterested type of Scot. He wished to make a competence but he was more set upon making machines work than upon rewards. He refused a baronetcy and showed no relish for the honors that accrue to talent. His face, as one looks at the Beechey portrait, is that of a dreamer, which he was, and of a fine, thoughtful, unselfish man. Indeed his face bears as much looking at as any I can think of in the annals of Scotland.

James Watt had started as a mechanic, but he seems to have been received into the company of the talented of Scotland not only because of his achievements but by right of good fellowship. They were an extraordinarily sociable lot, these thinking men of Scotland, as appears constantly in Jupiter Carlyle's recollections of them. Of Hume Carlyle wrote: "For innocent fun and agreeable raillery I never knew his match," and even those who disliked his opinions succumbed readily to the man when they met him. Carlyle tells us that Adam Ferguson had a boundless vein of humor. Hutton is said to have been as amusing as any of them and full of high spirits as well. Not as much could be said for Adam Smith, who was, however, a friendly old soul and who was widely liked, but interested people by the range and incisiveness of his conversation rather than by his humor. Black was a formal person who commanded respect and admiration and yet had much give and take. Robertson was the only man in the lot that might have been called pompous and his pomposity was only skin deep. When Benjamin Franklin came to Scotland in 1759 he met most of the men I have been talking about and they seem to have enjoyed him and he them. He characterized his visit as "six weeks of the densest happiness I have met with in any part of my life."

They were a disinterested and independent group. Hume was willing to endure the disapproval of the Kirk and of kirkly people, to miss professorships and honors on account of his religious opinions, and cherished no grudges. Adam Smith was not afraid to avow his admiration for the republican form of government and was never concerned to be on the prevailing side. Robertson and Adam Ferguson both came to the rescue of John Home, when as a minister he produced the play *Douglas* and shocked the Scottish Kirk. That lively old butterfly, Jupiter Carlyle, also dared to support Home. The truth is that most of the men I have mentioned were seldom in the good books of the Kirk. But they were such fine men that not much could be done by the Kirk. Their helpfulness to one another, their absence of jealousies, with one or possibly two exceptions, is worthy of note.

Their influence upon Scotland was beyond estimate. They must have raised the intellectual temperature of the whole nation. They were at the center of the country, and their words and writings were broadcast. Some of them had university chairs in which they could affect the talent of the coming generation, and others by their writings had influence upon their own generation. They were in touch with a considerable part of the nobility of Scotland and with the judges and eminent figures at the bar, all of whom they were likely to meet in the various clubs. Those men may not have accepted all the new opinions put forth but they were likely to imbibe some of the liberalism implied, and did so in fact. One wonders how much the lairds and the burgh classes, the merchants in country towns, were affected, and one does not know. But it is usually true that country towns quickly take their cue from the cities near by and it is hard to believe that Stirling and Kilmarnock, Dumfries and Dundee and Perth did not feel the influence of the thinking leaders of Edinburgh and Glasgow. The very fact that the Moderates were able so long to keep the upper hand in the Kirk, that Robertson remained Moderator of the Kirk for years, means that the liberal outlook of the two cities must have had weight in smaller places.

We have to remember what a long jump forward beyond the religious struggles and wars of the seventeenth century these men represented. Where is that old Scottish passion of the Covenanters, where is the zeal of the Presbyterians and of the Scottish Episcopalians? Among the men we have been talking about there seems to have been little passion or zeal save to find out truth. Is there something about the passion for truth that is expulsive of other passions? Francis Hutcheson, whose teachings at Glasgow in the early part of the eighteenth century did so much to set free the spirit of inquiry, had been of great use in putting even moral questions on a common-sense basis. But men who dealt with economic and historical and scientific subjects were in fields so new and earthy that it was easy for them to break away from the old theological furors. It was not so difficult to become open minded when you were making your way into matters that had not been discussed before, and once you gained the habit of utter open-mindedness, you continued to exercise it even upon those subjects upon which men had formerly held to fast convictions. The old Highlander, Adam Ferguson, who taught moral philosophy at Edinburgh, might reasonably have been expected to retain some of the passion that belonged to his breed, but he had consorted too much with Black and Hume and Adam Smith.

Hence this group of men showed an aspect of Scottish character never sufficiently recognized, the ability to examine a matter from all sides and to form independent judgments. It was the more easy to do so when you were in association constantly with other men who were seeking out truth without regard to old premises. It had been hard to

225

do when men went to the works of theology for their first principles. Now instead of staiting with first principles they were engaged in observation and were searching for principles out of that observation. The inductive method set forth by Bacon was being put in practice. Newton was studied earlier in Scottish than in English universities. Scottish curiosity was taking a new form and was being raised in degree into intellectual inquiry. The inquiring Scot found no fences to bar his pursuit of the unknown. Causation was in his blood and he could seek for it with no premises to hold him back. He would examine the causes of what he saw about him. The Lammermuir shepherd had long pondered on the ways of God and man. His cousins in Edinburgh and Glasgow pondered on the ways of man and nature, and with no limits set to their thinking.

XXI

ALLAN RAMSAY, FERGUSSON, AND BURNS

BEFORE I deal with the second great age of Scotland, I think it best to turn aside and discuss three poets: Allan Ramsay, Robert Fergusson, and Robert Burns. Each of them was typically Scottish, each of them dealt with typically Scottish themes. Yet none of them can be really fitted into the two great ages of Scotland. Ramsay preceded the first Periclean Age and Fergusson, though he did not precede it, was not part of an important intellectual group. As for Robert Burns, he flourished really between the two periods of intellectual and literary activity in Scotland and had little relation to either of them.

Allan Ramsay (1686–1758) is known in Scottish literature as the precursor of Burns and as a collector of Scottish poetry. He published four volumes of Scottish poems and songs, tampering a good deal with their texts and possibly improving some of them. He added two volumes of his own work. Much of those six volumes I have read and I have learned something of Scottish life from them, but it would be exaggerating to say that I have been stirred by the poems of Ramsay. Yet with some of them I am glad to have become acquainted. Ramsay used rhythms and verse forms which Burns was to imitate. He had a philosophy which ran dead against the Presbyterian teaching, a philosophy that was old Scots: Let's enjoy this world while we can.

> Play up there, lassie, some blythe Scottish tune,
> Syne all be blythe, when wind and wit gae round.

One could give many examples:

> Be blythe, and let the world e'en shog,   *jog*
>   As it thinks fit.

227

Ne'er fash about your neist year's state,   *bother, next*
Nor with superior powers debate,
Nor cantrapes cast to ken your fate;   *incantations*
  There's ills anew   *enough*
To cram our days, which soon grow late;
  Let's live just now.

Then left about the bumper whirl
  And toom the horn:
Grip fast the hours which hasty hurl,   *empty*
  The morn's the morn.

In these lines, as in all his writings, are to be seen the thoughts and philosophy of Horace, phrased in Ramsay's own Doric.

There are an uncommon number of poems about fair lasses, about Nell, Bessy, Anne, Betty, Christy, Mary, Katy, Tibby, Nanny, etc., lasses whose charms are delineated somewhat realistically, but without much attempt to indicate particular character. Even the titles of his love lyrics anticipate Burns, as: "An Thou Wert My Ain Thing," "And I'll Awa to Bonny Tweedside," "The Sodger Laddie," "I'll Ne'er Leave Thee," "O'er the Moor to Maggie," "Thro' the Wood, Laddie," "Fy! Gae Rub Her O'er wi' Strae [Straw]," "For the Sake of Somebody," "The Lass of Patie's Mill." The lasses seem generally to have been characterized by good eyes, high spirits, and good figures. One gathers that most of them met the lads halfway, and were eager to marry lest they lead apes (the medieval notion about old maids) in hell. One infers that they were unwilling to wait long for marriage lest something worse befall and they be forced to "mount the stool" of penitence.

Yet Ramsay makes Minerva say of marriage:

Those near related to the brutal kind
Ken naething of the wedlock of the mind.
Tis I can make a life a honeymoon
And mould a love shall last like that aboon.   *above*

Ramsay was the recorder of the vulgarities of village life. We are shown the bride, the tailor, the miller, and all the other men and women eating, drinking, and playing high jinks:

> Was ne'er in Scotland heard or seen
>   Sic banquettin and drinkin,
> Sic revelling and battles keen,
>   Sic dancin and sic jinkin.
> And unco work that fell at e'en
>   When lasses were half-winkin,
> They lost their feet and baith their e'en
>   And maidenhead gaed linkin   *passing quickly*
>   Aff a' that day.

Ramsay went into the bawdy house and showed Lucky Spence giving her dying advice to the inmates:

> There's ae sair cross attends the craft,
> That curst correction-house, where aft
> Wild hangy's tawze ye'er riggins
>   saft   *hangman's rope, limbs*
>   Makes black and blue
> Enough to put a body daft;
>   But what'll ye say.   *there is no help for it*

The rougher aspects of Scottish life Ramsay knew all about and he managed to convey the very tone of rollicking and maudlin scenes, no easy thing to do. He delighted to present the Scot, male and female, released from inhibition and fairly letting go. The two cantos that he added to the medieval "Christis Kirk on the Green" are more rollicking and vulgar than the first canto had been, and in the same Scots tradition. When the Scots broke over the fence they went far afield. They did in the good old days and they still did in Ramsay's time.

Such scenes Ramsay could picture, and yet, like a true Scot, he supported caution:

Nor, with neglecting prudent care,
Do skaith to your succeeding heir;   *harm*
Thus steering cannily through life,
Your joys shall lasting be and rife.
Give a' your passions room to reel,
As lang as reason guides the wheel;
Desires, tho' ardent, are nae crime,
When they harmoniously keep time.

Robert Fergusson (1750–74) deserves mention because he, like Ramsay, was an inspiration to Burns and anticipated some of Burns's best poems, and because he was the poet of Edinburgh and its streets and crowds. His "Hallow-Fair," his "To the Tron-Kirk Bell," his "Mutual Complaint of Plain-stanes and Causeway," his "Caller Oysters" are all scenes in early eighteenth-century Edinburgh. So too is "Leith Races," which was an anticipation of Burns's "Holy Fair." There were pure Scottish life and character in its description of the debating society:

There's lang and dreech contesting;   *tedious*
For now they're near the point in view,
   Now ten miles frae the question
      In hand that night.

In his "Auld Reekie" he dealt with the Scottish Sunday and Scottish respectability:

On Sunday here, an alter'd scene
O' men and manners meets our ein:
Ane wad maist trow some people chose   *believe*
To change their faces wi' their clo'es,
And fain wad gar ilk neighbour think   *cause*
They thirst for goodness, as for drink.

In his "Elegy on John Hogg," porter at St. Andrews, he touches on Scottish qualities:

230

Nae dominie or wise mess John   *minister*
Was better lear'd in Solomon;   *learned*
He cited proverbs one by one
    Ilk vice to tame;
He gar'd each sinner sigh an' groan   *made*
    And fear hell's flame.

John was thrifty:

For John ay lo'ed to turn the pence,
Thought poortith was a great offence;   *poverty*
"What recks, tho' ye ken mood and tense,
    "A hungry wyme . . ."   *stomach*
"For gowd wad wi' them baith dispense,   *gold*
    At ony time.

In the "Farmer's Ingle," which was not as good a poem as the one modeled on it, Burns's "Cotter's Saturday Night," the Scottish scenes were rendered with verve and concreteness. He described the good dame warning her children of witches and warlocks and

O' gaists that win in glen and kirkyard drear.
    . . .
For weel she trows that fiends and fairies be   *believes*
    Sent frae the de'il to fleetch us to our ills.   *coax*

But then Fergusson goes on in his most enlightened manner:

O mock no this, my friends! but rather mourn,
Ye in life's brawest spring wi' reason clear,
Wi' eild our idle fancies a' return,   *age*
And dim our dolefu' days wi' bairnly fear;
The mind ay cradled when the grave is near.

In his "Braid Claith" Fergusson satirized Scottish respectability. Broadcloth, he declares,

Makes mony kail-worms butterflies,
Gies mony a doctor his degrees
   For little skaith,   *expense*
In short, you may be what you please
   Wi' gude Braid Claith.

Fergusson was a Scot in his regret for the lost glories of his country:

   To Holy-rood house, let me stray,
   And gie to musing a' the day;
   Lamenting what auld Scotland knew,
   Bien days forever frae her view.   *pleasant*
               . . .

   For O, waes me! the thistle springs
   In domicile o' ancient kings,
   Without a patriot to regrete
   Our palace and our ancient state.

Robert Burns (1759–96) the greatest of Scottish lyric poets, belongs in the direct line from Allan Ramsay and Fergusson. He concerns us nearly, for his poems and songs have more significance to the Scots than many battles or several Stuart kings. His writings were a series of revelations of the Scottish people as they really were, and he himself was a representative specimen of the Scottish peasantry. Sooner or later that stock was bound to have produced such a spokesman.

He was the oldest son of a family that was hard put to it to scratch a living from poor acres. The years from fourteen to twenty-three were taken up with the hardest kind of drudgery on the land, drudgery that strained his constitution and that must have left a clever, pleasure-loving lad ready to break over, when he could find a way. He had a remarkable father who talked men's talk to his boys and taught them a great deal, and who with four other farmers engaged a schoolmaster for their lads. From that teacher Robert learned much, and incidentally about words and sentences.

What was equally important in his development was that, like many Scottish peasants, he had a few books in the house and access to others, many of them poetry, and that he read and reread them intently. To a considerable degree he lived in a world created out of those books. He had no advantage of talented men with whom to talk; his associates were ploughmen and those he met in the village tavern, though some of them were no doubt men of active minds.

There must have been hundreds of such country boys in Scotland. But there was about him an intensity and a zest for pleasure that marked him among his fellows. Men who observed his eyes said that they were like living coals. He had listened to old Scottish songs and he had a sense of rhythm and of music that was as well developed as his sense of words. He was capable of great feeling and he had time to recollect that feeling, although seldom in tranquillity, and to put it in language fit to be remembered. His first poems were rhymes such as all sorts of rhyming chaps in his community were making, but they presently reached a level above that of the other rhymesters. He had an old Scottish eye for detail and he was writing with old tunes in mind. He could take old songs and transform them from vulgar and halting words into lilting lines.

He dealt with matters in which the common folk were interested, with lovers, with fairs and festivals, with ghosts and brownies, with ministers and elders, with God and the De'il. He went into the field, like the old Scots poets, and made persons out of horses and dogs, sheep and pigs and hares, and even a wee, sleekit, timorous mouse. As for his songs, they were about Jean and Mary and Clarinda, who were all fair and lively and friendly, inclined to meetings with the lads among the heather. I don't remember a noble woman nobly planned, nor one who could talk the talk of men and touch with thrilling fingers, nor one who was her lover's "joy inwart" and "the well of womanhood," nor one who was "baith fair and guid and womanly." We must not ask Burns to be other than himself, a sentimental soul who had a penchant *à l'adorable moitié du genre humain*. He was straight in the sentimental tradition of the Scots makers of songs, but far from the traditions of the earlier poets who had reflected about womankind. There was a softness about him in regard to women such as you find in novels of Scottish life.

Burns was the first poet in modern Scotland to show a feeling for human equality. Certainly it is not to be found in Allan Ramsay nor in Fergusson and but little of it in the Scottish verse of the sixteenth and seventeenth centuries. It is true that John Barbour back in the fourteenth century did recognize the worth and dignity of the individual of whatever class, and that other early poets betrayed pride in the common man and even belief that he was not essentially different from his betters. The dignity of the individual was a fundamental faith with Burns, but he knew also, as did many among his kind, that his class was getting the worst of it, and that something was wrong in the world. From boyhood Burns had been aware of class distinctions and had seen lads of the gentry draw away from him as he grew up. As a young man he had modeled himself upon a friend of like birth who had been given a "genteel education." He did not undervalue good breeding, but he had that bitterness about the more fortunate that an intelligent peasant at the end of the eighteenth century was likely to feel. In "Man Was Made to Mourn," he wrote:

> If I'm design'd yon lordling's slave,
>   By Nature's law design'd,
> Why was an independent wish
>   E'er planted in my mind?
> If not, why am I subject to
> His cruelty or scorn?

But it was in "For A' That and A' That" that we find the creed of Burns most clearly set forth:

The rank is but the guinea's stamp;
    The man's the gowd for a' that.   *gold*

.   .   .

The honest man tho' e'er so poor,
    Is king o' men for a' that.

Ye see yon birkie ca'd a lord,   *fellow*
    Wha struts and stares, and a' that;
Tho' hundreds worship at his word,
    He's but a coif for a' that   *ninny*
For a' that and a' that,
    His riband, star and a' that,
The man of independent mind
    He looks an' laughs at a' that

In these lines Burns was expressing ideas that were in the air. He saw clearly what his class was enduring: "The neglected many, whose nerves, whose sinews, whose days, whose thoughts, whose independence, whose peace, nay whose very gratification and enjoyments are sacrificed and sold to these few bloated minions of fortune." What he said was being thought by many of the farm laborers and by the workers in factories as well. His verses so pat and quotable made vague aspirations concrete and easily remembered.

The superstitions of the Scottish peasantry come into Burns's poems. As a boy he had listened to an old woman who had resided in his family. "She had, I suppose, the largest collection in the country, of tales and songs concerning devils, ghosts, fairies, brownies, witches, warlocks, spunkies, kelpies, elf-candles, deadlights, wraiths, apparitions, cantraips, enchanted towers, giants, dragons and other trumpery. This cultivated the latent seeds of poesy; but had so strong an effect on my imagination that to this hour, in my nocturnal rambles, I sometimes keep a sharp look-out in suspicious places." He knew all the phantasmagoria of Scotland. It comes out in "Tam O'Shanter":

And, vow! Tam saw an unco sight!
   Warlock and witches in a dance;
Nae cotillon brent new frae France,   *brand*
But hornpipes, jigs, strathspeys, and reels,
Put life and mettle in their heels.

      •   •   •

There sat Auld Nick, in shape o' beast,
A touzie tyke, black, grim, and large!   *a shaggy dog*
To gie them music was his charge;
He screw'd the pipes and gart them skirl.   *caused*
Till roof and rafters a' did dirl   *ring*
Coffins stood round like open presses,
That shaw'd the dead in their last dresses;
And, by some devilish contraip sleight,   *magic trick*
Each in his cauld hand held a light.

All such lore was stuff for the poet, even if Burns believed none of it. It was so worked into the ballads and literature of the country, so involved from ancient times with the daily life of the people that the poet could not neglect it, nor for that matter can the observer of Scottish character. The Scots have never quite shaken off the beliefs of their primitive ancestors. The enlightened Scot is likely to be skeptical of the supernatural but is still afraid of too much good fortune at one time.

Burns was a Scot in his interest in character, probing curiously to the motives and impulses of the villagers about him. What a galaxy of his acquaintances otherwise forgotten will be remembered only because he held them up to laughter! He could be hard on people and then suddenly kindly, as is the way with some Scots. He was as skilled a satirist as Sir David Lyndsay of pre-Reformation times. Indeed his humor had usually a satiric touch to it, at the least, and when not satiric was bantering.

He had the old Scottish penchant for details. Take this from "Tam o' Shanter":

   Weel mounted on his gray mare Meg,
  A better never lifted leg,

Allan Ramsay, Fergusson, and Burns

Tam skelpit on thro' dub and mire,   *ran, slush*
Despising wind, and rain, and fire;
Whiles holding fast his guid blue bonnet;
Whiles crooning o'er some auld Scots sonnet;
Whiles glow'ring round wi' prudent cares,
Lest bogles catch him unawares;
Kirk-Alloway was drawing nigh,
Whare ghaists and houlets nightly cry.

By this time he was cross the ford,
Whare in the snaw, the chapman smoor'd   *smothered*
And past the birks and meikle stane,
Whare drunken Charlie brak's neck-bane:
And thro' the whins, and by the cairn,
Whare hunters fand the murder'd bairn;
And near the thorn, aboon the well,
Whare Mungo's mither hang'd hersel.

Such details are exactly those a Scottish peasant would recall.

Burns's poems must have done much to undermine the fearful hold of the Kirk upon the people of Scotland. His sympathies were on the side of the Moderate preachers. He was an enlightened man and was naturally somewhat rationalistic. The inquisitorial methods of the Kirk revolted him. Had he not himself suffered from the elders? In his "Address to the Unco Guid" he said:

O ye wha are sae guid yoursel',
    Sae pious and sae holy,
Ye've nought to do but mark and tell
    Your neibour's fauts and folly.

Against the Kirk of Scotland he had several counts. He hated its proscription of the pleasures of the people. He hated all the hypocrisy that went with the unco guid. It will be remembered that in "Holy Willie's Prayer" that estimable character had shown his zeal against swearing, drinking, singing, and dancing. In the same breath Willie confessed to the Lord

237

certain episodes with Meg and with Lizzy's lass, but since
he was one of the "elect" he knew that all would be well.

> I bless and praise Thy matchless might,
> When thousands Thou has left in night,
> That I am here before Thy sight,
>   For gifts an' grace,
> A burning and a shining light
>   To a' this place.

The doctrine of foreordination Burns put in its worst light:

> O Thou, that in the Heavens does dwell,
> Wha, as it pleases best Thysel',
> Sends ane to heaven and ten to hell,
>   A' for Thy glory,
> And no for ony guid or ill
>   They've done before Thee!

In "The Holy Fair" he takes off the preachers:

> Now a' the congregation o'er
>   Is silent expectation;
> For Moodie speels the holy door,   *climbs*
>   Wi' tidings o' damnation.
>   . . .
>
> Hear how he clears the points o' faith
>   Wi' rattlin' and wi' thumpin'!
> Now meekly calm, now wild in wrath,
>   He's stampin' an' he's jumpin'!
> His lengthen'd chin, his turn'd-up snout,
>   His eldritch squeal an' gestures,   *weird*
> O how they fire the heart devout
>   Like cantharidian plasters,
>   On sic a day.
>   . . .
>
> A vast, unbottom'd boundless pit,
>   Fill'd fou o' lowin' brimstane,
> Whase ragin' flame, an' scorchin' heat,
>   Wad melt the hardest whun-stane!

The half-asleep start up wi' fear,
 An' think they hear it roarin'
When presently it does appear,
 'Twas but some neebor snorin',
  Asleep that day

Like Allan Ramsay, Burns believed in making the most of all the joys to be had, and "just now." It was a tradition that went back to early Scottish poetry and, I think, belongs in the Scottish temperament, in spite of all that the successors of John Knox did to destroy it. Burns praises the virtues of John Barleycorn:

'Twill make a man forget his woe,
 'Twill heighten all his joy;
'Twill make the widow's heart to sing,
 Tho' the tear were in her eye

In "Halloween" he exalts the simple pleasures of the poor:

Wi' merry sangs an' friendly cracks,	
I wat they did na weary;	
And unco tales an' funny jokes,	*strange*
Their sports were cheap an' cheery	

      . . .

Syne wi' a social glass o' strunt	*liquor*
They parted aff careerin	*cheerfully*
Fu' blythe that night	

It will be seen that Burns was passionate in his views, perhaps the most passionate of all the Scots poets. The gods who bestowed the *praefervidum ingenium* upon the Scots had not overlooked Ayrshire. Yet he was like his countrymen in his capacity intellectually to look at the other side of a question, while of course retaining his own strong convictions. With all his passion he had a mind that could see into the heart of things.

What's done we partly may compute,
But know not what's resisted.

No one has ever been able to find all the sources of the songs written by Burns. It has already been said that he owed much to Fergusson and Ramsay. Those two poets themselves owed much to older Scottish songs. Burns made himself a master of Scottish country songs, and took old tunes and fragments of the many versions of the words, used a line here and a line there, and made a new song that was his own. William Allan Neilson in his wise little book, *Burns and How to Know Him,* shows how the Reformation had harmed poetry and song. Under the influence of the Presbyterian ministers "art and song were suppressed, and Scotland was left a very mirthless country." Human nature could not be suppressed, Neilson continues, and when whiskey had "relaxed the awe of the kirk session, the 'wee sinfu' fiddle' was produced, and song and dance broke forth. It was under such clandestine conditions that the traditional songs of Scotland had been handed down for some generations before Burns's day, and the conditions had gravely affected their character. The melodies could not be stained, but the words had degenerated until they had lost most of whatever imaginative quality they had possessed, and had acquired only grossness."

Burns made over the songs for a popular songbook, did it against time, and without pay. It was necessary that he should offer versions fit for young lasses to sing. He did his job well. He took poor verses and transformed them into songs that will never be forgotten. He mixed up the old and his own so well that we can only guess what was Burns and what was much older. I cannot accept the interpretation of a famous Burns critic that he was in the true line of Dunbar, Henryson, and Sir David Lyndsay. Some of their verse forms and rhythms he did appropriate. Burns had the same feeling for concrete details as Dunbar, something of the same vein of satire as Lyndsay, but he had nothing of Henryson, so far as I can judge. His love lyrics had none of that deep reflection to be found in some of the anonymous love poems of the sixteenth century which I have mentioned or quoted. He was a songster and a maker-over of songs, the best handicrafts-man in the history of lyric literature. As Sir Walter Scott was to take the episodes and characters of Scottish history and lore, the odd tales and weird narratives, and fuse them into a body of fiction, Burns took old refrains and made them into songs that will always be sung.

Washington Irving tells of a visit to Ayr: "I found a poor Scotch carpenter at work among the ruins of Kirk Alloway, which was to be converted into a schoolhouse. Finding the purpose of my visit, he left his work, sat down with me on a grassy grave, close by where Burns' father was buried, and talked of the poet, whom he had known personally. He said his songs were familiar to the poorest and most illiterate of the country folk. And it seemed to him as if the country had grown more beautiful since Burns had written his bonnie little songs about it."

That we can well believe. He was of the common people and spoke for them. It was their own voice refined and strengthened that spoke to them in those songs. They saw not only their countryside in a new poetic light but their seemingly drab lives.

He was a typical Scot in a dozen ways. And so his country-men have long decided. They do not forget the Wizard of the North but they dote upon the Ayrshire ploughman. From Perth to Saskatoon and Hobart, they meet on January 25 and sing the songs of Burns and drink the barleycorn he praised.

XXII

THE SECOND PERICLEAN AGE: THE EDIN-
BURGH REVIEW AND SIR WALTER SCOTT

THE second Periclean Age may be bounded roughly by the years 1802 and 1832, that is, from the establishment of the *Edinburgh Review* to the death of Sir Walter Scott. There were not as many great men as in the earlier Periclean Age, but there was a galaxy of young men who co-operated in a considerable undertaking, and there was above all Sir Walter. He was sometimes called the Wizard of the North, as Edinburgh was alluded to as the Athens of the North.

A glance at the Edinburgh of the time reminds us of the characteristics of the age. The old Edinburgh along High Street still had its high buildings where families were hived in apartments and from which for centuries the slops had been thrown out of the windows upon the street below. Off that old "mile" from the castle to Holyrood were wynds and narrow, ugly, irregular streets. But across the deep valley bed of the old North Loch (where the railway runs today, concealed by public gardens) a new Edinburgh was growing up with fine commodious houses opening on wide thoroughfares. In one of those houses on North Castle Street lived Walter Scott, whose attention, however, was to be focused on the old town where he was born. He looked to the old Scotland, but the *Edinburgh Review* and its young editors looked to a new. There was much of the old feudal world that still smelled of the midden, a world full of prejudices and narrow views. There was a new Scotland in the making, a sophisticated Scotland with old ladies of spirit and young men chock-full of ideas and projects.

The factors that made the age of Adam Smith, Hume, and Robertson were still operating. Times were so good that a leisure class was growing up in Edinburgh, Glasgow, and outside of those cities. As peace and prosperity continue in a country there is an increase in the number of talented men that seems to be in almost geometrical progression. More than ever before talented boys were gaining a chance. They were crowding to all the four universities and especially to those in the two centers of Edinburgh and Glasgow. Most of them were still poor lads trying to better themselves, but some of them, more than ever before, were sons of those not too hard pressed and had some bookish and intellectual traditions behind them. The boys from such families had enough resources to be able to turn round, to think, and to check upon thinking.

The chances for talent were improved by the slackening of the hold of the Kirk. Less and less was the attention of the Scottish mind riveted upon eternity. Allan Ramsay's philosophy of living "just now" was an attitude toward life that men found it easy to accept, and the growing wealth of the country did not lessen the willingness to accept it. There was a great deal of natural talent in Scotland that had been obscured by wars and religious struggles. Now it was finding the chance to make itself felt.

It is true of course that a considerable amount of talent was lost by emigration to England. Young Scots were moving on the English universities and were likely afterward to settle in London, as William Murray who became a judge and the first Earl of Mansfield. Other young men such as Tobias Smollett found their way to London. Scots were finding their way into the military and naval services, into government posts and into the East India Company. When Lord Bute was carrying on the government for George III he showed a preference for his countrymen.

But I am concerned here with the young men who stayed in Scotland and gave the country its second great period of flowering. Before, however, dealing with those men I must indicate something about the background of that period.

In the late eighteenth century England and Scotland were

very different in respect to politics. The English had begun to realize the glories of their constitution. Political thinkers in France and England had extolled it. Not without reason the English had come to believe that they had in some mysterious way, wholly creditable to themselves, developed the best form of government known to man, and French writers had encouraged them so to believe. The parliamentary system of representative rule by which a portion of the people voted for members of Parliament, and the politically minded gentry and aristocracy, with some little help from the bourgeoisie, filled many of the seats in Parliament, dominated the cabinet, and controlled policy, seemed well-nigh perfection. Kings had been put gracefully into the background and the liberties of the subject had been protected against the tyranny of the government. In local affairs the country gentlemen as justices of peace exercised benign sway.

Since the Union the Scots had learned something of the parliamentary system, though they had not really wakened to its possibilities nor to its superiority over other systems of government. The Scottish Parliament had been unimportant and the Scots could never take the duties of members of Parliament with the seriousness of the English. It had become Scottish national policy for the Scottish members of the House of Commons to vote with the government. In that way it was believed that the Scots could receive most favors in the way of patronage. For thirty years in the late eighteenth and early nineteenth century Henry Dundas (later Lord Melville) as Lord Advocate and as Keeper of the Signet and later as Home Secretary, President of the Board of Control, Secretary of War, and First Lord of the Admiralty, through patronage and the management of elections was the real power in Scotland. The Scottish Whigs did not like the arrangement and got few favors, but there was surprisingly little general complaint from Scotland.

The representative system did not mean to them what it meant to the English. They had seen no centuries-long struggle for the rights of the subject against the crown. They had no mind to resist the crown, these people who in medieval days had been set upon freedom. Freedom slowly broadening down from precedent to precedent was an idea not understood north of the Cheviots. The struggles of Scotland had been mainly ecclesiastical and were so still. Men fought in the General Assembly over patronage, over whether the parishioners should choose their own ministers or have them imposed upon them by patrons. Parliament was not in their blood. That a Scot should rule them was, however, important in their eyes. The Duke of Lauderdale who had ruled Scotland with a high hand in the reign of Charles II offended chiefly in that he lent himself to an anti-Covenanting policy. But he was at any rate a Scot. Henry Dundas as ruler of Scotland gave Scotland the jobs that Scots wanted and saw to it that Scottish interests were looked after. Furthermore he was by birth a member of the Scottish ruling class, part of the group of important families to whom Scottish loyalty had been given for hundreds of years. As for those families, they knew on which side their bread was buttered; they accepted graciously posts in the government for their sons and took the Tory line.

Thus Toryism was rampant in Edinburgh. It was not only the nobility who attached themselves to the Tory cause but a large proportion of the advocate class and indeed of the professional classes generally. The ruling classes accepted it the more readily when the excesses of the French Revolution began to alarm propertied people everywhere. The reader may recall how conservatives in our country were ready after the Russian Revolution to dub any American of liberal views a Bolshevik. So Scottish Tories distrusted anyone of Whig inclinations.

They showed their suspicion of Whigs by overlooking them socially. Many of the ablest men in Scotland were Whigs, especially in the younger generation, but not only were political doors shut to them until the Whigs came into power, but social doors as well. Whigs and Tories hated one another with an old Scottish passion, hated one another too much to meet at parties. The Scots still carried old feudal loyalties and dislikes into political matters. Sir Walter Scott, when he went to London, was surprised to see how much more flexible and good-natured English society was. Tories and Whigs fought one another at Westminster but met at the same dinners and jostled one another at the same "routs." Scott himself was an old-fashioned Tory who was wary of Whigs and could be unfair to them, but he admired the easier ways of the English who did not allow politics to interfere too much with natural human relations. Sir Walter was foolish enough to back an Edinburgh scandal sheet got out by some hotheaded young Tories denouncing certain Whigs, he was foolish enough to write a song in which he seemed in one line to exult over the coming death of that great Whig, Charles James Fox. The old Border hatreds still lingered in his naturally generous blood.

The judicial set-up of the period was on no higher a level than the political. The judges, who were of course the leaders of the legal profession, were cocks-of-the-walk in Edinburgh. The town spent its time in telling stories about them. Whenever four men were gathered together in the Outer House, that is, in the Law Courts in the Parliament House, Edinburgh, and were seen to be laughing, it was a fair guess that a story was being told about Lord Eskgrove. Lord Eskgrove with his odd way of walking and of speaking lent himself to such stories. He was learned in the law but without any deep understanding of it, or without any least feeling for fairness. Anything that was liberal or new was abomination to him. The whole body of judges with only occasional exceptions was conservative, passionately so. They were moreover men remarkable for their coarseness of language, for their partisanship, and for their unfairness in dealing with the accused and particularly with those accused of political crimes or of any form of radicalism. They were given to extravagant statement. Some of them had much knowledge, a few of them had considerable power of reasoning, but they used those powers in behalf of whatever prejudice they had, and their prejudices were legion. They were characters highly endowed with eccentricity, and one suspects that they developed their eccentricities, as college dons sometimes do, in order to be the more talked about.

There was in Scotland no tradition of dispensing exact justice such as was believed to be characteristic of the English bench. In England the judges no doubt had their prejudices like other beings, but they had to look to the decisions of the judges who had gone before. They were held in check by the accumulated wisdom of their predecessors. The shadow of those great judges was always behind every judge when he was rendering a decision. His decisions would be part of the sum total of English law and he had to take pains to be sure that they were in line with what had gone before. He was forced to be a traditionalist. The Scots had no common law. They depended upon civil law, and there was no long tradition of great judges and of a great body of decisions. Lord Braxfield, who was deemed a "giant of the bench," was said to ask only of the prosecution that they bring before him the victims and he would find the law to hang them, and he took solid satisfaction in taunting the men he was about to sentence. "It may be doubted," wrote Cockburn, "if he was ever so much in his element as when tauntingly repelling the last despairing claim of a wretched culprit, and sending him to Botany Bay or the gallows with an insulting jest; over which he would chuckle the more from observing that correct people were shocked." To a very eloquent culprit at the bar he once said: "Ye're a vera clever chiel, but ye wad be nane the waur o' a hanging." Even Lord Kames, who was known as an intellectual man and something of a philosopher, showed cruelty on the bench. He was trying for murder a man with whom in better days he had played chess. When the man was brought in by the jury as guilty, Lord Kames turned to him and exclaimed: "That's checkmate to you, Matthew."

In 1793 and '94 various men were brought before the

judges for radical activities. I need only mention the now celebrated case of Thomas Muir. Muir had gone to Glasgow University, had finished his legal studies at Edinburgh and had been admitted to the Faculty of Advocates, that is, to the Scottish bar. He had taken part in establishing in Scotland societies like that of the London Society of the Friends of the People, an organization designed to promote parliamentary reform. The reform, by which wider franchise was to be given and members selected on the basis of districts of equal population, seems to us to have nothing radical about it but it seemed to the conservatives a dangerous plan, smelling of the French Revolution. When Muir took a trip to France he was believed without reason to be making plots with revolutionaries there. As soon as he returned to Edinburgh he was accused of exciting a spirit of disloyalty and of recommending Thomas Paine's *Rights of Man*. The High Court of Judiciary in Edinburgh condemned him to transportation for fourteen years. England had been passing through a period of nervousness as a result of the French Revolution when men of even moderate views were suspect, but England took no action that I can recall so outrageous as this. One of the jurors who had condemned Muir had the grace later to state that the jurors had all been "mad." It is pleasant to know that in the 1840's, when parliamentary reform had been accepted, a monument was put up to Thomas Muir on Calton Hill.

The quality of justice administered in Scotland is another evidence of how slowly Scotland shook off the undisciplined ways of her past. The passionateness of the old Scots was still evident in the judges.

In both politics and the judiciary the Scottish picture was rather discouraging. Yet the intellectual life of the time was promising. The old interest in philosophy was still alive and the interest that had been developing during the eighteenth century in economics was in the early nineteenth century becoming general in Scotland. England had her Malthus, her Bentham, and her Ricardo, three considerable names, and

Scotland had none to match them since Adam Smith, but the interest in economics was, I think, as widespread as in England. Scots took to figures and statistics as squirrels to nuts. They were equally interested in science, as can be proved from the nature of the articles in their periodicals and by the courses offered in the universities.

For Scottish intellectual life more than English can be traced back to the universities. Glasgow and Edinburgh were flourishing institutions and sooner or later a large number of the talented young men of Scotland took some of their training at Edinburgh and many of the best of them were members of a discussion group known as the Speculative Society. Groups not only formed in societies but gathered round professors such as John Playfair and Dugald Stewart.

John Playfair had been at first a professor of mathematics, and then was elected to the chair of natural sciences. He became a single-minded geologist, hunting rocks up and down the rough surface of Scotland and teaching his students to interpret their meaning. The theories of Hutton about rocks had only recently been put forth, and Playfair wrote an explanation of the Huttonian doctrines which became a classic in the field and which had in it something of Playfair as well as of Hutton. The value to young Scots of a man who went afield and asked his students to search for meaning in the outcrops of stone can hardly be overestimated. There were not as yet and were not to be for some time such men in the English universities.

Dugald Stewart, who was professor of moral philosophy in Edinburgh from 1785 to 1809, had a remarkable influence on a large body of students, including many of those who were to make the next generation illustrious. He was hardly an original mind, nor was he indeed a man of profound insight, but he preached the beauties of literature and the duties of the good life to his students with such eloquence and persuasiveness that they never lost the impression made. He was a perfect example of how useful a teacher can be, even if less than a first-rate mind. A true academic, he leaned to the

liberal side and yet was cautious about "dangerous opinions."
Now and then he gave a course in economics, and in that
course there was not much exact theory nor many figures
but an application of philosophical principles to economic
situations which I am told by an American economic thinker
is still worth the perusal of economists.

Stewart's students were devoted to him and it is said that
some of them would repeat his courses and continue in his
classroom for five years. He was the center of a circle that
included Brougham, Horner, Jeffrey, and Sydney Smith, the
men who were to establish the *Edinburgh Review*. Others
moved in and around that circle. Lord Henry Petty, son of
Lord Shelburne, and later third Marquis of Lansdowne, had
been sent by his father to Edinburgh rather than Oxford, on
the advice of Jeremy Bentham. Henry John Temple, later the
Lord Palmerston of mid-nineteenth-century fame, attended
Stewart's courses and lived in his home. In his autobiography
Palmerston declared of his training in Edinburgh that he
there laid the foundations for whatever useful knowledge
and habits of mind he possessed. In close association with
Playfair was Lord Webb Seymour, brother of the Duke of
Somerset, who had left England and settled in Edinburgh,
devoting himself to geology and to the study of philosophic
principles. He was always engaged in making preparations
toward some great conclusions which would benefit mankind. "Leave me," he used to declare to his jesting but loving
friends, "exempt from the casualties of human life and I am
almost secure of my object."

So much for the political, judicial, and intellectual backgrounds of the early nineteenth century in Scotland. I come
now to deal with the period itself, with its two marked features, the establishment of the *Edinburgh Review*, and Sir
Walter Scott.

The *Edinburgh Review* was founded by a group of young
men who had studied with the same professors and belonged
to the same Speculative Society, at the suggestion of Sydney
Smith, an Englishman residing at the time in Edinburgh,

Sydney Smith edited the first numbers and contributed many articles. Francis Jeffrey and Sydney Smith were assisted by Henry Brougham and Francis Horner. They and their friends wrote the articles, Jeffrey, who soon became the chief editor, and Brougham each writing two or three articles apiece in a single number. The *Edinburgh* was the first of the great political quarterlies, and long remained the outstanding one. The range of the articles was wider than had ever been customary before. Literature had the first place and next to literature politics, but economics and science were treated in the light of all the new ideas that were then in the air. It is probable that both science and economics had a better hearing because the *Edinburgh* was directed from the north.

Two subjects that had long been staple in magazines were seldom discussed in the *Edinburgh Review,* antiquarianism and religion. The young men who sent forth this new periodical were only slightly interested in the past and in that collecting of curious bits of antiquity which was the hobby of English gentlemen and Scottish nobles. As for religion, the editors were curiously indifferent to it, and were criticized for so being. One thinks of the Scots as never indifferent to religious subjects, but these young men, none of whom could have been pinned down as a rationalist or an agnostic, were too much interested in this world and its improvement to be concerned with the next. Reform was in the air. Parliamentary reform was being talked about. There was much that needed changing, and the French Revolution had set young men thinking of what needed to be done. The *Edinburgh Review* staff were anything but revolutionary, but they believed in change and a good deal of it and were not afraid to say so.

The reviewers were far better paid than ever before, from £15 to £25 a sheet of sixteen pages. The reviews were written on a higher level of criticism than had been known up to that time. The principles that should govern criticism and those by which political action should be appraised were stated with a clearness and an impartiality never before attempted in British periodicals, which had often gloried in their partisanship. Not that the *Review* articles were always fair. Jeffrey and Brougham, like many other Scots, were men of strong convictions and could state them with vigor. If their opinions have not always been justified by the verdict of posterity, they were nevertheless grounded upon careful consideration at the time. That the little group of able and widely read young men compared notes and criticized one another's performances before publication made, no doubt, for moderation and wisdom.

There was another aspect of the *Review* that was new. French, German, and Italian writings of the time were discussed and appraised, and English and Scottish writers were considered in terms of European thought. That was the Scotch of it, for the Scots by tradition had been European in outlook, thanks originally to the Auld Alliance and to the Scottish habit of seeking out far places and coming home again.

The burden of the *Review* soon fell on Jeffrey. Sydney Smith returned to England to be a country vicar and the darling of London salons. Brougham and Horner, both of them, settled in London, but continued to flood the magazine with their judgments and opinions. Jeffrey stayed by the magazine, wrote much himself, and took the supervision of all contributions. To his own surprise he found himself a great man, something an editor had never been before. He was an able lawyer and became a judicial figure, but he was above all a critic. He had a gift of fault finding and he made the most of it; he knew what was wrong, where there was a flaw in the logic, an unproved premise, or an overdrawn conclusion. Utmost clearness he demanded and orderliness of presentation. The mystic or romantic made no appeal to him. His opening sentence in reviewing Wordsworth's "Excursion," "This will never do," will be long remembered. The old Scottish talent for dialectic and close reasoning belonged to him as much as to any Scot. Moreover he could point out the false reasoning in an entertaining way so that the reader felt himself riding along with the reviewer in the hot pursuit of the fox.

Brougham, who became a leader in the Whig party and in the government and who might have been a statesman of significance had he been trusted by his colleagues, wrote some of the best articles ever printed in the *Edinburgh*, articles marked by breadth of knowledge and depth of understanding. Francis Horner was not so brilliant as Jeffrey and Brougham and was sometimes regarded as the dull member of the *Edinburgh* group, but he had force of reasoning and was a man of disinterestedness and fineness not too common in the everyday world of Scotland. His death at thirty-nine was a loss to the *Edinburgh* and to British politics.

Sydney Smith had hoped that the new periodical would be distinguished by its wit and humor. Himself an overflowing spring of high spirits and humor, he used to say that one could get a joke through a Scotsman's head only by a surgical operation. His Edinburgh friends could not measure up to him in lightness. Jeffrey and Brougham could be satirical, even amusingly satirical, in the best Scottish fashion, but there was nothing mellow about their humor. Horner was a serious chiel with nothing light handed about him. But the *Edinburgh* was seldom dull. It dealt with subjects which were in the air and about which people in Edinburgh at their continuous series of dinners and evening gatherings were talking. It put the best talk and thought of Edinburgh into print.

The *Review* was read as much in London as in Edinburgh. It was read as well in the provincial cities such as Manchester, a Whig center, and Birmingham. It was read on the Continent and in the New World. The thoughts of Scotland had from the early eighteenth century been influential in the Thirteen Colonies and now Scottish comment was read in the new republic of the West.

The *Edinburgh* was Whig in its general outlook from the beginning and yet had among its contributors such Tories as Sir Walter Scott. As time went on it became more and more Whiggish, and Scott refused to contribute. He joined with others in establishing in London the *Quarterly Review* as a Tory periodical which should oppose the *Edinburgh*.

I suppose in our day we would speak of the clique that established the *Edinburgh* as indicative of a revolt of youth. The men who founded the *Edinburgh* were in the twenties and early thirties, Horner being only twenty-four. They were young men with not too much to do, since as Whigs they could not hope to find much law practice in Edinburgh (all of them save Sydney Smith had been trained in the law). None of them, unless possibly Brougham, was of the intellectual stature of Adam Smith and David Hume; none of them left such a mark as Joseph Black and James Watt. But taken together they were pretty formidable. They made their magazine formidable. They gave a tone to Scottish life and offered to Britain what Scotland had to give.

Sir Walter Scott belongs by himself as an example of a typical intellectual movement. He was indeed almost a movement in himself and his influence radiated over much of western Europe. Burns had been the climax of the new poetic movement, the skilled workman who put Scottish songs into the forms they have retained, and added many of his own unforgettable lyrics. Scott was not such a lyric genius as Burns, but he was a man of greater breadth and made a greater disturbance in the waters of European literature. Both were able to do what collectors seldom do, create new literature for men to enjoy.

Scott was fortunate in his youth. Many summers he spent upon the Border. As a child he had made an impression upon his elders. Mrs. Cockburn in a letter describes him as a six-year-old boy. He told the aunt who took him to bed that he liked Mrs. Cockburn, "for I think she is a virtuoso like myself." His aunt asked him what was a virtuoso? "Don't you know?" he answered. "Why, it's one that wishes and will know everything." He was out to know everything, this lame boy. He roamed the Border and later many parts of the Highlands persuading old women to sing him ballads and old men to tell him tales.

He was more than a collector of antiques in the way of song and story. Like many imaginative youngsters he moved in a secret world of his own, a world where he dreamed of great men and great deeds. But for his lameness he might have been a soldier, at least so he thought himself. The dreaming boy often becomes a man of action, and Walter Scott was one of those dreamers who had to find an outlet for his dreams either in action or in some other way. As it happened he found it in fiction. His impulse toward acton was released in his business ventures that turned out so unhappily.

His family inheritance, as Grierson points out, was not too promising. His sister was a neurotic who died early, his brothers were none of them successful or well poised. He was himself undoubtedly a high-strung lad whose nerves were stabilized by his out-of-door experience and by other influences. His natural gayety, evident in all the letters of his young manhood, was perhaps an element in saving this invalid boy for a hard-working life of creative activity. He had withal a variety of interests that must have been a wholesome sedative.

He tried his hand at rhymed narratives that embodied aspects of Scottish history, character, and scenery, and at length turned his efforts to novels, putting into them as much Scottish lore, superstition, and history as he knew, and that was a great deal. His country, he feared, was losing its individuality and was becoming Anglicized. He saw that what was most Scottish in manners and character was disappearing or being transformed into something nearly English. Those manners and characters he sought to put down before they were gone so that the kingdom of Scotland, "once proud and independent," might not be utterly forgotten. In so doing he had many moments of doubt. John Buchan and others have quoted a passage from his writings that seems significant: "What a life mine has been, half-educated, almost wholly neglected or left to myself, stuffing my head with most nonsensical trash." Did he mean that Scottish history and traditions were nonsensical trash? Were they then, since Scotland was no longer a nation and even its language fading out, not worth dealing with? Sir Walter was wrapped up in the past of his country and all its lore. Nothing else lay so close to his inner, secret life. But at the same time he was loyal to the British crown and that loyalty meant that he had accepted facts. The history he dealt in was broken off, the language his characters spoke was becoming obsolete. He was throwing his energies away on a lost cause.

The nonsensical trash he stuffed himself with he transmuted into what was neither nonsense nor trash. He bestowed upon the world a whole gallery of Scottish characters and scenes. As none before or since he understood the inwardness and mystery of Scottish character. His Nicol Jarvies, his Dumbiedikes, his Jeanie Deanses were but personifications of Scottish character in general and in particular. We may leave out his novels about lion-hearted kings and bold dukes of Burgundy and we shall miss little. It was about Caledonia stern and wild that he was fitted to speak and his scenes and tales will last when all the Bonnie Brier Bushes and Little Ministers are only material for theses. The Scots, nearly all of them with whom I have happened to talk, have spoken of him as their Shakespeare, at first to my astonishment. Shakespeare gave the world a great gallery of characters of universal validity, Scott gave it a gallery of characters of complete Scottish validity. Scots alone can really appreciate the force and poetry of the words those characters utter.

His books were widely read. He made Scotland a kind of center of the world. The wynds of Auld Reekie, the shores of Fife, the kyles of Bute, Stirling Castle, and Ben Cruachan were suddenly of interest to men in France, Germany, and Italy, in Ontario and Kentucky. They have been ever since, though in a less degree in the last thirty years. Sir Walter put the map of Scotland into the consciousness of reading people in every part of the world. Today the agencies that rush the tourists by boat and coach over the Trossachs are concerned to indicate the places connected with the poems and novels of the one Sir Walter.

He romanticized his episodes but he did not romanticize Scottish character, which he understood. There was much about it to praise and much to blame. Better than any other Scot that has ever written he knew the weaknesses of his countrymen. He had been much in England and had caught the flavor of English life and could make valid comparisons and see his own people in perspective. He recognized the parochialism of the Scots and their capacity for hatred and revenge. Yet he set the world to admiring the Scots, he gave them a position as a people of significance.

He belonged of course to the Tory circles of Edinburgh, as was natural to one of his ancestry and proclivities. But he was too good natured to be extreme about it, though twice, as we have seen, his conservative passion got the better of him. The new winds of reform that were beginning to blow over Scotland seemed threatening to him. He feared that the social structure he knew might be overturned. When he was hooted and even stoned by an election crowd in Jedburgh he felt it deeply and lived it over on his deathbed. To have fellow Scots turn against him was too much. The truth is that he had outlived the generation to which he properly belonged. Scottish feudalism was dying and the laird of Abbotsford was part of a feudal setting.

He deserves to be remembered not only for the Scottish characters and scenes he left us but for himself. A larger Scottish soul had seldom dwelt in a house of clay. John Knox, George Buchanan, and Andrew Melville had been men of weight and intelligence, but Sir Walter was cast in a larger mold than any of the three. He was a man of breadth of knowledge, of curiosity about places and times and people, of sympathy and large-hearted humanity. Great mistakes he did make in his business enterprises, but men had done that before. He atoned for it. A tired, sick, old man, he set his unresting pen at work to cover more sheets that he might pay his debts. He was a great Scottish gentleman. He exemplified the height to which Scottish character could attain.

XXIII

SOCIETY AND TALK

IT has been seen from previous chapters that there had
been growing up in Edinburgh something that could
be called society. That society at the close of the eighteenth century and in the early nineteenth century exhibited
a good deal of what was thoroughly Scottish. The men and
women who made it up were gregarious, spirited, and concerned with ideas. There was nevertheless a certain formalism about them.

It was a society recruited largely from the professional
classes, from lawyers and judges, physicians, ministers,
schoolmasters, and professors. There was a sprinkling of
lairds among them. Sir Robert Keith, returned from diplomatic service in Vienna, complained that the talk of the
lairds was mostly of dung and bullocks. As for the ministers,
one cannot read Jupiter Carlyle without realizing that the
best of them added to the dignity and weight of society.
They were likely to be reading men, more in touch perhaps
with new books and ideas than the lawyers, who had sharp
but often unreceptive minds. As for the professors, they
were of course purveyors of ideas and their influence upon
society, direct and indirect through their students, was of
importance.

It was a much more professional society than that of London or Paris, where aristocrats dominated the life of the
city. In London the great Whig families and others with
their town houses and country houses not far away set the
tone. The court was in London and Parliament brought there
a selected circle of the most interesting men and women
in the British Isles. Scotland had no court or parliament and
her great nobility flocked to London. Hence Edinburgh
society was necessarily a somewhat bourgeois society, al-

though dominated by the professions, exhibiting some of the stiffness and formality characteristic of such a group in most times and places. Yet Edinburgh had a special local wine to its fare. One who reads the diaries and letters of that day is impressed with the variety of types that appeared in the Scottish capital. Highland chiefs and Lowland drovers, ministers from the Hebrides and soldiers back from America, men from shops and ships, from castles and manses, went back and forth in the streets of the Old Town and the New Town. It was a happy center where many ranks and many minds touched. The burghers could watch Scotland go by. They were prepared to tolerate the idiosyncrasies of all, especially those of high birth. The ranks of the burghers included printers, booksellers, publishers, and occasional nabobs returned from the East. There was variety of type even among those who remained continuously in town.

We may be sure that there were many social strata. Mrs. Elizabeth Grant of Rothiemurchus speaks in her memoirs of those groups and says that they were not always intimate with one another. We have already seen in an earlier chapter that Whigs were largely excluded from the houses of the Tories. There were families of course, living part of the year in the country and part in Edinburgh, who deemed themselves a cut above others, and there were little groups that held to themselves, as in any city at any time. This is to be said, however, that Edinburgh was probably less dominated by families of wealth and position than many cities. "People live," wrote Louis Simond, who knew his France and North America and was qualified to make comparisons, "without fear of losing what they had or much hope of improving their fortune otherwise than by prudence and economy." The results were good, he thought. To him the city gave an impression of peace and tranquillity.

It was a time of pretension in England. Witness the characters that cross the pages of Jane Austen and meet in Bath. England was full of the new rich and the richer old rich. Whether Scottish society was as pretentious as English

I have not the information to determine. There are few novels of Scottish life in this time. Those of John Galt that I have read do not offer us pretentious characters, but it takes rather a special gift of observation upon the part of a novelist to portray such people. I doubt if Edinburgh was as pretentious as Bath, but the two places are not really comparable. There were few in Edinburgh who had the means to make a show and there was little point in any case in putting on airs in a town where everyone knew about everyone else. Yet the Scottish well to do have seldom been skilful in concealing their advantages. It is possible that among the newly successful of the manufacturing and industrial groups in Glasgow and in the larger provincial towns there may have been a good deal of pretension. But such groups would have been so well snubbed by the landed and professional classes of the time that they could not have raised their heads very high.

The reader of the chapters that have preceded will be convinced, I think, that the society laid a good deal of emphasis upon brains and talent. "My good fortune will be very great," wrote Sydney Smith to Francis Jeffrey, "if I should ever again fall into the society of so many liberal, correct and instructed men and live with them on such terms of friendship, as I have done with you, and you know whom in Edinburgh."

In that society women played an increasing role, as they did in London and in Paris. Indeed the great ladies of Edinburgh may in some slight degree be compared with the women of the French salons. Oliver Goldsmith had been impressed with them. Cockburn spoke of the old ladies as strongheaded, warmhearted, and high spirited. "The fire of their tempers not always latent, merry even in solitude; very resolute; indifferent about the modes and habits of the modern world; and adhering to their own ways, so as to stand out, like primitive rocks, above ordinary society. Their prominent qualities of sense, humor, affection, and spirit, were embodied in curious outsides." One gathers that they were old fashioned in respect to clothes, and indeed there is no time or place in Scottish history when and where women were distinctly smart in their attire. These ladies Cockburn mentions we would call "originals," and the young people of our generation would say that they "had a line." Few of them were beauties; at least they are not mentioned as such. None of them were really bluestockings in the approved sense of that word. They were creatures full of lore and whimsicalities, spirited females who seem to have given society life and color and who were remembered with pleasure long after they had left the scene. Some of the younger women had good looks, naturalness, and engaging ways that, when they visited London, conquered the southern metropolis, the more easily because they were more open hearted and friendly than the young women of the same quality in London.

Not everyone was as enthusiastic about them as Cockburn. Francis Horner, who went to London to practise law, wrote to friends at home that he found the English ladies whom he met at dinners more intelligent than those he had known in Edinburgh. It is to be remembered that Horner, a great success in London, probably touched in that city a higher circle of society than he had known as a young Whig in Edinburgh.

The reader of Sir Walter Scott's letters cannot but see for himself how many great ladies there were in Scotland, mostly in country houses to be sure, who were intelligent women and who took as much interest in literary matters as their husbands did. Not all of them were really intellectual: they would not have made the fuss over David Hume that they made over the courtly Sir Walter. It was the poet and antiquary and agreeable conversationalist that appealed to them in Sir Walter. The Scots have always been at least as much interested in literary folk as the English. The Scottish women of society, most of them with some flair for poetry, lionized the Ayrshire peasant. It is not only in Scott's correspondence but in all the letters of the time that the importance of the great ladies of Scotland can be recognized.

Where did women gain the education that fitted them for the part they played? The answer is not easy, and I am not sure of it in any case. In the parish schools the girls appear to have studied with the boys and in some of those schools the boys went directly from the school to the university. There were burgh schools or grammar schools in most of the towns and to some of them, especially in the smaller burghs, girls seem to have been admitted. To the academies that grew up in the eighteenth century, which emphasized science and commercial subjects, the girls were not admitted. But in a few of the burghs there were separate burgh schools for girls. As for the daughters of the families who lived in country houses and castles, they had in some instances been trained by their fathers or by a minister in the community. We may imagine that the daughters of the professional classes in such a city as Edinburgh received some education in Latin from their fathers or from private teachers at home. Walter Scott gives a slight clue as to that. In a ballad which he probably made up he tells about his gay goshawk, that is, his son, and his turtle-doo, that is, his daughter:

> I have learned my gay gosshawk
> Right well to back a steed;
> And sae ha'e I my turtle-doo
> As weill to write and read.
>
> And I ha'e learnt my gay gosshawk
> To weild baith gun and sword;
> And sae ha'e I my turtle-doo
> To read the Latin word

One cannot use the heroines of novels with too much assurance, but such a character as Diana Vernon in *Rob Roy* cannot be overlooked. Di Vernon was of course an English-woman in the novel but we may be reasonably sure that Sir Walter was drawing her picture from some Scottish woman he had known, probably out of a country house. It will be recalled that Diana had been brought up to read Latin authors and of course French. The young women in the country houses, such as Anne Lindsay, who at twenty-one composed to an old tune the words of "Auld Robin Gray," and her sister, Elizabeth, became familiar with the books stowed away in passages around the house. They were brought up on the annals of their families, on the old rhymes and ballads that mentioned their forebears. They listened to old songs and they took to rhyming and making songs themselves. The story of the Scottish gentlewomen of the eighteenth century who wrote good songs would make an interesting chapter. The Scottish country family was addicted to antiquarianism of a poetical kind. The works of the poets, Scottish and English, were well known to the families or to some of the more lively of those families, and the women could not but profit from it. Those daughters and wives were probably more knowing and intuitive than trained in orderly processes of thought. Women with inquiring and lively minds who have not been closely trained but who pore over many books are likely to be whimsical and spirited, and that is just what they were. Such of the men folk of the same group as had not been brought up to one of the professions were likely to be a good deal the same.

A French traveler in Scotland in the early nineteenth century wrote that the Scots looked upon their wives as mortals and did not overwhelm them with compliments, but he asserted that the women received a more durable homage, that given them for their qualities of the heart. Women seemed to him in Scotland to share the work and the hospitality of the land. That impression could be confirmed from diaries and letters. It seems to me that Scottish diarists and letter writers talked about women and admired their qualities more than did English diarists and letter writers.

There were many unmarried women in Scotland. For a long time young Scotsmen had been going to England and to the far parts of the earth while the women stayed at home, and the result was a large proportion of unmarried women. But the unmarried woman of the diaries and biographies was able to look out for herself. Consolation she found in books, in the fine arts, in enriching her soul. Other consolations were hers, if she were of the well-to-do classes. The old maids of Edinburgh went out to dinners and gave dinners, and some of them were very much figures in the life of the town.

Walter C. Smith, a minor poet of the mid- to late-nineteenth century, gives a picture of one of those old maids of a time slightly earlier than his own. Miss Penelope Leith was of a high-Tory outlook.

> Her politics were of the age
> Of Claverhouse or Bolingbroke;
> Still at the Dutchman she would rage,
> And still of gallant Grahame she spoke.
> She swore 'twas right that Whigs should die
> Psalm-snivelling in the wind and rain.

That is to say, she thought the Covenanters got what was coming to them. She had a Scottish willingness to display her opinions. She loved to play cards on Sunday, and close by the window, that the Whigs passing from the kirk might stare at her unhallowed occupation.

She was always at fairs, buying highland cattle. Old clothes she wore,

> the same brocade
> With lace of Valenciennes or Ghent,
> More dainty by her darning made.

She was a snob of course.

> A stately lady; to the poor
> Her manner was without reproach;
> But from the Causeway she was sure
> To snub the Provost in his coach;

> In pride of birth she did not seek
> Her scorn of upstarts to conceal,
> But of a Baillie's wife would speak
> As if she bore the fisher's creel.
> She said it kept them in their place,
> Their fathers were of low degree.

I have been talking largely of women who took part in society. Other women there were in Edinburgh who never saw the inside of the houses of the wellborn but who were no less endowed with high spirits and liveliness than their betters. Edward Topham, as a young man just out of Cambridge, visited Edinburgh in 1774 and described a party at an oyster bar, where women drank brandy punch with the men. He thought the women more entertaining than those he had met and known in England and praised them for their vivacity and fondness for repartee and for their unaffected good nature. The women he met at the oyster bar were probably representative of the middle classes in Edinburgh. We have already seen in dealing with Allan Ramsay, Fergusson, and Burns that there was plenty of spirit too among the women of the lower classes; they were lively and hoydenish.

What did the Scots talk about when they came together? It is hard to be precise upon that point, for the historian is seldom furnished among his sources with stenographic reports of conversation. He is forced to piece together from fragments in letters and journals and autobiographies the subjects which people had on their minds and presumably canvassed when they foregathered. He can be certain that the form of conversation was different from the language of the letters and memoirs. Occasionally, indeed, in letters Henry Cockburn and others took a light and bantering tone that may have resembled in some degree the tone of their table talk. There was a certain humor about it that we can just barely catch across the generations. They were lighthearted in those days and no doubt amused one another.

If their humor seems a bit heavy footed to us, it is because humor depends so much upon the time and place and is easily dated. Universal humor is something rare. We have been told that high spirits were the mark of the Edinburgh group and we must accept it. We may perhaps assume that those high spirits were often accentuated by the liquor which enlivened conversation if it did not necessarily improve its quality.

Most matters of discussion sooner or later went back to Scottish history and, though the Scots were not yet students of their own history in any scientific or philosophical way, they were amateur antiquaries, alert to solve the puzzles of past incidents, to learn every last detail about the personalities that created the incident. The old figures, the old traditions, the old couplets and ballads, the old epitaphs, all such matters interested them.

For the Scots have always been concerned with personal episodes and they liked best those that revealed love and loyalty or long hate. Signal retributions interested them and sudden deaths and foreshadowings of death, last words, and the return of ghosts. Such marginalia upon life they treasured and passed on. Often the stories they preserved were funny, but sometimes they were weird and uncanny. In many cases they were merely odd stories of men and women caught in embarrassing situations and what they said or did. If those sayings were in broad Scots, so much the better.

We talk about trade and business conditions and so did the Scots. They had seen the results of English discrimination upon Scottish business; they had observed the beneficial effects of the Union upon the trade of their country; they had seen Glasgow flourishing and their large country towns becoming centers of industry. They were becoming to a considerable degree citizens of the world, as is evident in the diaries, and the commercial relations between themselves and other parts of the world naturally interested them. They were realizing as never before that the relations of trade and politics required constant examination and re-examination.

The conclusions of Adam Smith had furnished them with a whole body of ideas that deserved discussion and criticism. There was the possibility of philosophy in economics that naturally attracted the Scottish mind.

But there was more pure philosophy in religious questions and the Scots never got far away from them. Whenever Scots were talking with one another they were likely to consider man's chief end and the answers were not always precisely those of the Shorter Catechism. They were profoundly interested in the bases of moral principles. The teachings of Thomas Reid and Francis Hutcheson had affected not only the students of those two philosophers but the grandsons of those students. David Hume in mid-eighteenth century had offered theories to which the godly were uneasily seeking answers even in the early nineteenth century. More immediate religious questions were up, and above all, the question of patronage. The right of congregations to name their own minister had been fought over since the Reformation and was not yet settled; it was a fundamental matter never far from the minds of those who believed in it and of those who opposed it.

Politics, except the politics of the Kirk, was not much talked upon. Certainly the Scots of that period had no such avidity for politics as the English; their experience with politics had been so much less. Moreover Scottish politics was not very important and the politics of Westminster was a good way off. The figures of Pitt and Fox, of Liverpool and Castlereagh and Canning were not as often mentioned in the letters and memoirs of Scotland as might be expected. The Scots had accepted the Union, they were reconciled to the Hanoverian kings and had transmuted the Jacobite faith into myths and songs. Political matters they left largely to the Dundas family and whatever Scots in London might have Scottish affairs in charge.

Nor was their conversation much concerned, so far as I can make out, with the arts, with painting and sculpture and architecture. One great painter they had in Scotland,

Sir Henry Raeburn, and one considerable landscape painter, Alexander Nasmyth, and they exported the Adam brothers to England. It is true that the plans for the New Town in Edinburgh and the buildings there erected stimulated some interest in architecture. The Royal Scottish Academy was founded in 1826. But there was as yet no consuming interest in matters artistic, not even on the part of those who inhabited the houses with plenty of wall space. The truth is that few of the noble families had the means to indulge themselves in works of art, and there was no long tradition of patronage of the arts.

A certain amount of the diversion of Edinburgh folk was given to formal dinners. It was on such occasions that a good deal of formalism revealed itself. Henry Cockburn tells us how much he disliked the rounds of toasts at these affairs. I cannot quite understand all Cockburn's details and I am afraid that the reader will not understand them, but I am going to give them in his words:

Every glass during dinner required to be dedicated to the health of someone. It was thought sottish and rude to take wine without this . . . And the person asked to take wine was not invited by anything so slovenly as a look, combined with putting of the hand upon the bottle. . . . It was a much more serious affair. For one thing the wine was very rarely on the table. It had to be called for; and in order to let the servant know to whom he was to carry it, the caller was obliged to specify his partner aloud. All this required some premeditation and courage. Hence timid men never ventured on so bold a step at all; but were glad to escape by only drinking when they were invited. As this ceremony was a mark of respect, the landlord or any other person who thought himself the great man, was generally graciously pleased to perform it to everyone present. But he and others were always at liberty to abridge the severity of the duty by performing it by platoons. They took a brace, or two brace, of ladies or of gentlemen, or of both, and got them all engaged at once, and proclaiming to the sideboard—"A glass of sherry for Miss Dundas, Mrs. Murray, and Miss Hope, and a glass of port for Mr. Hume and one for me," he slew them by coveys. And all the parties to the contract were bound to acknowledge each other distinctly. No nods or grins, or indifference; but a direct look at the object, the audible uttering of the very words—"Your very good health" accompanied by a respectful inclination of the head, a gentle attraction of the right hand towards the heart, and a gratified smile. . . . No sooner was the table cleared, and the after-dinner glasses set down, than it became necessary for each person, following the landlord, to drink the health of every other person present individually. Thus, where there were ten people, there were ninety healths drunk. . . . This prandial nuisance was horrible. But it was nothing to what followed. For after dinner, and before the ladies retired, there generally began what were called "rounds" of toasts; when each gentleman named an absent lady, and each lady an absent gentleman, separately; or one person was required to give an absent lady, and another person was required to match a gentleman with that lady, and the pair named were toasted, generally with allusions and jokes about the fitness of the union. And worst of all, there were "senti-ments." These were short, epigrammatic sentences, expressive of moral feelings and virtues, and were thought refined and elegant productions. . . . The glasses being filled, a person was asked for his or for her sentiment, when this or something similar was committed: "May the pleasures of the evening bear the reflections of the morning," or "May the friends of our youth be the compan-ions of our old age." Or "Delicate pleasures to susceptible minds." "May the honest heart never feel distress." . . . But the proper *sentiment* was a high and pure production; a moral motto. . . . Hence, even after an easier age began to sneer at the display, the correct course was to receive the sentiment. . . . But it was a dreadful oppression on the timid, or the awkward. They used to shudder, ladies particularly—for nobody was spared, when their turn in the *round* approached. Many a struggle and blush did it cost; but this seemed only to excite the tyranny of the masters of the craft; and compliance could never be avoided except by more torture than yielding.

Cockburn tells us that the new generation laughed away such sentiments, although he observes that they continued to be used in male parties, and he notes that Sir Walter in presiding over the Bannatyne Club insisted upon rounds.

But it is evident from the literature of the time that these Scottish customs were giving way to a freer social life that was more like that of the English. It is only fair to say that I have seen a little evidence that a generation or so earlier the custom of rounds of toasts was known in England. But by this time English society had become pleasantly informal, and we may be sure that reports filtered through to Edinburgh of the ways of London and in particular of the Holland House circle.

Such reports roused no jealousy. The Scots were content with their society, more than content. They believed it a superior society. Did they not have many men who attracted the attention of the world? They developed a whole body of tradition about those men and about many Scots whom the world has forgotten. In that way they remained, in spite of the absence of a parliament, a nation with a capital and conscious of itself.

XXIV

DECLINE OF THE ARTS AND
RISE OF MACHINERY

THE death of Sir Walter Scott marked the end of an era in Scotland. The second third of the nineteenth century, when English civilization was flourishing as seldom before, witnessed the obscuration of Scottish creative activity, save in business. In politics, in language, in literature, and in the arts Scotland as a nation played a minor part. Humanitarianism which, although not an art, is an indication of the creative activity of highly civilized people, had been a marked feature of the late eighteenth and early nineteenth century in England. It had hardly touched Scotland by the 1830's and '40's. Much of the best talent of Scotland was being funneled to England and so lost to the national expression of Scotland. The energies of the country were being taken up with business. Business caught and absorbed much of the brains and imagination of Scottish youth. The dominance of business affected every class. Indeed there was no class, social or professional, that was able to make headway against the Scot who was making money.

In politics the Scots, as Scots, were less important, because they were so largely drawn into the English orbit. It will be recalled that during the last quarter of the eighteenth century and the first quarter of the nineteenth the Scottish representatives at Westminster had been merely an annex of the Tory party. Almost as a group the Scottish members of Parliament had followed Henry Dundas (who became the first Lord Melville) in voting for Tory measures, and had received their reward in favors for friends and relatives. Political principles Scotland had none save to win the loaves and fishes for her nationals. The disgrace of Lord Melville in 1805 and later the temporary ascendancy of the

Whigs lessened for a short time the subordination of Scotland to the Tories. But Robert Dundas (the second Lord Melville) gained almost the same oversight of Scottish affairs as his father, in return for throwing the Scottish votes to the Tory party. There were less than 3,500 men in all the Scottish counties who had the right to vote for members of Parliament and it was said that Dundas had them all ticketed and a record kept of what each of them wanted and who were his friends and associates. The electorate in the burghs is said to have been less than 1,500. It was little wonder that the Dundas family had Scottish representation in the hollow of its hands.

Long before the end of the Dundas regime in 1827, however, the people of Scotland were beginning to be restive. The French Revolution cannot be said to have set the heather on fire but it had started the peat burning underground. Liberal opinions had filtered into Scotland from England. Such men as Henry Erskine, the Scottish version of Charles James Fox, and the young men on the *Edinburgh Review* had exerted influence. Even a segment of the aristocracy had embraced liberal principles. Burns had voiced democratic sentiments that were in the air. The bitter conditions that followed Waterloo, unemployment and low wages, increased the discontent which began to express itself in public meetings, in riots, and occasionally in conspiracies. The new radicals were for a time suspicious of the old Scottish Whigs but slowly radicals and Whigs learned how to work together.

With the Scottish Reform Bill in 1832, that followed within months the First Reform Bill in England, the Scots in large numbers were given the vote. The result is not surprising. The new Scottish representation was predominantly Liberal. The drift of Scotland toward the Liberal party continued through the century. There were other reasons why Scotland should vote Liberal. The Liberal party became in England the voice of the Nonconformist conscience, and Scottish Presbyterians were naturally sympathetic with English Nonconformists. Furthermore the position of Gladstone in the Liberal party and his eventual leadership of it strengthened the hold of the party upon Scotland. Gladstone was himself of Scottish merchant stock, and in his moral earnestness and passion for what he conceived was right, he was more Scottish even than in his ancestry. His fervid language the Scots understood. They believed in him.

For its support of the Liberal party Scotland received few of the rewards that the Dundas family had distributed in an earlier time. It had only the consolation of being often on the side of reform and in line with the progress of events. While in the early part of the century such Scots as Thomas Erskine, Francis Horner, and Henry Brougham had become figures at Westminster, and, while toward the end of the nineteenth century many Scots held cabinet offices, the long middle period saw only a few Scots prominent in British politics.

Meanwhile what was left of the Scottish language was giving way to English. The schools were making efforts even at the elementary level to teach the children to speak and read the English of England. Families with aspirations for their children took pains to see that they discarded early the Scottish accent and Scottish words unknown in English. The middle classes in burgh towns realized that they could widen their business opportunities by pronouncng and using words as the English used them. No doubt there were still many older inhabitants in the smaller towns and in the country districts who continued to speak in the language of their fathers. No doubt many of the best people in Scotland even in professional homes and in castles clung to Scottish idiom in their own homes. But the trend of Scotland was toward the English of England.

That the Scots had to write a language somewhat different from that learned in childhood was a handicap to them, especially if they aspired to literary craftsmanship. Skilled writers they could hardly hope to become in a language unfamiliar to them from youth. A man may write well in the language he has always known because he feels in that language. If he grows up with one language and then has to state his thoughts in another, he may put them clearly enough but not with utmost ease and facility. He will fail to use idiom as one born to it, he will just miss those shadings and overtones that belong to the best writing. Certainly he will be unable to give his words the emotional content to be found in literature. Robert Burns could indite good English verse but when he was stirred by imagination he fell back into the Scottish tongue. If Joseph Conrad and George Santayana would seem to be exceptions to the statement that a man cannot write well save in his original tongue, it may be said that even their best English wants something of naturalness. The Scots had not yet learned to write the English language as the English wrote it. As they came more and more to write in English they ceased to write so well. Scottish literature went into eclipse.

There was more to the failure of the Scots to write literature than the mere difficulty of writing the language. The old language had become hard to read and so the Scots were cut off from their traditions. The prose of Lindsay of Pitscottie, of John Knox, and of James Melville was becoming hard to understand and had been relegated to the back shelves. The fifteenth- and sixteenth-century poets were no longer part of the Scots' spiritual equipment. The Scots had been parted from their heritage. From the death of Sir Walter Scott to the emergence of Robert Louis Stevenson there was little prose in Scotland that can be compared with that written in England and hardly any significant poetry. I can think of less than a score of Scottish poems written during that time that deserve to be remembered.

There were other reasons no doubt why Scottish literature failed to materialize. A great deal of the talent of Scotland was taken up with the new machinery, even some of the talent of those who went to the universities. Moreover the universities of Scotland were not commanding the brains they gained so easily in an earlier time. The promising youngsters of Scotland were taking the road to Oxford and Cambridge and, on graduating from those English institutions, were entering the British Civil Service or the professions in England. For a time, as we have seen, Edinburgh had offered those who settled there a society of thinking men and good enough talk to have given stimulus to any mind. That had all gone by the board. Sir Walter had not been dead many years before Edinburgh was on its way to becoming a bourgeois center with memories and traditions but little intellectual life of its own. As one reads through the memoirs, letters, and travel records of Henry Cockburn one soon realizes the heavy change that had come over the capital of Scotland. It had been coming even before the death of Scott. Edinburgh was becoming, as someone said, a pack of cards with the face cards left out.

When a Scottish writer did emerge, Thomas Carlyle, who gained his start in writing for the *Edinburgh Review*, he soon moved on London and became the sage of Chelsea. It is true that he remained in many ways a Scot. His message about the importance of the individual was right out of his Calvinistic background, though his emphasis upon heroes was from his German reading and travel. His prose with its new-minted words and phrases was that of a man who had made his own way in English and had been influenced not a little by the German language. He was as vigorous and passionate as John Knox. He was not ordained, but he was hardly less a preacher than Knox. The fiercely democratic feeling which runs through his earlier writing was derived from his Ecclefechan milieu, and reminds us of that of Burns. Both men came from the southwest counties out of the old Covenanting country. Hume Brown calls Carlyle one of the four great Scottish personalities of all time. It would seem nearer the truth to call him an important British prose writer, whose message is now slightly dated.

One man in early Victorian times may be mentioned as part of the story of Scottish literature. John Galt (1779–1839), who wrote *Annals of the Parish* and other good novels of Scottish life, will be remembered for those books and perhaps even more for one moving poem often attributed to him, the "Canadian Boat Song."

The arts flourished even less than literature. After the death of Sir Henry Raeburn and of Sir David Wilkie there were no painters of distinction, nor any significant school of Scottish painting until the close of the nineteenth century. Within a recent time Scottish etchers have become among the best known in the world. As for music, the land which had developed tunes and airs the like of which no other country could claim had during the larger part of the nineteenth century little to offer in new airs or in musical composition. At the beginning of the new century Mrs. Kennedy-Fraser's collection of the *Songs of the Hebrides* proved that Scotland's old resources in music had not been exhausted.

There was as yet no evidence of a humanitarian movement in Scotland. From the last decades of the eighteenth century England had been deeply affected by the work of philanthropists and humanitarians. By the middle of the century indeed charity schools had been widely established, hospitals increased in number and improved in facilities, a Foundling Hospital had been built and better arrangements made for infants left to the care of the parish. In the latter part of the century John Howard was exposing prison conditions, in the new century Wilberforce was starting a Society for Bettering the Conditions of the Poor and, with Zachary Macaulay and other Evangelicals of the Clapham Sect, was agitating against slavery in British possessions. Few stories are more thrilling than that of the growth of humanitarianism in England. Evangelicals and Quakers played a large role in it but many Dissenters took part.

One may ask why the Scots had not become interested in humanitarianism. Why were they behind the English in considering the lot of the oppressed? Today they are quite as given as the English to humanitarianism in all its many aspects. Why were the Evangelicals in Scotland less awake than those in England? The answer is not easy. Were the

277

old-style Presbyterians so impressed with the immediacy of the next world that this world seemed of little account? Was it that they deemed the sufferings of the distressed a fit means of punishing them for their sins? Was it that they were so concerned with morals that they thought too little of happiness? Or that they were so aware of the sins of their fellows that they failed in that love for them which leads to helpfulness? I am not prepared to say.

In England the humanitarian movement drew its support and leadership to a considerable degree from an educated and enlightened bourgeoisie. G. M. Trevelyan pays his respects again and again to the eighteenth-century English aristocracy as perhaps the most enlightened aristocracy in the history of the world. It might be urged that the English *haute bourgeoisie* was a class even more to be admired. They were possibly less enlightened but more sympathetic with distress. Their humanitarianism had long roots. Back in Elizabethan England there had been a few signs of humanitarianism and in the seventeenth century many signs. At that time the men who made money in business endowed almshouses and covered England with the evidence in Jacobean brick of their good-will to their fellows. In the late eighteenth century they were coming to the front in aid of the children, the poor, the sick, the imprisoned, and the enslaved. If their help had much of patronage about it, that was the custom of the time.

Did Scotland have no such class that might have supported humanitarianism? There was beginning to be a well-to-do bourgeoisie in Edinburgh, Glasgow, and in some of the larger towns. Compared with the English bourgeoisie they were a much less wealthy and cultivated class. They had no old tradition of humanitarianism, and in such matters tradition is a great deal. They, or their ancestors, had recently been too hard pressed themselves to give attention to the troubles of others. The bourgeoisie of Scotland were in this period little touched by the universities and not much in contact with the thinkers of the time and with the best of the professional classes. From such circles they might have picked up liberal ideas that would have made them susceptible to humanitarian impulses. They were too much occupied in gaining bawbees to look beyond their counting houses and suburban residences.

The energies of Scotland were going into new machinery and new manufacturing. It was a time of great engineers and of men who developed new enterprises. Never before had there been such engineers. Thomas Telford from an Eskdale village made himself, without special training, one of the most useful men of his generation. "Telford's is a happy life," wrote Robert Southey, the poet, who had known him and had traveled with him on his engineering tours, "everywhere making roads, building bridges, forming canals and creating harbors—works of sure, solid, permanent utility; everywhere employing a great number of persons, selecting the most meritorious, and putting them forward in the world in his own way." One cannot go about either Scotland or England without crossing bridges that Telford built. The great Caledonian Canal that bisects north Scotland was carried out according to his plan and under his oversight. Hardly less important was John Rennie, a protégé of James Watt. Rennie designed machines, laid out canals, made docks and harbors and built bridges, including the beautiful Waterloo Bridge that has just recently been rebuilt. Robert Stevenson, the grandfather of Robert Louis, designed more than twenty lighthouses and superintended the building of the famous lighthouse on Bell Rock (the "Inchcape Rock"). James Nasmyth invented the steam hammer. Robert Napier put steam engines into ships. William Fairbairn set going a machine for riveting boiler plates by steam power. David Mushet discovered blackband ironstone and proved its value for furnaces. James B. Neilson established the hot blast for smelting iron, which multiplied by three the amount of iron produced by a given amount of coal. Such inventions and discoveries and many others sprang out of Scottish imagination and initiative.

These men who prepared the way for an industrial Scotland were not the sons of the great. Of course James Nasmyth was the son of a famous landscape painter and Robert Stevenson was the son of a West India merchant. But Telford was the son of a sheep herder in Eskdale, John Rennie of a farmer at Phantassie in Haddingtonshire, Sir William Fairbairn of a farm laborer, Neilson of a millwright, and Napier of a blacksmith.

When one examines the stories of the great engineering works, the chemical manufacturers, the metallurgical and ship-building enterprises, and the manufacturing of cottons and woolens, one discovers that the manufacturers made much of their own machinery. One observes further that many of those manufacturers were originally—or else their fathers were—metal workers, blacksmiths, and millwrights, skilled workmen who made chances for themselves and out of little businesses developed great concerns. People in Oxford can remember when Lord Nuffield kept a bicycle shop, and his story is a more recent version of that of many a Scottish manufacturer. The Scots have a proverb, "Hand in use is the father of affluence." Enterprising men found it the more easy to build up manufacturing concerns because they could draw for help on a large reservoir of mechanics and machinists which Scotland already possessed. Every village had its men skilled in one trade and another. It was said in the Highlands that there every man was jack-of-all-trades, and there were many such men in the Lowlands and in the north of England who could quickly turn their hands to a new kind of skill. The Industrial Revolution was made possible in Scotland by the mechanical talent that was available in the old village industry.

It is not too much to say that the Industrial Revolution in Scotland was largely brought on by Scottish invention and discovery. Indeed Scottish invention had much to do with the Industrial Revolution in England. It must be said, however, that Scottish invention was pretty closely associated with invention and mechanical development in the north of England. George Stephenson was an Englishman born close to the Border. James Watt had become associated with an Englishman, Matthew Boulton, and that association was typical. Enterprising and mechanically minded Scots and north-country Englishmen of much the same type co-operated to create the great new enterprises in Britain. And Scottish engineers and inventors played their full half in the development.

Machinery made Scotland over. The manufacture of iron, the making of steam engines and of ships, the making of cotton and of woolen goods, of shawls and rugs, and a hundred other commodities went on over much of south and southeast Scotland. Those goods were shipped to England, to the Continent, to the New World, to Australia, New Zealand, and India. Scotland was profiting from her connection with the British Empire. The Industrial Revolution centered in the valley of the Clyde, in the country that has sometimes been dubbed Glasgovia. While there was manufacturing in other parts of the country, at Falkirk, Edinburgh, at Dundee and Aberdeen, at Kilmarnock and Dumfries, the new forms of Scottish business were to an extraordinary degree concentrated in and around the growing city on the Clyde.

The history of the Industrial Revolution in Scotland has not been written in detail, and in particular the aspect of it that concerns the working classes. Henry Hamilton has dealt with the rise of the various kinds of enterprises. He has hardly touched upon the men who worked in those enterprises. Marwick has supplemented him and given us some information about the workers. But if we knew the story completely, we could not in these pages go over it in detail. We all know a good deal about the evils that happened in England, we know of the sudden drift of men and women from the country, where they had friends, to the new cities; we know of the long hours and the miserable conditions under which they worked, and of the burdens imposed upon women and children. Those evils have been slightly exaggerated by a generation of social reformers and sympathetic historians who picked out the worst as typical. But the abuses were real. The Industrial Revolution left a lasting mark upon the physique of the English working classes that can still be recognized in any northern city.

So little study comparatively has been given to the same movement in Scotland that we must walk warily. But it is at once evident that the Scottish Industrial Revolution was in some respects worse than the English because it came upon Scotland more suddenly than upon England and because the Scots had less machinery for enforcing the care of the poor than the English. In the late sixteenth century the Scots passed legislation much resembling the Elizabethan Poor Laws of England. Legislation was not enough. The Scots government had not the means of pushing local authorities that the English had developed. The kirk sessions were not compelled to make assessments for the poor and in most cases trusted to voluntary grants which were never nearly enough. Toward the end of the eighteenth century and in the early nineteenth compulsory assessment became more common, but kirk sessions and the heritors, upon whom the burden of payment largely rested, were thrifty, and the poor got the worst of it. In the country the great nobles had a tradition of caring for their impoverished tenants, but nobles were few and far between and many of them in the late eighteenth century were away in London much of the time and left matters to stewards who were less generous. The clan system too had taken care of many of the poor in the Highlands but that was breaking up in the eighteenth century. Fletcher of Saltoun, writing at the beginning of that century, had estimated that there were two hundred thousand beggars in Scotland. His estimate must have been an exaggeration but beggars and hopeless poor there were aplenty then and later.

The problem of poverty had not been solved by parish relief and not even greatly ameliorated. As late as the early nineteenth century there was stiff opposition to compulsory relief. The famous Thomas Chalmers, who led the Disruption of 1843, for conscience's sake opposed bitterly the principle of compulsory assessment. By that time, however, there were physicians and liberal-minded men who compared conditions in Scotland and England to the advantage of the English and declared that the whole system of relief in Scotland must be worked over. In 1843 a commission of seven gentlemen of competency was appointed to make an inquiry into the practical operation of the Scottish Poor Laws and as a result in 1845 an act was passed that made over the whole system of the treatment of the poor in Scotland and set up sufficient machinery to carry it out.

When, with age or illness, any of the thousands of men and women who had begun flocking to the towns and going to work on the new machines lost their jobs, the miserly parish grants failed utterly to meet the needs. Furthermore the employers, the new manufacturing class, were often Lowlanders of the old Anglian stock, hardheaded and close as the kirk sessions. They drew their workers in a considerable degree from the Highlanders moving into Glasgow, men whom they did not understand or like, and from the "wild Irish," whom they had always distrusted. They believed in long hours for their workers, who seemed to them naturally lax. Short hours, they feared, would promote "idle habits." There was no custom or theory of short hours. The manufacturers may have known of the theories of their fellow countryman of an earlier generation, Adam Smith, but whether they did or not, they had heard of laissez faire, let well enough alone, don't interfere with economic laws. Laissez faire was in the air and hard to resist. It was the most logical of theories, it suited admirably the ideas of manufacturers who were only too pleased to find economic laws on their side. It was not all laissez faire. Many of the manufacturers were paternalistic in their attitude toward their employees, provided cottages for them, and looked after them as feudal lords might have done, but kept them strictly under control and would have resented interference by the State. The new factory acts which kindhearted English country gentlemen and Evangelical humanitarians were pushing in Parliament would have seemed to them an interference with their rights.

The machine age was hard enough on the English working classes but it was harder on the Scottish workers. The tens of thousands of men and women who rushed into the new factories had lived before miserably in the Highlands or in the Lowlands, and they accepted hovels in Glasgow without sunlight and sanitation and fresh air as part of their lot. The Irish who flocked across St. George's Channel had always lived wretchedly. They were said to be easily contented with bad conditions and were blamed for pulling the Scots down after them. They helped to fill the increasing slums of Glasgow and the near-by towns.

The Scottish manufacturer—or his father before him—had often been a handicraftsman of some kind, as we have seen, and by his own inventiveness or enterprise improved his position and become a small-scale or even a large-scale manufacturer. In more cases he was a small man who grasped a business chance in his community made possible by the new inventions. He was likely to be a narrow, hard-bitten man of little culture or breadth of view, passionate in his pursuit of his expanding schemes, and with little time to spare for other things. His early experience had been parochial and his business connections did not much widen his outlook.

He and his kind transformed Scotland within two generations. The talk of his friends was of machines and ships and markets. Scotland was on the up and up. Businessmen became the predominant feature of the Scottish landscape. They were in the front of the picture, and professional people ceased to be as important as they had been in the Periclean Ages. Business ruled the roast.

XXV

EARLY VICTORIAN SCOTS

HENRY COCKBURN, the Scottish judge, on his circuits round Scotland in the 1830's and '40's had much to say of the country. Everywhere he saw old castles and churches going to pieces for want of any care either by local authorities or by the lord who owned the land and would not waste money he could spend in London. It hurt Cockburn to see the memorials of old Scotland disappearing. The old was going and the new was conspicuous. He could not go far without running into the ugliness of the new manufacturing towns and the crowded tenements that had grown up within them. He loved the natural scenery of Scotland, the mountains, the glens, the lochs, and the long grassy slopes of moors. He was glad, too, to see nature improved by man, plantations of trees that had been set to clothe the bare hills and the diversification of crops that gave the fields color and interest. But he saw also many ugly towns with unattractive houses and untidy grounds. He knew England from a coach and he could not escape the impression that the Scots were a people without taste or a feeling for beauty. He may have made allowance in his mind for the Scottish want of taste by remembering that they had less money to spend on improvements, but he did not make that allowance in his record. His impression of the ugliness of Scottish villages and houses is confirmed by the earlier account of Dorothy Wordsworth, who could not but see the dinginess outside and the dirt inside the houses. There were other Scots who came back from journeys in England to lament the drabness of the Scottish countryside.

Cockburn could not help comparing what was and what had been: "Whoever wishes to see the contrast between the Scotch past and the Scottish present should look on Melrose and Galashiels, and on Jedburgh and Hawick, mouldering ruins, attesting the predominance of a single worship, and that the papal, and connected with great national occurrences, solitude, poverty and silence, on the one side; and but a few miles off, manufactures, bustle, wealth, population, and newness on the other; the solitary ruins sink the modern vulgarities into contempt. Both are best, but each in its place. Trade cannot mix itself with the sacred haunts of visible antiquity without profaning or destroying them, and should therefore keep to its own place. And I suppose it is from conscious shame that it generally does so."

Cockburn resented a little the new Scotland of business enterprise, and had on the whole surprisingly little to say about businessmen. He saw his old friends of the aristocracy and of the professions. The new manufacturers, who were making Scotland over, seem not to have been within his acquaintance or that of his associates.

Yet those businessmen were important, perhaps as important as any men in Scotland in the nineteenth century. As they set the machines going and kept them going they formed at first a new and little recognized bourgeoisie. Many of them adopted the strictest Presbyterian views. To keep the Sabbath, to know the Catechism, to conform to the tenets of the Kirk, satisfied their conscience and ministered to a formalism they understood.

The Books of Discipline had had a good deal to say about the poor. But the new businessmen of Scotland had not delved into the roots of Presbyterianism and their minds were not on the poor nor on the abuses of overworked and underpaid labor. They did not even think of those abuses. Abuses are seldom recognized until they have been abuses for a good while. What the manufacturers realized was that the accumulation of money led easily to larger accumulations. Prosperity was to be had for taking thought and they were ready to glorify God in that way. Did not the Old Testament abound in examples of patriarchs who had flocks and herds and served God? There were texts aplenty to indicate that prosperity was proof of the favor of the Almighty.

It is not to be supposed that the business classes were all alike. Many of them were, as we have seen, inventors and engineers with an aptitude for machinery and with zeal for finding out new methods of saving human effort. Some of the best imagination in Scotland was going into the development of heavy industry and shipping and cloth making. Men with imagination are fond of going their own way; they are likely to refuse to accept set patterns and to look out on the world from their own fresh, individual slant. Such men there were in Scotland, and while few of them at first saw the inside of the houses of the old great, they could not be denied importance in their communities and some of them have become part of the honor roll of Scotland.

But there were other businessmen, as we have already noted, acquisitive chaps who followed in the wake of the inventive and imaginative and got in on the flowing tide of business activity and were carried far. It is not easy to find the sources that tell us about them. May I be permitted to guess that some of them may have been like a certain type of Scot to be found today often far from his native heath in port towns over the world? They are easily good fellows with a certain kindling enthusiasm that is attractive. They trade upon their Scottishness, attend Burns celebrations, and sing Jacobite songs. They play games and talk about brands of Highland whiskey and, when they have sampled them, become communicative. They know what fortunes or salaries their associates enjoy and rate them accordingly. The type is Scottish but may be found among other peoples.

Eventually of course there developed from the manufacturing and industrial families a new set of aristocrats who took on the manners and codes of an older society. In England the manufacturers were accepted by the gentry, if not at once, within a generation or so, especially if they built houses in the country and made suitable contributions to the hunts. In Scotland the families of old position were slow to accept the new people, however wealthy. So high and impenetrable was the fence against the newly rich that they sometimes moved to England where they were more likely to be welcomed than in their own country. Money talked more loudly possibly in England than in Scotland. The old privileged classes in Scotland were more democratic in dealing with tenants and in meeting servants and humble folk of every kind than were the same classes in England. But they were more reserved toward those who might claim equality. Blue blood went far in a land where there had been few rich. A nonaffluent aristocracy holds to its exclusiveness. The English aristocracy usually had money and found it natural to associate with those who lived and played games and spent money as they did. Being, many of them, huntin'-fishin'-shootin' people of the country, they did not associate so readily as Scottish landed folk with professional people of the town. The Scots noble was often too intelligent and bookish to cut himself off from men of similar tastes. But businessmen were beyond his acquaintance. This failure to accept the new classes of the business world until their sons and grandsons had taken up professions and public service meant some loss to the strength and freshness of Scottish national life. For a long while the manufacturing classes were unable to win a place in the Scottish picture beside the nobility and the professional classes.

The ministers had a more palpable influence on the community. By the nineteenth century they were receiving fairly good pay. They were in many instances men who had bettered themselves, who had come from homes where pennies were scarce and made their way with effort through one of the universities. At the university they had specialized in philosophy, logic, theology, and biblical studies. Usually the minister before going to the university had had some training in the classics and he might, at the university, have had a course or two in the Greek Testament, but in general he had not been much exposed to the older humanities. Henry Cockburn often attended church services, as he made his judicial rounds of the country, and used to complain of the ranting

sermons he heard. He found the ministers tedious, uneducated, and illiberal. It is true that the minister was likely to
be a conservative and rather narrow and evangelical. Mod-
eratism was on the wane and even Thomas Chalmers had
been converted to Evangelicalism. The whole drift in the
Established Scottish Church and in the various nonestab-
lished kirks was toward the preaching of the gospel. The Old
Testament was not used as much for texts as formerly.

Less than in a former time was the minister the proclaimer
of thou-shalt-not, but he was nonetheless the voice of Scottish conscience, the walking embodiment of Scottish morality. As a minister he was expected, as he had long been, to
carry himself with the dignity and sobriety of conduct of one
whose mind was centered on matters of high import. It was
not for him to laugh at the contradictions and whimsicalities
of man's behavior and he was not likely to have done so in
any case. His grave carriage guaranteed him respect and influence in a community that preferred that its spiritual
advisers be men of ostentatious want of levity. Yet while his
influence was considerable it was probably less than in an
earlier day.

Unlike a pleasant type of English parson he was seldom
an antiquarian or an amateur in some branch of humane
learning. He was possibly less cultivated on the average than
the English clergyman, and usually less interested in the arts
and literature. His study was not a little on the Bible and he
pored over commentaries upon it. It was generally believed
in the North that he was a more intellectual man than his
English confrere and that in preaching he made sharper distinctions and reasoned more closely.

I am not sure that he was as often the friendly counselor of
his parishioners as the English clergyman. He was not afraid
to give them spiritual advice, to rebuke them for dereliction,
for breaking the Sabbath or failing to attend church services.
He was hardly the same genial figure in the village. Yet he
was compact of moral courage and willing to make sacrifices
on behalf of his faith. In the novels and memoirs he comes

out rather well as a man of strong character. Had he been also a man of wide range of learning and of breadth of view he might have been a force to resist the growing Philistinism of the time.

The dominie or schoolmaster had always been a useful and respected person in the community. In the nineteenth century there were more dominies than ever before and some of them were better paid than they had been in the eighteenth century. Others were still drawing incomes inferior to those of farm laborers. There was still a dearth of schools; at the beginning of the nineteenth century there were fifty thousand children in Scotland, it was said, who had no chance of schooling. Nevertheless there were many grammar schools and academies in the burghs, and parish schools over much of the country. The Society for the Propagation of the Gospel, as we have seen, and the General Assembly had been setting up schools in the Highlands. Where there was no school, parents joined together to pay for a schoolmaster or schoolmistress, or some unoccupied man in the community set up a school on his own, perhaps a "stickit minister," that is a minister who had failed to be appointed to a church.

John Kerr, a Government Inspector of Education who went from place to place observing the schools, tells of visiting the school of James Beattie in northern Aberdeenshire. Beattie made his living as a cobbler, and while engaged in making and repairing shoes taught the boys and girls the elements of reading, writing, and geography. The inspector was afraid that he might not be welcomed but was gladly received by Beattie. Kerr feared Beattie would not be pleased that a new school was being opened two miles away which would draw off his students, but James Beattie who at eighty-two was still making shoes and watching his students read was glad to know that a better school was to be set up: "Ay, if I werena an auld dune man, as I am, I wud hae been thankfu' for the new schule. I hae may be dune as weel's I could, but a' my teachin', though its better than naething, is no to be compared wi' what they get at a richt schule."

Early Victorian Scots

The inspector said to Beattie that he must have had a long education, and James replied: "I've been learnin a' my days, and I am as fond to learn as ever." When Beattie taught the children the letters he had to stop cobbling for the moment, but the Bible passages that he set them and the storybooks he put before them he knew so well that he could attend their recitation and go on with his handwork. He was proud of the fourteen hundred or so students he had turned out, some of whom wrote him and sent him presents from far parts of the world. He had started teaching with a basis of only eleven weeks' schooling himself and only because the parents in the village had asked him to do so. He had received no fees or any salary save that his neighbors worked his little croft for him.

There were hundreds of such men and women teachers who gave children a start in learning, usually for small fees. There were hundreds of others who, in the parish schools, taught the elementary subjects and more advanced subjects such as Latin. Most of the teachers in the grammar schools and in the academies were men who had been to the universities and who watched out for clever lads in their classes and fitted them for the university.

The dominie does not figure a great deal in the memoirs and novels of the time but there can be little doubt that his direct and indirect influence in forming character was important. Yet few Scottish boys seem in later life to have recalled their schoolmaster with pleasure, perhaps because he was an example of that life of hardship and poverty from which they were glad to have escaped. The autobiographies of the great men of Scotland, so far as I have read them, are full of praise for their professors at the universities, and have little to say about their teachers in childhood. Those professors carried with them a certain dignity and position. The schoolmaster was too poor to impress his pupils.

As for the humbler classes in the country, they were naturally not much noticed in the records of the time. Large numbers of them were drifting into the factories in the towns.

There were still, however, many farm laborers left in the country. Some of them were working on large farms where their condition was little better than that of serfdom, save that they could move on to another farm. Many men lived in wretched barracks, four in a shed, away from the farmhouse. Those who had families could go back to them once in two or three weeks for a day. These men had a "certain allowance of oat, barley and pea-meal," Cobbett tells us, "upon which they live, mixing it with water, or with milk, when they are allowed the use of a cow." On some of the large farms the married men were permitted to have their families with them. The married laborers lived in a sort of barracks. "It is a long shed, stone walls and pantile roof, and divided into a certain number of boothies, each having a door and one little window. Each distinct boothie is about seventeen feet one way and fifteen feet the other way. . . . There is no ceiling and no floor but the earth. In this place a man and his wife and family have to live." Cobbett and others were astonished that families could be brought up under such conditions, but he and others observed that the women tried to keep their places decent and were often self-respecting people. In Hugh Miller's recollections of his life as a workingman, he has a good deal to say about the barracks on the large farms, and it is evident that while the farm laborers and their families lived in great poverty and with scarcely enough to eat, they were so accustomed to poverty that they were not sorry for themselves and managed to get along, even to maintain their pride.

Not all farm laborers were as badly off as those Cobbett pictured, and yet Dorothy Wordsworth's description of farm laborers a bit earlier is not cheering. Luckily we have the autobiography of a workingman, Alexander Somerville, who went from place to place seeking work, and who describes his fellow laborers, their pay, their work, and their food. They seem to have been an impoverished class of people who had by no means lost their spirit or resourcefulness. Many of these bitterly poor people managed somehow to read books and to know the poems of Robert Burns and of Allan Ramsay. They had known grinding poverty for generations but chill penury had not repressed their noble rage nor frozen the genial current of their souls. They had maintained their courage. They prided themselves on their capacity for work and their ability to endure.

John Buchan in his autobiography has presented a glowing picture of the Border peasants whom he knew at a much later time. The Border shepherds were men of the long stride, he says, and clear eye; they were God fearing, decent in all their relations of life, and supreme masters of their craft. A fighting stock, he calls them, and men of independent mind. He says further that they had some aptitude for the graces of life. That may have been true by the end of the nineteenth century.

The peasant Scots one meets in books of the earlier part of the century had seldom learned the gentle manners, soft voices, and quiet behavior that villagers in the south had picked up from the families of the squire and the vicar. Some of them were rough rather than gentle, ready to resort to violence to maintain their rights as they conceived them, and occasionally as passionate as their ancestors. They were likely to be more capable than the same class in England of holding their own in an argument. They knew how to start with a biblical premise and build up an argument. They seldom failed to be characters. However hard they worked, however much hardship they endured, they had time left for association with their fellows. They were a coming-on people, eager to talk with their neighbors and to quiz the stranger. The men and women whom Dorothy Wordsworth met in her peregrinations through Scotland and the fellow laborers with whom Alexander Somerville consorted were not all of them by any means God fearing and decent in all the relations of life, but they were often masters of their farming crafts and interesting men and women who had a way with them.

As for the working classes in the towns and cities, they were busy at the wheels of the new machinery and had little leisure for developing interesting character. Now and then a talented mechanic or machinist broke through into a managership or perhaps became a figure in his world. But a large proportion of the men in the shops lived in miserable conditions in long rows of ill-built houses. Their living conditions became worse as what were new tenements became old slums. The homes of their forebears had never been dwellings of beauty and neatness and they had been schooled by experience to expect little, but now they were forced into a drab existence that was worse than their forefathers had known.

Some of them were rough people. Hugh Miller, who had himself been for many years a mason and had watched his fellow workers with observant eyes, says that many of them were pretty barbarous people who had been held down only by the public opinion of their small communities in the country. In the city they found themselves limited by no neighborhood discipline, and all their wild instincts had opportunity. It is certain that the whole Clydeside district gained a reputation for wild and violent men. It may not have been merely slums and ill conditions that made them so. It may be that some of that old ferocity of their ancestors got its last fling when they moved into the city and away from the confinement of country opinion.

The seafaring people of Scotland were one of the groups that deserve a few paragraphs. Hugh Miller in telling of his seafaring forebears wrote that his grandfather's first wife was buried in the family burying place, "in which—so heavy were the drafts made by accident and violent death on the family —the remains of none of the male members had been deposited for more than a hundred years." His father went the way of the others. He had been bringing a load of kelp by sea around Cape Wrath and then around past the Moray Firth. A fellow townsman happened to be watching the boat from a point on the land and saw that the skipper was exhausting every nautical shift to keep away from the shore. The skipper seemed to have succeeded in getting round the cape and the watcher thought that once more his friend had been saved from the sea by his skill. But the boat was never seen again. Day after day his son would climb a point on the old coast line, "to look out wistfully after everyone else had given up hope for the sloop with the two stripes of white and the two square topsails." He had often before known the family elation when the father turned up after a dangerous trip and he could not give up. Those familiar with Scottish songs will remember "There's Nae Luck aboot the Hoose."

> But are ye sure the news is true?
> And are ye sure he's weel?
> Is this a time to talk o' wark?
> Ye jades, fling by your wheel.
>
> Is this a time to think o' wark,
> When Colin's at the door?
>
> His very foot has music in't
> As he comes up the stair:
>
> And will I see his face again?
> And will I hear him speak?

The Scots were a fishing and seafaring people and the story told in that song and the story told by Hugh Miller were both of them in the Scots tradition. On every coast of Scotland from Berwick to John o' Groats and from there to Cape Wrath and along all the Western Islands and between them and the west coast there were fishermen. And seamen went out on their missions of carrying goods from every port large and small. Good harbors until the nineteenth century were few, and lighthouses fewer, and storms were many, and sooner or later the seamen failed to reappear. It is not surprising that a good part of the lore of Scotland is connected with the adventures and misadventures of men at sea.

They were a sturdy lot of people; some of them did well and built stone houses fronting the water, and brought up sons to follow the sea and daughters to marry seamen and become early widows. Perhaps that inclination to take chances which appears again and again in Scottish character was due not only to the Norse stock of western Scotland and the islands but to the fact that so large a part of the population had to make its living by taking chances. When steamships came in, the element of chance in going to sea almost disappeared, but the Scots still went to sea. There is a saying that on any ship anywhere you have only to call down to the engine room, "Mac, are you there" and a Scottish voice will reply.

The men who owned or rented farms were doing well. Since the end of the eighteenth century scientific farming had been coming in and Scottish farmers were possibly even more aware than English of the new methods in agriculture. Throughout the nineteenth century more and more varieties of farm machinery were being introduced upon the larger farms and often even upon the smaller farms. The farmers were making money and becoming important members of the community. When Cobbett came to Scotland they wined and dined him and signed public letters to him. Many of the farmers were becoming something like entrepreneurs. As the farmer became an entrepreneur he tended to separate himself from those who worked for him. He made his friends among the neighboring farmers and among the middle classes, the business people in the near-by towns. His ideals and his outlook tended to approximate those of the Scottish bourgeoisie.

The lairds were less important in Scottish life, had always been, as we have seen, than the gentry in England. They had little of the prestige that went with "county" in England, they were not united by county ties and county association like the English gentry. They were not as cultivated as the English gentry had once been but possibly quite as cultivated as the hunting gentry of nineteenth-century England, if not as well bred. They had little of the English country gentleman's sense of noblesse oblige. They were really landlords, often hardly distinguishable from the large-scale farmers. They looked after their lands, gathered in the rents, and were sometimes rather hard boiled about it. They had, many of them, taken up the new farming on a large scale and were doing well at it, sending fat beeves to the London market, and raising in the Lowlands between the Clyde and the Border great crops of wheat and oats.

The Scottish nobility had of old been a great force in Scotland, as we have seen. But throughout the nineteenth century the influence of that class was diminishing. The great lordly seats still had some magic about them and there were Scottish lords who had influence not only because of their historic names but because they were men of character and intellect. A Duke of Argyll might be a member of Gladstone's government and influential in Scottish affairs because of his political position, but his real influence depended upon his abilities and his speeches and sometimes upon his writing. His seat, Inverary, was no longer the center of the west of Scotland, as it had been in the days of Montrose and those of Jeanie Deans. The Scottish nobles spent much of their year in London and sometimes on the Riviera and became too Anglicized in their outlook to sway the thought and feeling of Scotland.

Many of them, more in proportion, I suspect, than in England, were men of learning and wisdom. Their wives and daughters were women of spirit and liveliness, full of proverbs and of sad stories of birth and death and of the chances of this strange world. It is a delight to read the memoirs of Scottish noble families in the nineteenth century. Whereas many of the memoirs of English lords and ladies—by no means all—contain accounts of their travels, of the embassies in which they were guests, of the continental great with whom they dined, of the race meets they attended, and the gracious words uttered to them by sovereigns, the memoirs of Scottish families are crowded with quaint and homely characters from the neighborhood. The Scottish lords and ladies were likely themselves to be quaint characters. Strong characters too they were, who knew their own minds and could express them, but who knew much else. They knew about their neighbors below the castle and about the courtship of the new minister. They had looked on the grassy slopes of the Lammermuirs and smelled the pines above the pass. They remembered Montrose's dying words and the Testament of the Bruce.

The Scots noble had some weight in the General Assembly of Scotland; he expressed himself in letters to the *Scotsman* or to the London *Times;* he took the chair at public meetings and made a long speech about conditions in the Highlands; he served on railway boards and public commissions; now and then he published a volume on some subject that possibly bore few traces of the amateur.

Fine figures the Scots nobles have been in modern Scottish life, and often useful figures. Few of them have been gifted with political skill, though the eighth Duke of Argyll was not without considerable political acumen. The late Lord Rosebery became Prime Minister, but proved a better public speaker than leader. The Scottish nobles have little history behind them of fighting for causes and of bringing about political reforms. Their ancestors, as we have seen, had gone their own way, or made short-term alliances with their neighbors, for military reasons. The modern Scottish noble has contented himself with being a great figure. That influence possessed by his forebears is no longer his birthright. The Scottish noble is passing, as all nobility is passing.

XXVI

NINETEENTH-CENTURY HIGHLANDERS

I HAVE traced the Highlanders from century to century and have commented here and there on their character. By the nineteenth century they were becoming less important as Highlanders. They still exhibited the antique courtesy, the friendly easy manners, and the natural sympathy that had always been theirs. They still lived in miserable cottages in the glens, they still remained a problem, as the poor are always a problem.

The charm and virtues of the Highlanders had been published to the world and not with understatement. Their old faults were somewhat glossed over by a romantic generation. An attentive reading of the memoirs of Highland aristocrats and of others convinces one that not all the crofters in the glens were nature's gentlemen. Some of them had a way of leaving the hard work in the fields to their women, as had been their custom in the old days when men did the hunting and fighting and women the work in the fields. They were not only indolent but unprogressive. Petty thievery and deceit were not unknown. If cattle stealing had become difficult under the new sway of law, sheep stealing on a small scale was still carried on, and many a household lived on mutton not raised at home. In respect to exact statement the Highlander was not always skilful. He was too eager to please and too imaginative to be matter of fact.

The faults of the Highlanders as well as their virtues had been well known to the great Sir Walter and set down honestly. He endowed them nevertheless with a glamour which has never wholly worn off. His narrative poems and his novels turned English tourists north by the thousands. Those tourists saw usually what Sir Walter had told them to see. To some of them the Highlander appeared the incarnation of the noble savage celebrated in the eighteenth century. He came into his own when George IV visited Edinburgh in 1822 and was received by Sir Walter who was in charge of ceremonies. The king toasted the chieftains and clans of Scotland, as if they constituted Scotland. Royalty continued to show partiality to the Highlands. Queen Victoria bought a house in the Highlands and built a castle. Her movements in that romantic country were recorded by the newspapers, and by herself, and did not diminish popular interest. The Highlands became fashionable.

But as they became popular they lost their old character. It has already been noted how in the late eighteenth and early nineteenth century many Highlanders had been evicted from their habitations to make way for sheep. In the later nineteenth century more of them were pushed off the land so that deer might flourish and English sportsmen might have a happy hunting ground. The north of Scotland became a gathering place of wealthy Southrons and even of occasional Americans who followed in the wake of the English sportsmen. Highland gillies guided the sportsmen in pursuing the deer, Highland beaters drove the grouse in front of the guns, Highland pipers entertained the weary sportsmen in the long evenings, and Highland games gave them an excuse for pleasant patronage. The engaging manners of the Highlanders infatuated the English sportsman, who believed that he was seeing the MacGregor on his native heath. He was pleased and amused at the gillie's want of servility and his readiness to talk back. What good stories he would tell in London about that gillie! The gillie knew very well the value of being a Highland character. The sportsman accepted the pipers and the Highland games as right out of Walter Scott and told his friends in London about "MacCrimmon's Lament" and "Lochaber No More." His bright new Highland tartan he displayed to his associates. Had not one of his great-aunts been married to a Macdonald?

The casual tripper of the late nineteenth century could have his Highlands too. There were pictures of swaggering

Highlanders in costume, there were kilted men who played bagpipes on the corner and passed the hat. There were Highland whiskeys of an extraordinary tradition to be had at a price. Highland regiments in kilts were to be seen marching up to the castle with the band playing "Wae's Me for Prince Charlie," and "Will Ye No Come Back Again?" The tripper bought a picture of Flora Macdonald and went over the sea to Skye.

There were still, however, Highlanders who were not on show, who fished in the loch or cultivated their little holdings. They were a fertile race and not all the evictions or movements to Lowland factories or emigration to Canada had rid the glens of crofters. There was seldom much glamour about the Highlander in the glen. He had in many cases become a good Presbyterian who kept the Sabbath and had been persuaded by his minister to have done with ballads and songs and dances.

The nineteenth century saw efforts to ameliorate the conditions of the crofters. Some of them had made their way or had been driven down to the coast and learned slowly the dangerous trade of fishing. A kelp industry was started; that is, seaweed or what was called seaware, was gathered along the shore and sold inland as a fertilizer. But in 1825 the duty on barilla, a sodium carbonate, was removed, and barilla competed too successfully against the kelp. At a much later time an aluminum manufacture was established near Fort William, and Lord Leverhulme did his best to set up a great manufacturing plant on Skye. The making of rough woolen cloths of various sorts proved more profitable.

But the tourist trade, kelp, and Highland industries were not enough. In '46 the Highlands suffered from a potato famine similar to that in Ireland. The crofters had never been good farmers and had little capacity to improve. They were suspicious of new ways of planting and of new crops. All farmers are conservative, but the Lowland farmer had shown himself as progressive as any in Britain, while the Highland farmer has been utterly opposed to any change.

If the Lowlanders continued to look down upon the High-landers as a poverty-stricken and unprogressive people, they had to recognize that the Highlanders had become part of the Scottish saga. Some of the Lowlanders had indeed come to understand their neighbors to the north and to appreciate their virtues, now that those neighbors were no longer able to make forays into the south and lift cattle or start risings for kings from over the water. That the Highlanders had been considerably Presbyterianized made them more acceptable to the Lowlanders. They could now discuss Kirk matters at the General Assembly with Highland ministers and elders. Highland ministers who had come south were often filling Lowland charges. The Highlands and the Lowlands were no longer two nations held together by geography. The Lowlanders had penetrated into the fastnesses of the north and the Highlanders had crowded into the Lowland cities.

The Highlanders were Scots who had their full share in making up the Scottish national character. There were certain Highland characteristics which in some degree became Scottish characteristics.

A. G. Macdonnell in *My Scotland* would say that the sense of drama was one of those Highland qualities that influenced Scotland. He spends pages in developing the thesis that the Highlanders were a people given to drama, with a backdrop of mountains for scenery. Yes, of course. All Scots have a sense of drama, as the chroniclers of that country prove. The wight Wallace went from one hairbreadth escape to another, as Blind Harry told the story. Who was Lindsay of Pitscottie but an historian who could weave dramatic tales about the rise and fall of kings? Who was Mary, Queen of Scots, but a fey lady, moving on a stage of lovers, murder, battle, and prison, to her appointed doom? The Covenanters were hunted men who made their exits with fine apostrophes to this world and the next. I see no reason to believe that the Highlanders were much more given to drama than the Lowlanders. It was not for the Highlanders to impose a sense of drama on people who already had it. Macdonnell had suffered, as many others, from the strutting Highlanders provided for the tourist trade. Dorothy Wordsworth's Highlanders were gentle-spoken, ingratiating cottagers whose drama in their little homes had to do only with food and weather, with birth and death.

But imagination was easily one of those characteristics which the Highlanders lent to their Lowland brothers. We must not suppose that all Lowlanders were without imagination. The Lowlander was more Gael than anything else and he dreamt dreams and saw visions. What the Highlanders did in mixing with the Lowlanders was to reinforce that old Gaelic strain, to accentuate the natural tendency to project the mind. Highland imagination by itself was likely to be aimless; when joined with Lowland steadfastness it proved most useful. David Livingstone whose forebears were part Highland and part Lowland was an example of how useful the combination could be. In his mind's eye he saw problems to be answered by exploration and by Lowland persistence was able to find the answers.

The Scots have been more than imaginative. They have been adventurous, sailing far seas and crossing many ranges. An examination of the names of explorers would lead one to believe that the Highlanders have been pre-eminent among Scottish explorers and one can readily understand why. As one reads the stories of the boyhood of such Highlanders as have told their stories, one realizes that unless they were held down by abject poverty the lads had a good time. They gathered eggs on the sides of sea cliffs; they found out caves along the sea and in the glens and made them rendezvous for their circles, they robbed bees of their honey; they watched the herring boats and peat boats come in and listened to sailors' stories. They caught otter, shot ptarmigans, and trapped martens. Few of these sports were unknown in the Lowlands but it was in the Highlands that they flourished and that boys had the best chance to learn adventure. That adventure was not only an outlet for the imagination; it taught the youngsters to initiate plans and to venture far and dangerously. Robert Louis Stevenson's heroes had a way of being Highland born.

Highland sensitiveness added much to Scottish character. "Their sense of the supernatural," says G. R. Blake, "raised them far above the barbarian and gave the race that exquisite sensitiveness which when mingled with that of the Lowlands doubled the receptiveness and sensibility of the Scottish people at large."

Highland mysticism and superstition slowly made their way south and touched the Lowlanders. The Highlanders had superstitions that went far back. Those superstitions became connected inevitably with their religion. When the Highlanders accepted Protestantism they gave up little of their beliefs in fairies, brownies, and water kelpies. They superimposed upon Presbyterianism their superstitious fears. To break the Sabbath, for example, became something terrible, because it invited supernatural revenge. Osgood Mackenzie tells how his uncle on Isle Ewe required that turnips should twice a day be barrowed to his cows but on the Sabbath the cattle men could not think of using a barrow since it had a wheel, and on that day carried the turnips in their arms to the cows. Such rigid observance of the Sabbath was encouraged by the Highland ministers. They made of the logical Calvinism a thing of mysticism and passion.

Highland loyalty was a quality that touched everything Scottish. There were no longer the Pretenders upon whom the Highlanders might expend their loyalty, and the clans in the nineteenth century were not of much significance. Yet the fierce loyalties of old were not extinguished. The tenants of a Highland laird could express that loyalty in almost medieval fashion. When Lady Mackenzie died suddenly up in the Highlands in 1832 word went out quickly for men between twenty and thirty to attend her funeral. Four companies of one hundred and twenty-five men apiece took turns in carrying the coffin over the rough country where roads were none or few. Twenty-four miles they carried the body of Lady Mackenzie the first day and forty the second, and a shorter distance the third to her burial place. The great procession walked in silence at about four miles an hour. There was nothing strange about such a funeral. Those of my readers who have read Scottish novels will remember the funeral processions where the coffins were carried through glens deep in snow and over mountains.

That incredible loyalty or affection toward superiors in rank, which can be seen in the memoirs of the Highland aristocracy, lasted to a late date. It was transmitted, I am inclined to believe, to the Lowlanders, many of whom incidentally were not so far away from the feudal and clan system themselves. It was an old quality of the Scots going back to the earliest time, but nevertheless as the Highlanders penetrated to the Lowlands and intermarried with the Lowlanders, as Highland virtues were extolled in the Lowlands, the virtue of loyalty was constantly reaccented. One reason the Scot got along so well in the world was because he was naturally loyal to his superior in work. It was not a loyalty assumed for a purpose. It was an old ingrained loyalty to one who happened to be in a superior position.

Highland courage had become known to the world, and Highland success in war, as we have earlier noted. That success had reflected glory upon Scotland, particularly as the outside world read of Highland regiments and identified the Highlands with Scotland. It is said that from 1797 to 1837 the Island of Skye alone, a small fraction of the Highlands, gave to the British army twenty-one lieutenant- and major-generals, forty-eight lieutenant-colonels and six hundred other commissioned officers, and ten thousand men in the ranks. The Scots had been warriors of old but the Highland glory in arms made all Scots conscious of their national prowess. It will be recalled that at the siege of Lucknow the first indication of relief was the far sound of the bagpipers playing "The Campbells Are Coming."

It is not unlikely that the Highlanders with their many talents reinforced Scottish life in the Lowlands at a time when it was beginning to suffer from the constant drain of

ability to England. More and more of the able youngsters
of the Lowlands were finding their way to the English universities and leaving the dull and less interesting scholars
behind them in the universities of the north. A university
takes its color to a considerable degree from the brilliant
men who gather in it; even the less talented, serious-minded
youth are affected by the dash and brains of their fellows.
The Scottish universities began to suffer from the earnest
young men who were making a struggle to get on. The ablest
young men in any country never have to fight hard to get
on; they are pushed on by the need for them. But when
some of those able young men are sifted out of a country and
the universities have to depend upon those left behind, the
situation is not good for the institutions or for the country
that must live intellectually from their product. Not only were
young scholars drifting south but so were some of the best
of the young professional men, lawyers, physicians, and professors. Leaders of Scottish business were accepting posts
in Manchester and Liverpool and in London. Much of what
we may call the entrepreneur talent was going south.

> For rrae the cottar to the laird
> We all run south.

But meanwhile the Highlanders were running south too,
many of them to the Universities of Glasgow and Edinburgh,
where there had always been a sprinkling of them. Sharp
minds there were in the Highlands, as there had always
been, that only needed a chance of training. Few of them
in the first part of the nineteenth century ventured as far
as Oxford and London. They reached the Lowlands and
must have brought fresh imagination and fresh passion for
learning to the universities as they brought new brains into
the professions and into business. They may well have done
something to revitalize Scotland at a time when it needed
such revitalization.

But it was Canada that profited most from the Highlanders. Although they had been deemed lazy at home, once they were in the New World they became an active and a successful people. A surprising number of the great men of Canada came from crofts in the Highlands. In Canada Highlanders pushed to the Arctic Sea and crossed the Rockies, Highlanders built great railways to connect the west with the east, Highlanders became famous physicians and lawyers. One wonders if the fundamental trouble with the Highlanders from an early day had not been that they had not had opportunity on their poor lands in the glens to do interesting things. Imaginative people will seldom exert themselves unless they can make plans and have the means to carry them out. In the New World they could make sweeping plans and hope to see them accomplished.

The history of the Highlanders really concludes in Canada. They looked back to the Old World but Canada became home for many of them. One of the best-known of Scottish poems deals with the Scot in Canada,

> From the lone sheiling on the misty island   *cottage*
>   Mountains divide us, and the waste of seas,
> Yet still the blood is strong, the heart is Highland,
>   And we in dreams behold the Hebrides.

XXVII

OLD TRAITS IN MODERN FORM

THE Scot of the nineteenth and twentieth centuries has still many of his old qualities left but with modifications imposed by the circumstances of the modern world. He is still to some degree the old warrior, showing violence now and then in a small way, keeping grudges and refusing to compromise, but accepting nevertheless some limitations upon his old ways. He is still compact of loyalties to his country and countrymen but a Briton nevertheless. His ancestors were sometimes given to boastfulness but he has only a deep and sufficient pride. He is still something of a villager, kindly and neighborly as of old, full of curiosity, recognizing the dignity of his fellows and democratic in his impulses, but he has lived more often in cities and his village outlook has been a good deal transformed.

The warrior in the Scot is still there. He has furnished so-called Highland regiments with the bravest of soldiers. In the Crimean War, in the Indian Mutiny, in the two World Wars, Scottish regiments have won fame that needs no telling.

Elsewhere than on the battlefield the warrior in the Scot is still faintly visible. He has not quite shuffled off the old violence in his nature. It has been said that to watch a Scots-English rugby match is to think the battle of Bannockburn is being fought again. Let an American happen of a Saturday night into a pub in a working-class quarter of Glasgow or Edinburgh and he will see in the temper of the crowd hints that the Scot has still some old inclination to truculence. It is only an inclination. The Scot is a fairly law-abiding person, and the daggers with which he was once expert will not appear. Civilization has tamed him and his violence is mostly in manner and conversation.

Yet he can still be quarrelsome and still keep grudges. In Scottish novels can be found characters who for comparatively trivial reasons have broken off old friendships and replaced them with enmities. One cannot read Scottish biographies without realizing the Scottish addiction to quarrels. The English who had to deal with Scots in the seventeenth century and in the nineteenth complained that they were constantly having tiffs with one another. It was Sir Walter who wrote that the Scot was a less trustworthy friend than the Englishman but that was to ask a high degree of faithfulness. The Englishman makes friends slowly and keeps them for life. There are still Scots who cherish grudges, there are even those who keep up old family antagonisms. For three hundred years possibly a Scot's connection may have been at odds with another family connection about some skirmish that happened in a remote glen. The memory of the wrong done there is part of the family pride. It is a genealogical anachronism, and the Scots love genealogy and are not worried about anachronisms. A charming and intelligent Scottish lady had much to say to me about a wicked lord who in the reign of Charles II had tricked her husband's family out of their lands. Her dislike of the lord's descendants, who lived not far away, was no doubt a trifle sentimental, a kind of spiritual heirloom, but it seemed to me sincere.

The Scot has not quite lost his old warrior desire for revenge. One can still detect in the modern Scot a yearning to have his own back. In 1919 when I was walking up Ben Nevis I was overtaken by a cultivated and delightful Highlander. We chatted about the Peace of Versailles and I admitted disappointment in the terms of the peace. It was a harsh peace and started a sore that would be a source of infection to all Europe. He was sharp in disagreement. The peace was not hard enough. "I do not believe," he said, "in a tooth for a tooth any more than you do. No, I believe in two teeth for a tooth and two eyes for an eye." There were many Scots, I soon discovered, who would have agreed with him; many indeed who were not Scots.

A warrior is seldom good at compromise and the Scot of
the Middle Ages, of the Reformation, and of the Covenanting
time had no skill, as we have earlier seen, in meeting his
opponent halfway. His stubbornness in sticking to his own
view was still to be seen in the nineteenth and twentieth
centuries whenever he touched politics. In politics a conscience is likely to be a liability, and it was often so with
the Scot. To the English political world his conscience
seemed an unpredictable element. As a member of Parliament he was many times a tribulation to party managers
and party whips. About a policy his party had taken up he
was likely to have some special reservations of his own and
he could not be persuaded to waive them. It is not to be
supposed that the Scots were as troublesome in Parliament
as the Irish. From the passage of the First Reform Bill (1832)
on there was practically speaking no such thing as a Scottish
group. It was individual Scots who found it hard to come
into an agreement. They would be tempted by accidental
convictions and by some inherited scruple to stray from the
path of party warfare into a fight of their own. The Scotsmen
who have won great political position have sometimes been
no better than the backbenchers. Lord Rosebery, as Prime
Minister, seemed to have a great future before him, but he
could not get along with old party leaders and found at
length that he must plow his own "lonely furrow." Campbell-
Bannerman took his own line and rendered himself fearfully
unpopular at the time of the South African War, but it happened that his courage enhanced his prestige later. Lord
Haldane was a man of wide and statesmanlike views, with
no trace of Scottish parochialism, but never really a party
man.

In general, however, the Scots have made up for their want
of political experience, and have mastered to a considerable
degree the give and take necessary to the working of the
party system. They were, most of them, in the nineteenth
century and up to the Great War, good Liberals, and loyalty
to party held them in line when nothing else would have

done so. Moreover the House of Commons has been an excellent training school in the arts of compromise, and the English parliamentary system a beautiful, smooth-running mechanism that the machine-loving Scot could not resist learning to manipulate, even if he had to throw over a stray conviction now and then. Some of those Scots who won high places learned about splitting differences. Arthur Balfour, who was only half a Scot, Bonar Law, and Ramsay Macdonald knew the ins and outs of politics at Westminster and just when to give way and when to stand firm. Many less significant figures from the north have been quick to learn.

Religion was another matter. There the Scottish conscience seemed almost as inflexible as in Reformation and Covenanting days. It will be recalled that the Scots had developed many kinds of Presbyterianism. The history of Scottish Calvinism in the eighteenth and nineteenth centuries is an interminable series of dissensions and separations. It is a story too complicated and too uninteresting to be told here. No one but a Scot, or a Scottish Canadian of the old school, could hope to explain the intricacies of the sectarian quarrels and separations. Each sect was hostile to every other and of course to the Established Kirk. Moreover each sect was able to command many consciences.

It was the Disruption of 1843 that proved how uncompromising the Scot could still show himself. It will be remembered that the First and Second Books of Discipline had provided for the election of ministers by the congregations and that the right had been whittled down and taken away by James VI and Charles I. It will be remembered further that during the eighteenth century the struggle about patronage went merrily on, the Moderates supporting the right of the patron rather than of the congregation to nominate the minister. In the nineteenth century the Evangelicals who had taken the place of the old High-flyers fought against patronage, maintaining the right of the congregations to elect their pastor and denying the right of the State to interfere in

311

Church matters. The issue came to a head in 1843 when Thomas Chalmers, the leader of the Evangelicals, and four hundred others walked out of the General Assembly. The pastors who followed Chalmers gave up their manses and incomes and were forced to put their hope in a new Kirk that would eventually support them. It was a brave step and made at a heavy cost to the individuals who took part. It has often been said that such a sacrifice on the part of so large a group could have been made in no other country. What the Disruption of 1843 proved was that upon matters of faith the Scotsman could still be the uncompromising creature he had been in Covenanting days.

In the twentieth century the Scots have shown more willingness to compromise. The dissident churches have been coming back into the main fold. There are several reasons that in some degree explain the reunion of Presbyterians. The Episcopalians are becoming more important, and, with immigration from Ireland, the Roman Catholic Church is increasing in numbers and influence. Furthermore the Scots have realized that since the country ceased to be a political entity, the Church of Scotland is the greatest visible tie of national feeling. The more inclusive that body is, the better; the more Scotland can speak.

The Scot of medieval times was full of loyalties, to feudal lord, to clan and family connection. The modern Scot has little loyalty to the laird to whom he may pay his rents. He is loyal to his family connection. But his greatest loyalty is reserved for his country and countrymen. Scotland has ceased to be a political unit, and might be looked upon as little more than a province of Britain, a collection of counties north of the Cheviots. One might well ask what there is to hold the loyalty of the Scots.

A good deal. There are to begin with two political symbols of Scottish nationhood, the General Assembly and the Scottish system of courts and law. The assembly, which is now inclusive of a large proportion of all Presbyterians, is an annual religious parliament, a meeting of representatives

312

from all over the country. There the best talent of Scotland, the great preachers and eminent laymen, professors, nobles, and others, as elected spokesmen have their say. They speak before a body of weight and dignity. The proceedings are carried on with ceremony and even with pomp. If they deal only with religious matters, it must be remembered that in Scotland religious matters cover a good deal of ground.

Scottish law is only less than the General Assembly a symbol of nationality. The courts have their center in the old historic capital, Edinburgh. Scottish law, while an outgrowth of civil law that was brought in from France and Holland and that has its roots in Roman law, developed in Scotland its own special forms that were not only elaborate and interesting but tied up closely with Scottish history. Because laws since the Union have been made at Westminster, there has been a tendency for Scottish and English law to be assimilated and for English law to modify Scots and vice versa. Nevertheless Scottish law remains a living inheritance. The decisions in Scottish courts are followed all over Scotland, and when those decisions have attracted notice from students of civil law on the Continent the Scot has been pleased. So long as he continues to live under Scottish law and under the jurisdiction of the General Assembly, he has some living relics of Scottish nationality to which he can render his loyalty.

There is much else to which he can be loyal.

He is devoted to the. earth of Scotland. Robert Louis Stevenson tells of the landing of the Black Watch regiment on the Galloway shore. For years they had been in foreign parts, and for the last few years in Ireland among men who spoke their language, who were of their own race, and who had treated them well. They were landing in the Lowlands among men who had disliked the Highlanders for hundreds of years, among people who did not even speak their language. Yet the Highlanders of the Black Watch knelt and kissed the soil of Scotland. The tradition of Scottish national-

313

ity was so strong that Scotland, every part of it, was home.

They are loyal to the past of their country, as if that were the surest basis of their nationhood, to Wallace and Bruce, to Mary Queen o' Scots, to John Knox and Andrew Melville, to Montrose, to Bonnie Prince Charlie and Flora Macdonald. Their battles and their heroes they have enveloped in a mist of romance. They have cherished their great figures and their minor figures as have few other nations. They have made of the memories of defeat, as we have seen earlier, part of the substance of their nationhood and character. Was not Scottish history a long ballad of sadness and defeat? Things seldom went well either for the country or for the person.

> Lang will his lady look
>   Frae the castle Doune,
> Ere she see the Earl of Moray
>   Come soundin through the toun.

Out of all their experience has come strength to endure. They look back to a good old time, like people in almost every country. That time soon passed.

> But Minstrel Burns cannot assuage
>   His grief while life endureth,
> To see the changes of this age,
>   That fleeting time procureth;
> For mony a place stands in hard case,
>   Where blyth folk ken'd nae sorrow,
> With Homes that dwelt on Leader-side,
>   And Scots that dwelt on Yarrow.

The Scotts alluded to were the Scotts of the family of which the Duke of Buccleuch (descended from the unfortunate Duke of Monmouth) was the head and of which Sir Walter was a cadet member. In the writings of Sir Walter there is, it will be recalled, the ever-present note of sadness over the past of his country, and a longing to bring alive the Scotland

314

of old. It is what many Scots would do. They would explain their past and justify their forefathers, like many other peoples. They become antiquaries and search out manuscripts that their children may not forget what Scotland was. They become poets and sing of Jacobites and Covenanters. Even the new poets of Glasgow are nostalgic of Scotland's past and have little to say about the Scotland of today and tomorrow. They have a *Heimweh* that seems to be a considerable part of Scottish loyalty.

Now and then one comes to wonder if that loyalty is not a trifle insistent. Is the Scot perhaps a bit fidgety in his aim to assert the historical glory of his country? Must he say something for the auld Mither lest she be forgotten?

It is part of the loyalty to country to be loyal to any Scotsman who has made good. The Scot who emerges in English law, in London journalism, in the English Church, in criticism and poetry, in colonial administration, or in politics at Westminster is an object of special interest in Scotland. They overlook no man who has done their nation credit, even if he be in Canada, Australia, New Zealand, or in the United States. Even the Englishman who had one Scottish grandmother is believed to be the better for it.

Yet the Scot is not unloyal to Britain. He likes the use of the word "Briton" and is annoyed at the constant use of the word "English" where "British" should be said. He is not as enthusiastic a man about the empire as the Englishman, but he moves out to that empire and helps develop it hardly less than the Englishman.

The boastfulness of the Scots was, it will be recalled, remarked upon by medieval writers. It was a natural weakness of the warriors of old. I do not remember that any nineteenth-century traveler, English, French, or German, has attributed to the Scots a facility in boasting; nor can I recall modern Scottish novels which bring out that weakness. What they do reveal is Scottish pride. The Scot is presented as not giving away his poverty or misfortune. He is shown as putting the best face on things. Under all circumstances he must hold his head high. There is a story in Barrie, I think, though I cannot put my finger on it, of an old woman who has at length to be taken to the poorhouse. As she is driven along the streets the villagers pull down their blinds that they may not see her disgrace and that she may suppose they do not know. The kindly folk would save her pride.

The Scot has remained something of the villager he was in the early days. He may live nowadays in Edinburgh or more probably in Glasgow, but he retains, as we have seen, a certain *kleinstädterei*. He has kept some of the pleasant and amusing qualities of his ancestors who did live in villages.

He is still an oncoming person, naturally friendly. No touch of English arrogance has ever been charged against a Scot. The kindliness of the Scots has been noticed by American, by Dutch, and by French travelers in Scotland. One of the visitors to Scotland spoke of the loving-kindness of the Scots, and another implied that their kindliness was even expressed in the lovely pleading quality of their language. Any American who has gone north after a sojourn in England feels at once the change of social climate. On trains, in hotels, and everywhere the Scot is, like the middle-western American, willing to pass the time of day and become casually acquainted. In country houses, in manses, in the homes of businessmen, and in the cottages of coalminers, the Scots will welcome you and treat you as worthy of their interest, and they will be neither patronizing nor servile. Even the Englishman, accustomed to other ways, delights in the friendliness of the Scot.

The Scot will take pains to do you a favor, will go to considerable trouble to make your way easy. He has a desire that you should like him and he will give you occasion for that liking. There is seldom an ulterior purpose in his friendliness. Yet he is not always unaware that favors might be returned. The old Scots woman declared that it was of no use to speak ill of the De'il. It might some day come in handy not to have done so.

The Scot has retained his natural kindness. But he is less a villager than once, and knows that in a world full of many types of people kindness and oncomingness may be overdone.

He has still some of his old village curiosity. His eager interest in his neighbors is hardly less evident in the nineteenth century than earlier. Read George Douglas Brown's *House with the Green Shutters,* the most unpleasant of all novels about Scottish life, but an antidote to the novels of the kailyard school. There you will see villagers watching one another with hawklike eyes, speculating upon what their neighbors have done and may do. Run through Barrie's *Window in Thrums.* The whole village is on the alert as to what is to happen at the manse the coming week end, i.e., who is coming to visit. From doors and windows the women peer to watch all comings and goings and then compare notes and arrive by shrewd inferences at conclusions. The ability of the Scottish villagers to use small bits of evidence upon which to base conclusions might well raise envy in historians. If novelists tell truth at all, the Scots have lost none of their interest in the doings and ways of all their fellows. It has been noticed by several travelers that the Scot is a man who loves to be upon the street. Even the American tourist in Edinburgh can hardly fail to see that the Scot likes to walk up and down his thoroughfares observing all that is going on and who is passing.

The Scot does not shed his curiosity even when he goes abroad. On ships he makes up to you and he is interested in you, in your position on your native heath, in how much money you make. He is not unfair about it. He is willing to tell you about his fortune and his way of life, and expects reciprocity in personal details.

But here I am talking, of course, about the less sophisticated Scot, who for some reason seems often to be found on boats, perhaps because he is a traveling man for some manu-

facturing concern in Glasgow or Dundee or a manager who
has gone out to look over the branch offices. Many other
Scots there are who have too good manners to betray any
curiosity. Even in their case I have fancied I could detect
the appraising eye. The Scot is of an inquiring mind and
looks closely about him. He would probe to a man's center
if he could. Men, not their deeds, are what he would know
about, but their deeds may reveal the man. He would know
the why and wherefore of those deeds. Why did Montrose
change sides in 1643? What was it in his character? All the
Calvinism of the Scot comes out in his interest in decisions.
The Scot must get at the inwardness of the man if it takes
volumes of writing. It took Lockhart five volumes, and
Boswell more, to explain a character, and who would call
for less?

But the Scot is curious not only about men. He is curious
about intellectual concepts. The flower in the crannied wall
or the stone that William Hutton picked up, if he can know
about them, may help him to find out what God and man is.
It is about God and man that he would know. It has been
well said that he is "forever curiously testing new opinions
and courting new impressions, never acquiescing in a facile
orthodoxy." It is a paradox that with all his solemn convictions the Scot is likely now and then to display a singular
open-mindedness, even about the tenets of his religion. Witness the success of the Moderates in the eighteenth century,
witness the advanced theological position of Scottish Presbyterians today. The curiosity of the Scot can be sublimated
into something thoroughly liberal.

He is still a villager who assumes that all men and women
are people. In the old days he was not so much a man of
democratic impulses as one who respected the individual.
When Burns declared a man's a man for a' that, he was
expressing the exact creed of Scotland. But there was little
democracy in the old feudal days, and even in the days of
the Reformation the good Presbyterian ministers, who strove
for a kind of democracy in Church government, had no great

318

regard for the lower classes, and those classes showed surprisingly little confidence in themselves. By the time of Burns, it will be remembered, there was arising among the more intelligent of the submerged classes a discontent with their position that became more vocal with every decade. The French Revolution had the best broadcasting station of the time, and its messages quickly touched Scotland. As the nineteenth century progressed the laboring classes made as much trouble for their masters as in any country.

The more fortunate classes, as we have seen in another connection, took not at all to the new manifestations of democracy. They were afraid of revolution and they believed, perhaps a bit more simply than the English, in their own rights and privileges. The Scot was less inclined than the Englishman to let idealism play hob with his own interests.

Moreover, the Scottish aristocrat tolerated little nonsense about democracy. He had a deep respect for the manhood of all Scots, he had never acquired the sense of superiority that has been consciously developed elsewhere; but he knew his worth. He could trace his genealogy, and it was fairer written than that of most of the English aristocracy. No people have cherished old family more than the Scots and they have more old families in proportion than the English. All Scots are worshipers of antiquity and especially of antiquities connected with their own family tree.

There is nothing surprising in the picture I have been drawing in this chapter. That the Scot of the nineteenth and twentieth centuries should have retained some of his earlier characteristics but have modified them to meet the new conditions of modern times is precisely what might have been expected. The Scot has possibly a more marked character than many other peoples and may have retained more of the old than some other peoples. That he has kept so much of the old Scot in spite of absorption in Britain is testimony to the strength of his type.

XXVIII

NEW TRAITS

IT is a mistake to suppose that national character once established remains the same. New conditions develop new characteristics. The Scotland of the nineteenth and twentieth centuries was a changed world. The Industrial Revolution had made many people rich and put many others to tending machines in factories. The Scotland that lived by hunting and fishing and raising meagre crops was gone. Lowland farming was a prosperous industry and fishing was becoming a large-scale business. Most Scots were living in towns and cities. It is little wonder that they began to reveal qualities of character that had not been evident before, or to have such qualities attributed to them. The sentimentality of the Scots is a modern development. Scottish humor is as old as Scotland and yet many of its manifestations have been evident only within the last century and a half. The closeness in money matters laid at the door of the Scots is a recent attribution. Even more recent is the charge that they are people on the make.

Sentimentality has been defined as the expression of an emotion that is insincere. Some of Burns's poems and letters addressed to Clarinda (Mrs. M'Lehose) might be used as examples of that definition. But sentimentality includes more than that. It is often forced emotion, and we see it when people spend more emotion than the matter calls for. Sentimentality is a want of proportion in the use of the feelings. There are always those who live in their feelings and allow the mind little control. It is an easily formed habit to make a luxury of the emotions and to feel more pity for the misfortunes of the heroine in a book or a play than is due, or than is aroused by real people in trouble. It is a weakness that has become more evident in modern times as the masses have become more vocal. When a large part of the population can read and when their reading is no longer confined to the Bible and a few great books, the susceptibility of the public to overdone emotion is greatly increased.

It would be a mistake, however, to suppose that sentimentality is a matter of class. The lonesome shepherd on the Cheviots may have had so much time for reflection that he has learned the proper limits of feeling, and the soft daughter of the nabob may have come to indulge in her emotions as in a drug. Indeed the very secure who have few forms of excitement may find it in sentimentalizing. In general we may trust those who have had the opportunity of education and reflection to eschew the sentimental without giving up sentiment.

The Scots were an emotional people to whom tears came easily, but so are most simple and unsophisticated people. The House of Commons at Westminster in 1628 fell to weeping at a critical point when tension was high. There was nothing sentimental about that display of feeling, nor about the tears shed by Wallace or Bruce or Mary Queen of Scots. Sufficient occasion there was for their tears. The Scots of that time, like many medieval people, were tempestuous and as easily swept by this emotion and that as children, but wholly sincere in them. Even today they are a naturally sympathetic people, interested in their neighbors and the troubles of those neighbors, giving sympathy gladly and expecting it in turn. It is easy for sympathy to become gush.

The English have held up sentimentality as the weakness of the Scots, sometimes in a slightly condescending way. But sentimentality was not unknown south of the Border. Early Victorian society was steeped in the sentimental. G. M. Young in *Early Victorian England* gives us a scene at Bowood when Thomas Moore was singing one of his softly reminiscent songs and the country-house audience fell to sobbing and one after another slipped out of the room. Humbler people wept over Little Nell.

The wave of sentimentality was as wide as western Europe.

Rousseau's expansive and enthusiastic benevolence led right on to disproportionate feeling. The late eighteenth century and the early nineteenth were full of such feeling. The Romantic movement and the Evangelical movement were in flower. Romanticists easily crossed the line from sentiment to sentimentality. The Evangelicals both in England and Scotland stressed the emotional in religion, and the Methodists in England, who were the Evangelicals outside the Church of England, offered to the common people a religion of enthusiasm and emotion that prepared the way for the sentimentalists. To a considerable degree the English in the later nineteenth and twentieth centuries outgrew sentimentality and during the same time the Scots developed more of it.

A good many Scottish novels of a rather recent date are full of overdone emotion. The kailyard school of writers who have pictured Scottish village life have sold us faked portraits, making nearly all their characters kind and good and thoughtful. They overdraw on the reader's sympathy, they ask admiration and pity for men and women whose troubles are easily induced and as quickly cured. The characters are reinforced with feeling, too sweet and good for acceptance —men reputed misers who give away money by stealth and prove all tenderness within, women whose devotion to their lawful spouses passes the laws of probability. All is loving-kindness. The whole group of villagers in Ian Maclaren's village of Drumtochty, with a few exceptions, are out of some secluded valley in heaven. Barrie's characters are not all of them so tender but they also live in a world of forced sentiment.

The music hall songs of Glasgow and Edinburgh, the songs of Harry Lauder and of his predecessors and successors are full of forced sentiment. Those lovers roaming in the gloaming do not convince us.* Examine most of the songbooks of modern Scotland and you will find mixed in

* But the Scots music-hall singers are less sentimental than our American crooners. I doubt if anything Scottish is as sentimental as our "soap operas."

with beautiful old songs many others that are sentimental in both words and music. The vogue of these in the world proves that the Scots are not the only sentimentalists.

The cults of the Scots of the last century are sentimental, as cults in other nations are likely to be. Consider the tears shed for Mary Queen of Scots and for Bonnie Prince Charlie; the cult of the kilt, which is not an ancient Scottish garb but rather modern Highland wear; the cult of haggis, and of Burns.

Remember that this sentimentality is not to be found in old Scottish literature, nor in that of the pre-Reformation nor of the Reformation. One has to admit that the old refrain, "Douglas, Douglas, Tender and True" has a sentimental ring to it, for Douglases, other than the good Sir James, did not enjoy a reputation either for tenderness or loyalty. But in the considerable body of early Scottish poetry and in the many ballads* there is a great deal of sentiment of the finest Scottish type and yet nothing soft. Why the anonymous composers of the ballads, presumably men of the people, never became sentimental is a subject worth much consideration that cannot be given here.

When we come down to the eighteenth century we find nothing sentimental in Robert Fergusson. Some of Allan Ramsay's lyrics and parts of his charming *The Gentle Shep-*

---

* Sometimes old ballads have been reinforced with modern additions that do not ring true. In the lovely ballad of "The Four Maries" there is sincerity and depth of feeling and not a word off key. But a last verse has been added in modern days:

I wish I could lie in oor ain kirkyard
Aneath the old yew tree

. . .

My brothers, my sister and me.

These touching lines, meant to be touching, are untrue in tone, and untrue to the rest of the ballad. Marie Hamilton was not born in Scotland. She says earlier in the ballad:

I charge ye all, ye mariners,
When ye sail owre the faem,
Let neither my father nor mother get wit
But that I'm coming hame.

herd have a shade too much sentiment. As for Burns he could be as hardminded as the medieval Scottish poets and yet at the mere mention of a bonny lassie he could work up emotion.*

Nor does the prose of the late eighteenth and early nineteenth century have as much sentimentality as might be expected. Henry Mackenzie's *Man of Feeling* embodies of course as much of it as could have been put in one volume, and Jane Porter's *Scottish Chiefs* is designed to bring tears in every chapter. Yet there was nothing sentimental about Jeffrey, Horner, and the *Edinburgh Review* group. The novels of Sir Walter were utterly free of overdone sentiment and the same may be said, so far as I have read them, of the novels of John Galt. To read the correspondence of Sir Walter and his friends, one would say that while there is much sentiment, there is little sentimentality in his wide circle. Nor do the biographies and other personal records of the time reveal it.

To explain the sentimentality that has been exhibited in recent Scotland is not easy. A good deal of it, I suspect, is characteristic of our times in many places. Yet it is a matter that has engaged the attention of modern Scottish critics. They have said a good deal that is interesting and worth repetition, but left a good deal still to say.

It will be remembered that the affectionate or weeping preachers could gather their hundreds of men and women for long, exciting sermons. They believed that weeping was a sign of grace, that one should approach the mercy seat in a state of spiritual excitement. They encouraged emotion until a large number of people came to associate emotional experience with the spiritual life. The more weeping the more God was manifesting himself to His own. It is true that there had been opposition to the weeping preachers and a

* There is a good deal to be said in extenuation of Burns. He took old songs that had become bawdy and made them over hurriedly into fit songs for publication. He substituted sentiment for obscenity and sometimes the sentiment was undue.

great deal of fun had been poked at them by those accounted ungodly. But by the end of the eighteenth century the ungodly had been forced to sing low. If the weeping ministers provoked fewer tears and roused less excitement than earlier, it was because manners were changing and well-bred listeners preferred restraint in the pulpit. But the habit of giving way to the emotions seemed still a virtue to the fervent, and the fervent were many.

The Scots had long been a passionate people. That passion they had put to use in wars against the English and religious struggles at home. It had occasioned heroism beyond estimate and cruelty not pleasant to think upon. When the wars were over and when religion of every kind was tolerated, there was no longer much occasion for passion. Yet Scottish intensity was still there and when used on small issues led right into overused emotion.

The want of good taste among the Scots may have had some connection with the display of unnecessary emotion. It will be remembered that Cockburn lamented the ill taste he saw in early nineteenth-century Scotland. He was thinking primarily of buildings and the grounds about them, but he could have found other kinds of evidence. Good taste is the ability to distinguish the beautiful from the ugly; it is the product of generations of civilization; it is connected with the sense of order and restraint; its presence saves men from slopping over. It is true of course that taste shifts from period to period and what is good taste in one time is regarded as bad taste later. Yet we must believe that slowly over the generations there become established certain canons of good taste that prevail, like common law, and have equal validity. The Scots had been too occupied for centuries in making a living to think about beauty and order and restraint. Moreover the Scottish villagers had no such examples before them as the English. The country people of England had gained some notion of good taste from the gentlefolk in the near-by manor house. That influence, as I have said before, it is hard to overestimate. Few knew better than the English country gentleman the wisdom of economy of emotion. The Scottish laird, who was the nearest thing in Scotland to the English country gentleman, was little different from other people in the community save in his larger income. He was not a model of good taste and restraint for the community.

Worse than the lairds were the Lowland businessmen of the early and middle nineteenth century. They were often men of crudity. It will be recalled that many of them were out of touch with the cultivated classes and had little notion of what constituted good taste. Their attention was narrowly directed toward one end and they were unaccustomed to taking out their emotions in poetry, music, and the arts. Intense men they usually were and likely to find the outlets for their strong feelings in excessive and overdone sentiment.

The increase of sentimentality in Scotland may be explained as in part due to the loss of old traditions, a loss already mentioned in another connection. The Scots had given up their old language and with it ready acquaintance with their own fine literature. That literature ceased to be a living reality to them. Yet it was really bone of their bone and flesh of their flesh from which they were separated. The old Scottish writers had exalted the finer qualities of women and the bravery of men; they had sung the rhythm of the seasons, green-mantled summer and wan winter. Dunbar, Barbour, Henryson, Gavin Douglas, Lyndsay of the Mount, and auld Maitland had been almost forgotten by the mass of the people because their poems were written in a tongue that was becoming unreadable. The old stories that constitute so much of a nation's lore and the old storytellers were practically out of the ken of many Scots of the nineteenth and twentieth centuries. The new song writers were not soaked in the old tradition. Women were no longer celebrated for their comfort and solace to men but for their bright eyes and swanlike necks. Nature was no longer closely observed, but the banks of Kelvin Grove were apostrophized in fervent epithets. When the Scots were cut off from their old

heritage and improvised, the result was sometimes sentimentality.

The longing for the old traditions in itself induced overdone sentiment. Consider the feelings of Southerners in our
country for the Old South of the plantations. They have
managed to build up a romantic picture of a golden age. In
the same way the Scots looked back romantically to the old
kingdom of Scotland and conceived of those times as grander
than they were.

The *Heimweh* was sometimes narrow and concrete. The
workers in the drab alleys of the new industrial cities were
only too ready to sing of the bonny bonny banks of Loch
Lomond. The banks and braes their ancestors had forsaken
to win city wages had gained for them a romantic glory the
crofters of old would scarcely have recognized. True sentiment it was, but easily overstated.

For true sentiment the Scots had and have in a high
degree. Read in the Scottish memoirs of the last hundred
years and you will meet much delightful and sincere emotion. The English have so trained themselves that they are
afraid even to express sentiment. The Scots are not afraid.
They have a gift for it. We cannot be surprised that the
gift in the hands of the unpractised has been sometimes
overplayed.

Humor is not a new characteristic of the Scots in the
nineteenth century but the wide extension of it is a new
phenomenon. The English like to joke about Scottish humor
as if there were no such thing, but that is because they do
not understand the Scots and their sense of fun any more than
the Scots understand English humor. The Scots do have their
own brand. It is not the quiet humor of the great English
tradition, not such humor as may be found in Isaak Walton
or Thomas Fuller or Dorothy Osborne, the diffused humor
that springs from an urbane outlook upon the world. Urbane
the Scots have never been, though the great Sir Walter and
Sir Henry Campbell-Bannerman might be put down as exceptions.

The Scot in History

There are three fairly old Scottish traditions of humor, the humor of the fantastic or grotesque, the humor of satire, and the humor of rollicking high spirits. The reader will remember the examples given of the medieval fantastic and grotesque. That kind can be found in modern times in Burns's "Tam o' Shanter," in James Hogg's "Witch of Fife," and in William Scott Bell's "The Witch's Ballad."[*] The satirical humor appears in many of the poems of Dunbar and of Lyndsay of the Mount, and in Burns's "Holy Willie's Prayer." The humor of rollicking high spirits is to be seen in such medieval poems as "Peblis to the Play," and in Fergusson, Allan Ramsay, and Burns. It is the violent fun of men who were letting themselves go, the high spirits to be found today in a Scottish tavern when the whiskey has been around several times. There is nothing like it among the English, nor, so far as I know, among the French. It sometimes becomes "wut" in Glasgow music halls where established institutions and famous men, even great figures of the Scottish past, are dealt with in irreverent and noisy fashion.

Most Scottish humor has no old tradition behind it. The humor of understatement, for example, is a modern Scottish manifestation. Whether Scots learned the possibilities of understatement from the English or the English from them, I do not know. But understatement seems to fit the Scottish character. The Scot has always been a cautious body and when he sets out to exercise caution in statement he can go far in resisting exaggeration. Sometimes, of course, he is not being funny at all, he merely seems funny to those who listen.

A common Scottish humor is that of friendly bantering The modern Scot loves nothing so much as to tease his cronies lightly. The Scot is more ready than the Englishman or the American to banter a stranger. His way with the stranger is a form of friendly intrusion that is hard to resist. I have known a Scottish speaker to pick out someone in the

[*] An example in modern Scottish verse of the fantastic that is entirely serious is James Hogg's "Kilmeny."

audience whom he could tease about some prejudice and then keep on making jibes at him for the pleasure of the audience. But usually his bantering is more intimate.

Scottish humor is concerned with little things, with little traits of character, with the countrifiedness or naïveté of other Scots, with their inexperience with cities and the great world, or with their matter-of-factness. When a stout woman given to illness was asked how she was keeping, she answered: "Ou, just middlin, there's ower muckle of me to be a' weel at ae time." The Scots are always telling stories of the cautiousness of brither Scots. When an old carpenter was offered a drink and asked whether he would have it then or at the end of his job, he replied: "Indeed, mem, there's been sic a power o' sudden deaths lately, that I'll just tak it now."

The Scot likes to pick on the incongruous in character. The story of the man who catches the lovers doing what they should not and objects not to what they are doing but to their doing it on the Sabbath day, is an example. The Scot who is telling the story is making fun of his own people and their predilection for Sabbath observance and for respectability. The unco guid are fair game for him. He has lived all his life among them and may have been one of them himself. Important people in undignified positions give him the same gratification. Drunken lairds and ministers uncertain in their steps afford him countless yarns. The Scot likes to laugh at those out of their accustomed characters.

He has an incredible number of stories about death and funerals. Death has always interested him and funerals have been one of his diversions, and he is making fun of himself in telling stories about them. The matter-of-factness of the dying who perhaps smell the meats cooking for the funeral, the eagerness of those attending the funeral for the food and drink that follow the burial, the reception of the dead at St. Peter's gate are all fair topics for jibes. When someone was comforting a sick old lady that she would, after the winter, enjoy the spring butter she replied: "Spring butter!

By that time I shall be buttering in heaven!" When she was really dying, Dean Ramsay tells us, and her friends were gathered round her bed, one of them remarked: "Her face has lost its color: it grows like a sheet of paper." "Then I'm sure it maun be broon [brown] paper," the dying woman answered. When the famous Miss Johnstone of Hawkhill was dying there was a great storm outside and she whispered: "Ech, sirs! What a nicht for me to be fleein' through the air."

Scottish stories are always told in "braid Scots." The burr gives an odd, intimate, country quality to the episode. A character that speaks in dialect is slightly amusing to start with, and the listener is prepared to smile. Vernacular always sharpens stories and Scottish vernacular does it better, I suspect, than any other. It seems at once to call up the figure of a canny, cautious body caught out by circumstances.

The vernacular Scottish stories are to be found in great number and better authenticated than most in Dean Ramsay's celebrated *Reminiscences of Scottish Life and Character*. That much reprinted work has been a reference manual for those who make speeches at Scottish gatherings. It is nothing less than a casebook for those who would analyze the qualities of Scottish humor. But there are many other books to which one might go. When one has read rather widely in the funny stories of Scotland, one whispers to one's self that Scottish humor is far behind English. English memoirs are often filled with the most quietly amusing accounts of men and situations. English humor is, much of it, a comment upon English or human ways. There is no one place at which you laugh but you smile all the time. Scottish memoirs are usually pretty serious with a certain admixture of interpolated Scottish stories, often stories of amusing or sharp repartee, for the Scot still loves his satire. I can read a whole chapter of Dean Ramsay's collection and find myself seldom overcome with laughter. There is a sameness to Scottish stories. Yet we have all known Scots who in conversation could keep us between smiles and laughter.

The average Scot has been afraid of his neighbors. He is not too sure of himself, he would do nothing that might give his community occasion to regard him as other than serious minded. He is afraid to let himself go unless the occasion calls for letting go, and then, as we have observed earlier, he can constitute himself the life of the party. But at other times sobriety of conduct is the only suitable wear. He can smile at himself and he can laugh at his neighbors, but he has been too much villager to catch the comedy of human behavior in general. That behavior he has been trained to consider in moral terms.

Scottish closeness or stinginess has been the quality of the Scots that the average man thinks of first. It seems to me one of the most recently observed characteristics. I can find hardly an allusion to Scottish closeness with money before the late eighteenth century. One medieval reference might be cited to show that the Scots were regarded by the French as canny about money. Aside from that sentence the only reference that I know earlier than the late eighteenth century is to be found in the writings of James Howell in the middle of the seventeenth century. Little that he met with in Scotland pleased him and their penuriousness roused his sarcasm as it might have done that of any well-to-do Englishman. The Scots had lived in a mountainous country with little good soil. They were a poor people and even when they had some property had little coin of the realm, and were loath to part with it. They were the more loath because they were accustomed in many cases to exchanging goods, to the old system of barter. At the same time the tenant farmers had to pay rent for their lands in cash and so treasured actual money and did their best to hold on to it. What is surprising is that the Scots were not earlier and more often accused of closeness.

When we come to the nineteenth and twentieth centuries all that is changed. The English have constantly rung the changes on Scottish thrift until the canniness of the Scots about money has been worked up into a world myth. My own experience is that the Scots are not as hardfisted as the Yorkshiremen or the Normans, but these are extreme instances. I am certain that you can buy more for your money in Edinburgh or in Glasgow than in London. It has been proved again and again that when it comes to contributions to charities and welfare work and especially to missionary effort, the Scots are fully as generous as the English. Wendeborn, a German minister, who knew his England and Scotland at the beginning of the nineteenth century, declared that the Scots were more charitable than the English and his opinion was confirmed by that of a French traveler. An American traveler who marked how forthgiving the English were in matters of charity was inclined to believe that the Scots were even more so.

That is not improbable. The Scots had an old tradition of giving, and in particular the members of the landed classes. They had hosts of connections, bearing often the same name, who were poor or destitute, and they were unwilling to allow them to starve. Sir Walter Scott said that in his early life the problem of the destitute person hardly existed in Scotland because there was always some head of his family who would find him a position or give him a pension. Sir Walter was overstating the case, for there was destitution in his day, before it and after. But there was also much charity.

It was the English who established the stinginess of the Scots and the Scots who furthered the idea. The English in the nineteenth century who were so impressed by Scottish closeness were many of them sporting people with money in their pockets who came north to fish and shoot and enjoy themselves. The careful ways of the Scots amused them and furnished them with stories to tell in their London clubs. To spend money easily was deemed by the new rich of England a hallmark of lordliness. The Scots have never known the ways of lordliness, not even the old nobility.

The Scots, laborers and farmers, professional people, lairds and great lords, all of them were careful with money and proud to be so. When the Englishman joked about Scottish thrift, he pleased the Scot. Thrift was a virtue with him and he found it agreeable to be twitted about his virtue. He went further, he went out of his way to impress the English with his thrift and found it amusing to develop a body of stories about it. Today those stories would fill a shelf of volumes and there are always new stories sent from Scotland. I have noticed that even Scots in America are sometimes at pains to live up to their national reputation and to be more thrifty than they would otherwise be, in order to please their fellows and to prove their Scottishness.

The Scots are better at taking a joke against themselves than the English. I remember English men and women gathered in a Paris hotel in 1919 when Ruth Draper gave some of her monologues. The one in which the Americans were taken off met with hilarity, even on the part of the few Americans there, but when Miss Draper gave her famous monologue of the English Garden Party, the silence that came over the assembly was impressive. I have never seen Miss Draper satirizing Scottish ways in Edinburgh but I can imagine the Scots laughing at her skit for days afterward.

That the Scots have a weakness for success and exert themselves to get on is a charge that might be made against many people. It is only when people succeed in their aims and are pleased with their success that others think much about it. Now the Scots have been extraordinarily successful as individuals and have recognized as much. They admit their penchant for success. Sir James Barrie has touched again and again upon the Scottish itch to get on. In *What Every Woman Knows* David Shand says to the Comtesse: "My lady, there are few more impressive sights in the world than a Scotsman on the make." A few pages further on Shand declares that the greatest moral attribute of a Scotsman is that he will do nothing which will damage his career.

No doubt Scotsmen, like others, have long been on the make, but the charge against them is not one that has been made throughout the centuries. There are times a good way back when one would expect that the charge might have been made. When Scots in droves followed Jamie VI to London and received their full share of the loaves and fishes he was so generous in bestowing upon his friends, the invaders were unpopular in London and made themselves thoroughly disliked. But I cannot recall that anyone suggested that it was a characteristic of the Scots to attempt to get on. There was a second time when the Scots reached a peak of unpopularity in England, and that was in the reign of George III when Lord Bute as Prime Minister was busy distributing offices to his fellow countrymen. The Scots were so disliked at that time that it was almost unsafe for one to appear on the streets or in a tavern. They were indeed regarded then as grasping people who took more than their share of the political favors. The English forgot perhaps that London was the capital of Scotland as well as of England and that the English had enjoyed most of the favors in the past. But they did not charge the Scots with being people addicted to the vice of pursuing success.

It was late in the nineteenth century that the Scottish taste for success and skill to command it began to be generally recognized. From the 1830's on, Scots were taking the Great North Road or the railway to London. By the last half of the century the movement of the Scots southward was easily noticeable. They were becoming eminent in English medicine, at the English bar, in the Anglican Church, in politics, and especially in business. The time was to come when people would whisper that the Caledonian Club in London was the inner sanctuary of the London financial world. Scotsmen were prominent in English life out of all proportion to their numbers. They were successful in every field and they worked together to help fellow Scots. Furthermore they savored success and sometimes they betrayed their pleasure in it.

They were more simple minded than the English in following the goddess of success. The Englishman did not give himself away. He accepted success as his natural right; he expected it and the less said about it the better. The Scot was likely to proclaim his ambitions to his friends as if to enjoy his victories in advance. When the successful Scot looked back upon his career he liked to trace the steps by which he mounted the ladder. The Englishman liked to forget those steps and assume that he had always been at the top.

If you wish to see a Scot on the make and enjoying it, you do not even have to go to a Barrie play. Read Lord Shaw's *Letters to Isabel,* an account of his life in the form of letters to his daughter. What a progress he made! Every step of his climb upward he marked, and paused to live over the scenes. One promotion succeeded another until he was forced, much against his will, to be sure, into the "gilded chamber." The reader likes of course to see the hero of a book get on but his desire becomes a little tempered in the case of Lord Shaw.

Lord Shaw is more naïve than most Scots. But his aspiration for a title is not wholly out of keeping with the character of certain Scots. The Scot likes not only success but the trappings of it. Again and again an Englishman who has done a good job in a remote station of India is satisfied to realize that the people in the know understand the import of his achievement. There are Scots of that kind too, but others less modest. The Scot wishes his fellow countrymen to know that he has made good and a title would indicate as much. It would be sweet to him when he returned to his native village.

For the Scot is very human about his success. The Englishman has long been disciplined to hide his feelings of pain or pride and manages sometimes even to hide his humanity. There have been young men aplenty in England on the make. The north-country Englishman is not wanting in capacity to see the main chance. The English in general have never been unwilling to recognize the roads to pomp and power, though they like to believe that it is the Americans who pursue success. Over the doors of many Oxford colleges and over Balliol in particular should be engraved on the college arms, "Put Your Best Foot Forward." It is a motto that many a don has inculcated into the minds of his protégés. He has taught the grammar of getting on from its nominative to its ablative. But he has done it with subtlety and has taught his young men to seek and win their honors with a minimum of fuss and feathers.

There is a good deal to be said in historical explanation of the Scotsman's craving for higher station. It will be recalled that in the Middle Ages Scottish merchants, Scottish scholars, and Scottish soldiers made their way to the far corners of Europe and even into the nearer parts of Asia seeking careers and finding them, becoming successful factors in wool, scholars of European reputation, generals in German and Russian armies. J. H. Burton in *The Scot Abroad* recounts the successful careers of Scots outside the British Isles. The wandering Scot has often been called restless. He had to be restless if he was to make anything of himself and he was often clever enough to know it.

His want of opportunity and restlessness in consequence developed versatility in him. He went not only from one place to another but from one kind of work to another, from one profession to another. As one reads in the *Dictionary of National Biography* the careers of miscellaneous successful Scots, one is impressed by the records, whether in the sixteenth century or in the nineteenth. Now a Scot was a minister, then a professor, and presently perhaps a government official. He was never afraid to try a new kind of work. Poor boys had learned how to trim their sails to the wind. Sir Walter Scott commented on that characteristic of his countrymen. The Scots, he said, were much less professional than the English, they were less expert in any one field. He might have added that they were fairly competent in many fields and shifted as they saw the chance. In that respect they remind one of Southerners in America who in hard days after the Civil War took up one profession after another, perhaps because they were so often of Scottish ancestry but more probably because they were in bad times dissatisfied with their progress in one field and looked over the fence into another field and presently jumped the fence, and perhaps later another fence. So it was with the Scots. Poor men have to look in every direction.

Things became better in Scotland in the eighteenth century and there was prosperity such as Scotland had never experienced since the Wars of Independence blighted the land. But even with some widely distributed prosperity the chances for a Scot to get ahead remained not too many. He might go into business and attain some means, and his chance of wealth became better with the Industrial Revolution. But in the eighteenth and indeed in the early nineteenth century the professions were crowded. The sons of the nobility and of the lairds went so generally into law that the legal profession was jammed. Medicine was a better opportunity but the training involved was long and expensive. As for the ministry it was pretty well filled up and a young man might have to wait before getting a charge, and find himself, when he received it, settled in some remote village.

The enterprising young Scotsman was often ill satisfied with his situation and looked toward England as he had once looked toward the Continent. In the early nineteenth century there were Scots who began to realize that their countrymen were doing well in London, gaining positions in large businesses, taking the lead in London medicine and law, and winning even great political prizes. The Scot, a citizen of a small and remote country, began to realize that he was possibly good enough to win position in one of the great world centres, perhaps in the politics of a nation that had just overcome Napoleon and that had more prestige and more wealth than any other. The possible prizes were such as Scots had never dreamed of, and dominies in the country and professors in universities no doubt pointed out to favorite pupils the success to be had for adventuring south.

The Scot had many qualifications for success in London. In the discipline of poverty he had been forced to be alert to his chances and he had been trained to be hard working. He was likely to have some notion as to the next thing that wanted doing. He has always been gifted with a practical imagination. Even his thrift stood him in good stead and was likely to furnish him with a small capital for the next step.

He came to believe that success was easier to attain in London than in Edinburgh or Glasgow, and that was true enough, for there was more money there and greater prizes to be won. Furthermore the Scot liked to flatter himself that the competition in London was less keen. His long-cherished suspicion that he was a better man than the Englishman became a blessed conviction. Was he not able to pass the English in any fair race? He was not unwilling to try. His caution and village timidity lessened and sometimes he became that assured northerner who was not always liked. He sent word to his friends and relatives, and they too took the train for King's Cross and found Scots in London to give them a lift. Once started they could take care of themselves.

One might suggest that it was the English who, by giving the Scots opportunities such as they had never had, developed in them the desire to get on. The Scots have been successful in England now for a good while, but they remember the hard circumstances of their background and enjoy their success more than the English. The people of that fortunate nation have been tasting success for hundreds of years and are more accustomed to it.

XXIX

THE SCOTS AND THE ENGLISH

THROUGHOUT this book I have been making incidental comparisons between the Scots and the English. England impinged always upon Scotland. There are few points in history where the English did not leave their marks upon Scotland and upon Scots, and so affect indirectly the ways and eventually the character of the people. The direct influence of English educational institutions and of English literature and the indirect influence of such English ideals as those of moderation and fairness have permeated Scottish life. Yet certain English ideals they have failed to accept. They have been unwilling to accept English heroes. They have held to their own heroes. On the whole they have shown themselves hard and resistant. They remain Scots. Today they are talking of restoring their national existence and of setting up a parliament of Scotland.

More than many other factors, English education has affected the Scots. For centuries occasional Scots have been finding their way to Oxford and Cambridge; in the eighteenth century a few began to go; from the middle of the nineteenth century on they have been going in such numbers as to constitute a threat to the influence of the Scottish universities. More recently the drift of Scottish boys of the upper middle and aristocratic classes to the English public schools has accentuated English influence.

Scottish education in burgh school and academy and at the university had tended to reinforce Scottish character. The boy met many others from his own town and then from all over Scotland and was shaped into a Scottish type. He was not stamped either at school or at the university in a way that made him very different from his fellows who had not been given his advantages. The university left its intellectual imprint upon him and gave him some head start over boys not so fortunate. But the boy who had made great sacrifices to attend the university and who had lived in narrow quarters and on mean fare in order to win his degree was not a changed person in manners and bearing. Nor were the more fortunate boys who had gone through the university with more pennies to spend much altered. There were not enough of them to constitute a class. The Scottish university man was rated to a considerable degree on his intellectual qualifications, and his training assured him no special position. When he went home on his holiday he was likely to help the farmer with his haying in the afternoon and to play cards up at the laird's in the evening.

The boy who went south to Cambridge or Oxford had a different experience. He was thrown among boys of a rather wealthier background and usually of more sophistication. He lived in college, as an English gentleman was expected to live, in surroundings of some comfort. He could not but be affected by such an experience; he was likely to shed some of his Scottish parochialism and some of his accent. But he had usually been caught too late to lose his essential Scottishness. If he had gone first to a Scottish university, as was often the case, and then proceeded to Oxford or Cambridge, he was even more certain to have retained his Scottish quality. A Scotsman he remained, with a difference.

It was when the wealthier and more important Scottish families began sending their sons to Eton and Winchester and other English public schools that English education began to do its work of Anglicizing Scottish youth. These boys who lived four years in an English school and three or more at an English university could hardly fail to become English in manners and outlook. They took on sometimes that reserve and quiet ability to dominate said to be important for young men who might go out to the East. The English university man with a public school behind him was a man set apart. He could not be mistaken for one not of his kind. It was perhaps fortunate for Scotland that many of the Scottish boys trained in English public schools and universities remained in England or went into the India Civil Service. But enough of them returned to Scotland to introduce a type that country had not known. The representatives of that type were often talented men whose influence was likely to be felt in the community.

So much is that true that the Scots have been concerned about the Anglicization of their youth. They have made efforts to improve the quality of Scottish academies and to give them such distinction that ambitious parents would prefer them to schools in England. I am not sure how successful that movement has been, or will be. The English public schools have offered more than exclusiveness and association with boys of family. They have offered an ampler life during the formative years. The same may be said of the English universities. To Scottish boys the English university was often an escape from the drab to the beautiful. Scottish universities, save St. Andrews (I have not seen Aberdeen), have not attractive exteriors. St. Andrews is seated in a town full of memories but there is something cold and somber about it. In the English quads there is an atmosphere that can hardly be found anywhere else in the world, and Scottish families have realized as much.

English literature has had an even more generally Anglicizing effect upon the Scots than English education. It has affected not only the youth but the whole reading class, and that includes much of Scotland. The Scots of a recent time were readers of Sir Walter, of Robert Louis Stevenson, and Burns, and of a few other Scottish writers such as Barrie. But that was a small part of their reading. They were devoted to Shakespeare and have almost adopted him as their own. They read Swift whose satire pleased them; they read Addison and Carlyle (a Scot by birth), and Walter Bagehot. Among modern English poets Tennyson and Browning were easily their favorites. I would guess that up to a recent period Tennyson was more often quoted than any other poet except Shakespeare. They took naturally to Tennyson's moral-

341

istic outlook and they enjoyed his romantic characters. King Arthur might have been a cousin of Bruce. Today Tennyson is obscured in Scotland as elsewhere. Browning's roughness and argumentative quality have appealed to the Scots, and his moralistic and religious philosophy. The Kipling of "M'Andrew's Hymn" and "The *Mary Gloster*" and of the Indian tales has been popular north of the Border. The Scots read English novels because there were so many of them and because they were better than Scottish novels. English plays were likely to be put on the boards in Edinburgh and Glasgow.

What is more surprising is that the Scots have taken English history and particularly English constitutional history into their university programs and have made those subjects an important part of the curriculum. The intricacies and beauty of evolution of the common law, of Parliament, and of the courts are matters that would interest the Scots. There was a system of law in Scotland that had its own special interest as an aspect of civil law but it was not carried overseas. There was a Scottish Parliament but save for two decades in history it played no considerable role. The Scottish constitution had little if any effect upon the outside world and is hardly worth the attention of the general student. The English constitution had world significance, it was transplanted with variations into many places, and its development has philosophy in it. The Scots have been curious to examine that philosophy. The history of English political thought is also a large and stimulating subject which the Scots have realized is worthy of the attention of the best students.

In poetry and prose, in historical and political thinking, the Scot has been drawn to depend for his intellectual nourishment upon the resources of the English, because they had so much more to offer. It is hard to overestimate the Anglicizing effect upon the Scots of the reading and study of English classics. The unconscious absorption of English ideals must have been great. More than we realize, we all learn as youngsters to fashion ourselves, as far as we can, upon the models of those we admire in books and to avoid the faults of those we dislike.

From the early eighteenth century to our time the Scots were not only reading English works of many kinds but they were observing the English in politics and business, in religious matters, and in many activities. One can detect in Scottish writing an implicit admiration of many English ways. There has been much to admire about the English. They won representative government at an early time when the Scots were still misgoverned by kings and warring nobles. They won orderly government at a time when the Scots had hardly shaken off the barbarism of the Middle Ages. When the Scots were at length united with the English, they were only beginning to be a law-abiding people, and in submission to law they were still far behind the English. It was a superior civilization the English possessed and, although the Scots seldom admitted as much, they knew it in their hearts. They could not have failed to observe the moderation and fairness of the English.

Moderation the English had learned in some degree, as I indicated in the chapter on the Reformation, from their reading and study of classical writers at grammar school and at the university. From the late sixteenth century on the young men who were to govern at Westminster and in the country were perhaps as much influenced by Roman writers as by the Bible. They learned from the Romans that restraint and moderation were virtues of transcendent value. The responsibility of the English governing classes sobered them; they thought about their reading and they put what they had learned into practice. Fairness was a virtue closely related to restraint and moderation, and fairness they had learned from their experience with the common law and with equity and from their experience in the country as justices of peace. Nicoll, the Scottish diarist, marveled, it will be remembered, at the justice administered by the English in Scotland during the Commonwealth. The Scots had known nothing like it.

They had been anything but a people cherishing moderation and fairness. Passion was in their blood, and Scottish judges, it will be remembered, as late as the end of the eighteenth century, gloried in their partisanship.

But slowly during their continuing association with the English the Scots saw much of the workings of British government. The English were given to making laws with pages of special clauses to cover special cases. The British civil servants, from the middle of the nineteenth century a professional class, carried out administrative policies with infinite pains to consider all the elements in the situation. More than any other people the English mastered the practice of moderation and fairness in carrying on government.

The Scots were not a stupid people; they could see for themselves the benefits of English ways, for Scotsmen were at Westminster and in the Civil Service. If the Scots in the nineteenth and twentieth centuries seem to have discarded some of their old passion and partisanship, it may be that association with the English has had something to do with it.

Many things the Scots have learned from the English that must have affected their whole outlook upon life and so their character. Certain English ideals they have resisted. They have not been willing to accept for their own the English ideal of the gentleman, nor that of the amateur. Nor have they acquired that good nature which is possibly the fundamental characteristic of the English.

I have already alluded to the English training of young men to be gentlemen. They have believed in the value of gentlemen, and not only as rulers of the silent, sullen peoples. They have believed that in their schools and universities they could gather talented boys of every class and transform them into gentlemen, and so fit them for government and for the professions. In the gentleman they have seen embodied certain standards of fairness, disinterestedness, truth-telling, and noblesse oblige.

The Scot is not unacquainted with the word gentleman. It

has been used among the aristocratic and professional classes since the eighteenth century and is, in its special sense, a palpable importation from England. The Scot has run into the type as well as the word. Many Scottish families, especially among the aristocracy, have for more than two centuries been looking toward England and living there a part of the year. When their sons go to an English university, or to Sandhurst or Woolwich, and enter the diplomatic service or the army, they are likely to bear the unmistakable marks of the English gentleman. But in general the Scot has never taken the term to heart, nor given it the connotation it has received in nineteenth-century England. He has retained his own Scottish manners and ways. He has no great faith in the usefulness of gentlemen. He has not acquired that deep respect for the type that even the sophisticated Englishman is seldom without. I have seen fine, competent Englishmen suffer all their days from the fear that they did not belong to the sacred type. The Scot has no such fears. He has always been too much a villager to put his trust in the saving grace of bearing and manners. He is satisfied to be a Scot.

The Scot takes less account of gentlemen because he has no cockney accent to reckon with. In England a cockney accent came to set one off as low class. In the seventeenth century, to be sure, good country gentlemen, at the very top of the gentlemanly class, in parts of England spoke with an accent not unlike modern cockney; but in some way, at some time, probably in the late eighteenth or early nineteenth century, there came to be established a proper accent, a special accent which gentlemen spoke. Alas for those who could not speak it! A sharp line of demarcation was set up, a line that could hardly be crossed. A man could not hope, unless his schoolteachers got hold of him early, to rid himself of the betraying dialect. In Scotland there was nothing of the kind. A strong Scottish accent would of course indicate that the man was country born, but so were most Scots, and who cared? Was there not something charming about the country Scots language that warmed the hearts of those who listened? Did not duchesses in the privacy of their castles break into it? The Scot did not hold it against a man that he came from the country and was of obscure parentage. Rather he liked to see a man make something of himself. A country accent was no bar to the esteem of one's fellows and to success.

The Scots have never been able to take to themselves the English ideal of the amateur. It is an old English ideal. I have not space here to trace its development and I am not sure that I have the knowledge. The English have long admired the man who could turn competently from one thing to another. But I suspect that it was out of their political experience that they acquired their great faith in the amateur. They found that they could take a man who stood high in a competitive examination in Greek literature and make him into a first-class civil servant, say in the Post Office. They found that a country gentleman with a knowledge of the growing of mangel-wurzels made an exceptional record as Secretary of State for War. It was a convenient belief, and the English made a touching faith out of it. If a man could do one thing well he could probably do something quite different equally well, and bring some new ideas into his new job. They thought well of a country parson who delved into local antiquities and made an historical find. They saluted with admiration the president of a chain of banks who translated Homer, the cabinet minister who gave the Gifford Lectures in philosophy, and the prime minister who won the Derby. Indeed they carry their faith farther. They have their suspicions of a man who is given up only to one job; they suspect him of Teutonic ancestry and of being too thorough. Life should be a series of games and a man should play several of them well. The sporting instinct is pretty deep in most Englishmen. They like a flutter now and then at something new. They are a little vain about being not too much in earnest.

This ideal of the Englishman has never appealed to the

Scot. He is not so often an amateur. In the old days, as has been pointed out, he shifted easily from one occupation to another and was often less narrowly professional than the Englishman. Today I think he is just as professional. But he does not take as naturally as the Englishman to a second occupation as an amateur. He is not really appreciative of the amateur spirit. Life is not a series of games for him but a race in which he will win if he can honestly, even if he has to cross to another track.

The good nature of the English is not unrelated to the amateur spirit. It is a quality of character the Scots have never attained unto. For at least four centuries foreigners of many kinds have credited the English with being a good-natured people, and the English are wont to admit the impeachment. They would attribute this virtue, I think, to their fondness for games. They have learned how to play the game with others; they have found it easier in the long run to accept defeat gracefully; there will be more games. Watch them at a cricket match or a rugby game or at the tennis matches at Wimbledon cheering a winning opponent. They have mastered the arts of gentle persuasion. I know of no speakers so skilful as those in the House of Commons in bringing over the opposition. They can state the case for their opponents with fairness and then go on in a good-natured way to show that the preponderating arguments are on their side. The very best of the Scots have picked up, I think, some of that good nature. Not so all of them. Witness the Clydeside members in the House of Commons. The Scots have been too passionate to be as good natured as the English. They look too much to the present. History has not allowed them the luxury of the long view. They have too many old prejudices not quite dimmed out.

There are few better indications of a nation's character than the heroes it chooses for its own. But it must be noticed that those heroes change from age to age, as new ideals come up in a nation. It might be expected that with progressive Anglicization the Scots would have taken on some of the English heroes. Not a bit of it. Hardly one has been admitted to their Valhalla.

Within the last two generations the English have been concerned with heroes. They tend to forget Henry II and Edward I and Dutch William; they say little nowadays about Fox and the two Pitts; they seem to have overlooked the great Peel. To judge from their newspapers of the years between the Great Wars, they have taken to their hearts Drake, Frobisher, Ralegh, and others of the half-pirate, half-gentleman type. One heard a great deal about the Devon seas and about Plymouth Hoe and the game of bowls.

But the Scots have been sailors too, and for a long time, brave sailormen who had to round Cape Wrath and capes farther away. Scottish sailors have even indulged in piracy now and then. But the Scots have made heroes out of none of them, unless we count Sir Patrick Spens, a mythical character in a ballad, who was drowned half way o'er to Aberdour. The Scots have been unable to work up an interest in Drake and Ralegh.

The English have long doted upon naval men. Nelson was a fine hero, and he signaled for every Englishman to do his duty. He did not mention the Scots, it is said in the north, because he kenn'd that they would do their duty. Nelson's shadow grew steadily longer as the English became conscious that Britannia ruled the waves. They have a great deal to say about the "Nelson touch." Now the Scots were part of Britain at the time of Trafalgar but they have shown little inclination to accept Nelson as one of their heroes. That is interesting too, for there was a Lady Hamilton in the Nelson saga and the Scots have a weakness for fair and frail ladies in their history.

The military heroes of Britain, Marlborough and, in particular, Wellington, are to some degree accepted in Scotland as British heroes. Yet while the hilltops of England have many monuments to the great duke, I happen to remember only one statue of Wellington in Scotland.

Nor have the Scots made heroes of the great imperialists. Clive and Ellenborough are seldom mentioned north of the Tweed, nor Cecil Rhodes, nor Curzon nor Milner. Nor is there any cult of Joseph Chamberlain, the cult that gave the English at length Neville; nor do fine ladies in Edinburgh worship Disraeli and wear primroses in token of it. The poet and storyteller of imperialism, Rudyard Kipling, is read, but the Scots have never said much about the white man's burden. The Scot has played his considerable role in the empire but he has not been one to think imperially, at least in the matter of heroes.

The Scots have their own heroes and have been reluctant to take on others. They have been men who could endure, who could watch spiders and take heart, who could escape from the stricken field and carry on from fastnesses in the Highlands, who could stand up to queens and kings and face exile or death, men who could suffer privation and fever to search out a dark continent, and women who were beautiful but unfortunate. They have asked of their heroes not success or glory but some moral or romantic quality. I think it is true to say that they have changed their heroes little from generation to generation.

Tenacious they have been of their heroes and of their ideals. They are no longer a political nation, but their Scottishness persists. Had they been conquered by the English they might have developed a continuous series of grievances, like the Irish, and certainly they would have made the way of their ruler hard. It was fortunate that they came into the Union of their own will, or at least by the will of their Parliament. More than their share they have had in the government at Westminster; it is their jest that they are the dominant partner.

We have seen throughout these chapters that the hardness of their life in earlier times developed a character of great resisting power. Invasion after invasion, the destruction of their towns, the burning of their homes, and the death of one or more of each family on the battlefield made them hate the

Southron, and that hatred bound them together. Edward I and his wars against Wallace and the Bruce awakened in them a great estimation of freedom and feeling for their own nation. Their religion did no less to make them a people of character. The Scots adopted Calvinism and made it over into a special Scottish religion with many thou-shalt-nots. Presbyterianism was an unlovely religion but it reinforced the tensile strength of Scottish character. The gradual coming together of the Highlands and the Lowlands made two nations one and gave the Scottish character a wider base. Lowland thoroughness and hardness and Highland imagination to quicken them combined into a character that has been of great use in the world and that has been impervious to assimilation by a greater neighbor.

The English were scarcely affected by the Scots save as individual Scots, as Adam Smith and Carlyle, as James Watt and the Hunter brothers, contributed to English civilization by their thoughts and inventions and discoveries. It is possible too that the English learned something from the Scots who invaded the London business world. It has also to be remembered that England had six northern counties, Northumberland, Cumberland, Westmorland, Durham, Lancashire, and Yorkshire, whose inhabitants were much like Lowland Scots in their stock, but with a different history. Those north-country men were as hard and canny and cautious as Lowlanders could be. The English did not need the Scots to give hardness to them. The Yorkshireman and his neighbors had done that already. They did not learn from the Scots because they had learned already from people much like them.

But to come back to the Scots, they have remained, in spite of all temptations to belong to other nations, a people of their own special kind. They treasure their traditions and they are somewhat afraid of losing them. It was that loss, it will be remembered, that preyed upon Sir Walter. They are beginning to talk of a possible restoration of the Scottish parliament. Such talk is more common from year to year.

More and more voices are heard in favor of it and some of them are influential voices. They say that Scotland has been getting the worst of it. The whole country has become a "depressed area." As business goes in for "rationalization" it closes out branch offices and works in Scotland. Manufacturers give up the Scottish plant and railways move their repair shops to England. Thus the Scottish laborer finds himself out of a job. Furthermore there is a general feeling in Scotland that Parliament with its present excess of work neglects measures that have to do with the north. Scotland suffers from being so far from the center of legislation. A Scottish parliament would be considering Scottish interests every day.

The people of Scotland are reluctant to ask for such a political change. Conservative Scots fear the Irish who have flocked across St. George's Channel in increasing numbers and have crowded into the Glasgow district. They remember that the Irish are Catholic and usually anti-British. They fear too the radicals of Clydeside who grow more vociferous from year to year.

But many Scots are inclined to believe that if various difficulties can be overcome, and they are many, Scotland might profit from the possession of its own parliament. Edinburgh would become again a proper political capital. They are certain that the English, with their broad-mindedness and good nature, would put little in the way once they were convinced that the Scots really wished a parliament of their own. Yet they realize that there is much to be said on the other side and will move cautiously.

INDEX

Adam, John, architect, 215

Adam, Robert, architect, 215, 217

Adam brothers, architects, 269

Adamson, Will, timidity of, 43

Addison, Joseph, read in Scotland, 202, 341

Adultery, in the 1st Book of Discipline, 127, 131; related to emotionalism, 176–177

Adventurousness, of Highlanders, 303–304

Aeneas Silvius, quoted, 52, 63, 64

Aildred of Rievaulx, quoted, 61

Aird, Francis, a weeping minister, 176

Albany, Duke of, executed by James I, 26

Alexander II, king, 9; conquers Argyle, 14; reign of, part of golden age, 14

Alexander III, king, 9; conquers Hebrides and Isle of Man, 14; court of, dominated by Normans, 14; reign of, part of golden age, 14; poem about, 15; troubles of, at end of reign, 15; death of, 15

Alexander, Duke of Albany, delight of, in change, 27

Alexander, James, a weeping minister, 175–176

Alexander, Sir William (later Earl of Stirling), quoted, 154

Amateur, ideal of, English and Scots compared as to, 346–347

Anarchy, in Scotland, causes of, 18

Ancrum Moor, skirmish of, 45

Anderston Club, 216

Angles, the, in Lowlands, 9; schoolboy story of, 10; influence of, in Scotland, 13, 64; loyalty of, 33; victory of, in language, 160

Annandale, Bruces given lands in, 13; men of, 42, 71–72, 79

"Anti-Burghers," the, sect, 203

Arbuthnot, Alexander, quoted, 51, 87, 94–95

Archibald, Bell-the-Cat, Earl of Angus, boast of, 109

Argyle, conquered by Alexander II, 14

Argyll, George Douglas Campbell, 8th Duke of, 297, 298

Aristocrat, Scottish, and democracy, 319

Armstrong, Johnny, reiver, 4; anti-English, 71–72

Army, British, Highlanders in, 200

Army, Scots, feeding of, 34; weakness of system, 35

"Auld Alliance," allusions to, 72

Bagehot, Walter, read in Scotland, 341

Baillie, Robert, quoted, 142 (2); letters of, character of, 166

Balfour, Arthur, Earl of, 311

Ballads, the, makers of, 65; democracy in, 91–92

Balliol, John, the Claimant, 16

Bannatyne Club, 270

Bannockburn, battle of, 16–17, 36, 69

Bannockburn, village of, 42

Barbados, Covenanters shipped to, 147

Barbarity, of Scots, 5

Barbour, John, poet, 326; *The Brus*, quoted, 31–32, 32–33, 34, 38, 41, 45, 70, 96–97; influence of, in creating a hero, 39; illustration from, 54; worth of individual taught by, 234

Barrie, Sir James, heroines of, 47; *Window in Thrums*, curiosity in, 317; *What Every Woman Knows*, quoted, 333–334; reading of, in Scotland, 341

Beaton, David, Cardinal, assassination of, 109

353

Index

man, 93; tenant, influence of, 23; called shiftless, 59–60; in mid-19th century, 296

Farming, daily work of, described, 60; hindered by war, 60–61

Fatalism, 153–155

Ferguson, Adam, philosopher, mentioned, 215, 218, 219, 220, 223, 225

Ferguson, Robert, poet, 224, 232, 234, 240, 266, 323, 328; quoted, 196 n.; account of, 230–232

Feudal jurisdictions, in the Highlands, 8, 90, 139; abolished, 191

"Field conventicles," 146–147, 149

'Fifteen, The. See Jacobite Risings

Fishing, stimulated by David I, 13

Fitzalans, the, given lands, 13

Flemings, the, in Lowlands, 9; influence of, in Scotland, 13

Fletcher, Andrew, of Saltoun, patriotism of, 186; estimate of beggars by, 282

Flodden Field, battle of, 37, 40, 50, 109; warning of James IV, before, 80–81; lesson from, 110

Food, plenty of, 64

Forbes, Duncan, President, advice of, as to recruiting Highlanders, 192

Fordun's Chronicle quoted, 13, 45, 50

Foreordination, 152–155; belief in, an incitement to action, 155; attitude of Burns toward, 238

Forrest, Henry, executed, 104

'Forty-five, The. See Jacobite Risings, 188–191

"Four Maries," song of, sentimental addition to, 323 n.

France, old alliance with, 17; traditional ally of Scotland, 18; influence of, on Scotland, 23–24

Franklin, Benjamin, in Scotland, 223–224

Fraser, Mrs. Kennedy. See Kennedy-Fraser, Mrs.

Fraser, Simon, addresses the army, 90

Freedom, aspiration for, 69–70; Scottish conception of, 244–245

French, Scots' dislike of, 72

Froissart, quoted, 34, 63

Funeral procession, in Highlands, 304–305

Gaelic language, disappearing, 159–160

Gaels, outweighed by other stocks, 13; loyalty of, 33; and the Angles, 64

Galloway, a center of disaffection, 19

Galt, John, 324; account of, 276–277

General Assembly, 125, 204; in 2d Book of Discipline, 133; packed, 140; called, 143; abolished, 146; becomes voice of Kirk, 148; influence of Moderates in, 203; struggles in, over patronage, 245; schools set up by, 290; a symbol of nationhood, 312–313

Genevan Bible, the, 159

Gentle Shepherd, The, by Allan Ramsay, 323

Gentleman, Scots attitude toward notion of, 344–346

Gentlewomen, song-writers among, 264

George IV, visit of, to Edinburgh, 300

Gladstone, and Scots, 274

"Glasgovia," industry centered in, 281

Glasgow, society of, character of, 261; condition of, 183; flourishing, 267; workers drawn into, 284; poets of, 315

Glasgow University, 249; Hutcheson at, 205; and Watt's steam engine, 222

Gold, 64

Goldsmith, Oliver, about Scottish women, 261

Good nature, English and Scots compared, as to, 347

Good taste, among Scots, 325–326

Index

Index

Lochs, Scotland divided by, 7–8

Lockhart, J. G., 318

Lollardry, foothold of, in Scotland, 103

Lords of the Articles, changes as to powers of, 137

Lords of the Congregation, 108, 125

Lord's Supper, the. *See* Communion

Lothian, won by Malcolm II, 12; agriculture in, 59; increasing prosperity in, 64

Low Countries, tracts coming from, 103

Lowlanders, a nation, 8; mixed stock of, 8–9; more suited to orderly government, 9; attitude of, toward Highlanders, 9, 193, 302; resemblance of, to north English, 9–10; disadvantages of, compared with north English, 10–11; influence of, upon Scotland, 24; and the Jacobite movements, 189; imagination of, 303

Lowlands, cut off by Grampians, 7; territory included by, 8; influence of Angles upon, 64; men from, with Wallace, 68; men from, at Bannockburn, 69; reinforced with Highland talent, 304–305

Loyalty in war, 32–33; versus treachery, 32 n.; weakness of, 33; of Highlanders, 197–198, 304–305; to Scotland, 312–315

Lyndsay, Sir David, of the Mount, poet, 47, 54, 65, 73, 236, 326, 328; quoted, 50, 52, 61, 63–64, 84, 89, 97 (2), 104, 107; story told by, 81; satirizes Church, 88; classical models, 115; and the drama, 161; Burns's relation to, 240

McAlpin, Kenneth, conquers Picts, 12

Macculloch, John, geologist, story of Highland curiosity by, 194–195

Macfarlane of Glentartan, loyalty of, 197–198

Macdonald of Ross, cruelty of, 27

Macdonald, Ramsay, 311

Macdonalds, the, wars of king with, 18

Macdonnell, A. G., quoted, 302

McGregor, servant of Bishop of Dunkeld, 3

Machinery, Scottish energies occupied with, 279

McKail, Hugh, martyr, 146

Mackenzie, Henry, *Man of Feeling*, sentimentality of, 324

Mackenzie, Osgood, quoted, 304

Maclaren, Ian (John Watson), the "Drumtochty" of, 322

Magus Moor, Archbishop Sharp assassinated at, 147

Mahoun's dancé in hell, 77

Maitland, Sir Richard ("auld"), 326; quoted, 85; as to revenge, 26

Maitland, William, of Lethington, problem of, 112–113; patriotism of, 186; denounced by Knox, 120

Maitland Quarto MS., quoted, 50, 94

Major, John, quoted, 28, 60, 104, 190 n.

"Makars," the, 73

Malcolm II, wins Lothian and Strathclyde, 12

Malcolm III (Canmore), ruled greater Scotland, 12; marriage of, 12–13; wife of, *see* Margaret

Malcolm IV, coming of Normans, 13

Malmesbury, William of, quoted, 5

Manorial life, 90

Manorial system, 59

Manrent, usage of, 19

Mansfield, William Murray, Lord, 243

Marchmont, Sir Patrick Hume, 1st Earl of, quoted, 184

Margaret, wife of Malcolm III, brings in English ways, 9; marriage of, 12–13; piety of, 54, 86

Marjory, daughter of Bruce, married to Robert the Steward, 20

Marjory, daughter of Earl of Carrick, encounter of, with Bruce, son of Claimant, 45

Marriage, affection in, 48–49; not

363

sacrosanct, 105; Allan Ramsay on, 228

Marwick, W. H., cited, 281

Mary of Lorraine, 122; appeal of, to churchmen, 109; attitude of Knox toward, 120 (2)

Mary, Queen of Scots, 302, 321; character of, 117; and Knox, 120, 121, 122; cult of, 323

Mathieson, W. L., quoted, 108, 118, 185

Melancholy, of Scots, 85

Meldrum, Squire, romantic story of, 47–48, 50, 53

Melville, Andrew, 156, 202, 203, 257; a hero, 69; humor of, 99; estimate of, 134–135; part of, in 2d Book of Discipline, 135

Melville, David, Earl of, quoted, 185

Melville, James, prose of, 275

Melville, Lord. See Melville, David, and see also Dundas, Henry, and Dundas, Robert

Mercat Cross, battle of, 144

Merchant, the successful, rise of, 61–62

Merchants, given privileges, by David I, 13; foreign business of, 61; want of capital of, 62

Merriment, of Scots, 82–85

Miller, Hugh, quoted, 292; observations of working classes by, 294; story of his father's death at sea, 294–295

Ministers, elected by church, 125; subject to discipline, 128; attitude of, toward democracy in church, 151; duties of, 151–152; behavior expected of, 152; 17th century, outlook of, 163; 17th century, sermons of, 163–164; emotionalism of, 164–165; quality of, 204; influence of, on songs, 240; in mid-19th century, 288–290

Moderates, the, account of, 202–211; aims of, 208; influence of English thought upon, 209; Burns in sympathy with, 237; Moderates in church, *temp* James VI, 141

Moderation, English and Scots compared as to, 343–344

Monasteries, Anglicizing effect of, 9; spread over Scotland, 86

Monboddo, James Burnet, Lord, 215

Monmouth, James Scott, Duke of, sent against Covenanters, 147

Montgomerie, Alexander, *The Cherry and the Slae*, quoted, 40–41

Montrose, James Graham, Marquis of, 298; a hero, 69; probable theory of, as to royal power, 138; change of side, 144, 318

Moray, Lord James Stewart, Earl of, denounced by Knox, 120

Morevilles, de, the, given lands, 13

Morton, James Douglas, 4th Earl of, regent, and Knox, 121 (2); threat of, to Melville, 135

Muir, Thomas, account of, 248

Mushet, David, metallurgist, 279

Napier, John, of Merchistoun, logarithms, invented by, 137

Napier, Robert, marine engineer, 279, 280

Nasmyth, Alexander, painter, 269

Nasmyth, James, engineer, 279, 280

National Covenant. See Covenant

Nationalism, beginnings of, 67–69; present revival of, 350–351

Nature, poets and, 82; delight in, distressing, 177

Navigation Act, English, effect of, upon Scotland, 183

Neilson, James B., inventor, 279, 280

Neilson, William Allan, quoted, 240

Nesbit, Sir Philip, executed, 144

Nevoy, minister, 144

Newbolt, Sir Henry, quoted, 162

Newburgh, William of, quoted, 5

"New Lights." See Moderates

New Testament, in English, 104; translation of, by Tyndale, 159

Nicol Jarvie, Bailie, character in Scott's *Rob Roy*, 256

Nicoll, John, diarist, 343; quoted, 145

Nobles, character of, 9, 21; few of,

Index

Wishart, George, martyr, 149

Witches, persecution of, 78

Wodrow, Robert, historian of Presbyterianism, 148, 158; quoted, 175–176 (5); alarmed at rise of Moderates, 202; comment of, upon evil influences of time, 181; interested in the new opinions, 210

Woman, willing to sacrifice her son, 44

Women, work in fields, 45; share of, in battle, 45; of Highlands, 45; part of, in courtship, 45–47; of chivalric romances, not found in Scottish poetry, 47; affection of, 48–49; homely virtues of, 49; comfort of, 49; faithfulness of, 50; Arbuthnot about, 51; subordination of, 51–52; and priests, 51, 54, 104; patience of, 52; liveliness of, 52; in repartee, 52–53; spiritedness of, 53; gayety of, 53; broad-mindedness of, 53; pity due to, 54; and religion, 54; in poems of Allan Ramsay, 228; in poems of Burns, 233–234; role of, in Edinburgh society, 261-262; of country houses, 262–264; of early 19th century, 264; unmarried, 264–265; in Edinburgh, 266

Worcester, battle of, 145

Wordsworth, Dorothy, impressions of village houses, 285; quoted, 292; Highlanders of, 303; observations of, on working people, 293

Working classes in towns, character of, 293–294

Wyntoun, Chronicle, quoted, 16, 32, 44, 78, 90, 95

Yorkshiremen versus Scots, in respect to thrift, 332

Young, G. M., *Early Victorian England*, quoted, 321